Praise for *Not If I Can Help It*

"An inspiring, intelligent memoir . . . Each episode carries a tremendous punch, as well as a searing lesson about the failings of society to help those in need. . . . Groff balances her book with warmth and humor."

—*Kirkus Reviews* (starred review)

"Groff's masterful storytelling skills sculpt profound meaning from even the most terrifying of narratives, gifting readers with a deep understanding of what is needed to protect abuse victims and their children . . . Explosive memoir of a family law attorney's fight for justice."

—*Publishers Weekly BookLife* [Editor's Pick]

"Stories of criminal lawyers are common, but stories of those who do the critical unsung work of poverty law are rarely told. In her humble, witty, and compelling voice, Meg Groff shares the inside story of what it is like to be a family law attorney for Legal Aid, including the fantastic victories and traumatic losses that accompany the specialty of representing victims of domestic violence. This book is a must-read for anyone who wants to know what doing good by being a lawyer looks like."

—Joan S. Meier, NFVLC Professor of Clinical Law
and Director of the National Family Violence Law Center
at George Washington School of Law

"Meg Groff has fought for the rights and needs of children and women in the toughest arena, and has lived to tell a heart-warming story."

—Amon Bentovim, M.D., child and adolescent psychiatrist,
Director of Child and Family Training, and Visiting Professor
at Royal Holloway, University of London

"*Not If I Can Help It* renews your faith in justice and those who fight tirelessly for it, while also breaking your heart. You come away inspired and outraged, with important insight into the terrifying reality of domestic violence."

—Sasha Drobnick, Appellate Litigation Director,
DV LEAP, Network for Victim Recovery of DC

"Everyone who reads this book will want Groff as their attorney-champion, but for now you will have to settle for her being your storyteller."

—Danielle Pollack, co-founder, National Safe Parents Organization
and policy manager, National Family Violence Law Center

"The condition of our family court system is a national crisis, and Meg Groff is a bright light in the darkness. *Not If I Can Help It* should be required reading for every judge, lawyer, and law school student in America.

—Tina Swithin, Family Court Advocate, author of
Divorcing a Narcissist, and founder of One Mom's Battle

"All the understanding, courage, and humor of a veteran warrior in the fight for social justice."

—Terry Bisson, Hugo Award-winning author of *Any Day Now*

Not If I Can Help It

A Family Lawyer's Battles for Justice
for Victims of Domestic Violence and the Poor

Meg Groff

Rivertowns
B O O K S
IRVINGTON, NEW YORK

Printed in the United States of America · March 2025 · I

Paperback edition ISBN-13: 978-1-953943-47-7
Hardcover edition ISBN-13: 978-1-953943-48-4
Ebook edition ISBN-13: 978-1-953943-49-1

LCCN Imprint Name: Rivertowns Books
Library of Congress Control Number: 2024944924

Rivertowns Books are available from all bookshops, other stores that carry books, and online retailers. Visit our website at www.river-towns-books.com. Orders and other correspondence may be addressed to:

Rivertowns Books
240 Locust Lane
Irvington, NY 10533
Email: info@rivertownsbooks.com

For my mother, Helen Satinsky Splaver, who badgered me into going to college, convinced me that I could be a lawyer, and taught me, from an early age, that we must never remain silent in the face of injustice

When will justice come? When those who are not injured are as outraged as those who are.

~ Unknown ~

The Golden Rule is of no use whatsoever unless you realize that it's your move.

~ Frank Crane ~

Contents

Preface

E very chapter in this book recounts a case drawn from my career as a family law attorney representing victims of domestic violence, children, and the poor. Some people are identified by their real names, but in many instances—including all of my clients—names have been changed to protect the innocent. Sometimes, physical descriptions of the parties involved and other identifying case details have been altered, but nothing fundamental is fiction; these are true stories about some of the memorable clients I have had the opportunity to represent, and about the battlefield of society and the law on which their cases have been fought. Some readers may find portions of this book triggering, as instances of violence against women and children are depicted.

The stories in this book are from the early years of my career, but the circumstances described and the problems presented remain relevant today. Stories like these continue to occur in great numbers, not only in my home state of Pennsylvania but all across America. Please read the Afterword, "Where Do We Go from Here?," to learn about where we now stand in the ongoing battle for the rights of domestic violence victims, children, and the poor, and what you can do to help.

Meg Groff
Doylestown, Pennsylvania
February 2025

1. Guardian Angel

The first time I saw the Bucks County courthouse, I wanted to run in the opposite direction. It loomed so large in the county square, and *ten* judges reigned inside. I know now that there are far bigger courthouses with many more judges, but I had been living in a rural county with a one-room courthouse and exactly one judge, so ten seemed like an awful lot of judges to me. It was less than a year since I had passed the bar exam and received my license to practice law, and already I was starting over. And now my new boss, David Tilove, had assigned me a contested custody case that was scheduled for trial in that looming courthouse in only five days.

David was in his early forties when I first met him, handsome in an offbeat way that made you wonder if only you were noticing. I would soon learn that he enjoyed the intellectual challenge of jousting with a hippie rebel who held strong opinions about the pursuit of justice in an unjust world. But in my first week working at the Bucks County Legal Aid Society, all I really knew about David Tilove was that he was Legal Aid's executive director. I had only done a handful of short hearings in that laidback one-room courthouse in Mifflin County, and I felt sure that going to trial here would be a very different experience.

I needed to talk to my new boss.

I stood at the open door to David's office, but he was deep in thought at his desk and didn't notice me standing there, so I knocked on the wall to get his attention. He raised his head, still half-distracted, and looked at me quizzically. "Hi," he said. "What's up?"

I walked into his office and took a seat. "I want to observe a custody hearing here before I do one," I stated firmly. "I'd like to take a day off so I can go to the courthouse to do that."

"Do you really think that's necessary? You can't learn to swim without jumping into the water," he responded.

"I think you shouldn't jump into water before knowing if you'll be landing in a tub or an ocean," I shot back.

That got David's full attention. He peered at me, and there was a long moment of silence (at least it seemed long to me at the time). Then he asked, "If you got hired for a factory job, would you demand a free day to watch the widgets being made?"

"No, I wouldn't," I said, "but people aren't widgets. If I mess up a custody case, it would matter a lot to my client, her children, and me."

My new boss smiled broadly. "Good closing argument," he said. "Take a day off. I insist."

It turned out that family law cases were not actually litigated in the stately main courthouse, but rather in a small, inconspicuous, grayish building across the street. So I went to family court to sit quietly in courtroom A-9, waiting to observe the custody hearing scheduled that day before the Honorable Edward G. Biester, Jr. I was wearing an old pair of blue jeans and a tie-dyed shirt, with a colorful bandana wrapped around my long red hair. It was 1984; the Sixties were long gone, but I was a dyed-in-the-wool hippie and still looked the part. Because I was only going to be an audience member, I felt no compulsion to be dressed like a lawyer, which I avoided every chance I got. In truth, I still didn't *feel* like a lawyer, and I disliked having to dress up like one. (Thoreau cautioned, "Distrust any endeavor that requires new clothes." His warning had nagged at me throughout three years of law school.)

So this was a "come-as-you-are" day when I would sit unobtrusively in the courtroom, quietly observing how custody hearings were conducted. I had gotten there early to ensure a good seat, and I expected to go unnoticed, just one of the crowd. But as ten a.m. approached, only three people straggled into the courtroom. One was obviously a lawyer, an aristocratic-looking gentleman who walked with a cane although he did not seem to need it. By his side was a short man with a grim face and angry eyes. The third person, a thin, middle-aged woman wearing a threadbare coat and clutching a Bible, was visibly trembling as she took the seat farthest away from the man and his lawyer.

Judge Biester entered the courtroom, heralded by the requisite court fanfare designed to signal the solemn gravity of such proceedings. Taking his seat, he said, "Let us begin."

The three other people in the courtroom came forward and stood before the bench.

"Do you have an attorney?" Judge Biester asked the woman.

"No," she said. "I can't afford one."

"Did you apply to Legal Aid?"

"Yes," she answered, her voice quavering, "but they had no one available to take my case."

When I heard her say that, I felt a storm of guilt. This poor woman—poor in every way—was trembling and alone in a court of law because Legal Aid supposedly had no one available to take her case. Yet here I was, sitting leisurely and carefree, taking the day off.

Judge Biester declared a twenty-minute recess to give the opposing sides an opportunity to talk to each other. "See if you can resolve this matter," he directed as he left the bench.

I rushed over to the woman and introduced myself. I was a new Legal Aid attorney, I explained, and although I couldn't do a hearing, I could help negotiate an agreement on her behalf. Would she want me to do that?

"I've been praying to God to send a guardian angel to guide me," she told me, "and, praise be to God, here you are!"

I looked even less like an angel than I looked like a lawyer, but I determined, then and there, to do the best I could to fill both positions.

The man's lawyer eyed me warily. I went over to him and informed him that I would be negotiating on the woman's behalf. He was clearly not pleased with this turn of events. "Are you her *lawyer*?" he demanded. Perhaps I should have hesitated, but I didn't. "Yes," I said. "I'm her lawyer."

I took the woman to a small alcove down the hall from the courtroom and asked her to tell me about her case as quickly as she could.

There was no time for nuance; the recess was only twenty minutes. I learned that she and her ex-husband were recovering alcoholics, and that they had one child, a teenage daughter, who had lived with her since the parties' separation two years earlier. She had always been the girl's primary caretaker. But her daughter had recently begun getting into trouble at home and at school, including being caught smoking marijuana. At the urging of her AA support group, the woman had "grounded" her daughter for three months in an application of "tough love." Her daughter responded by running to her father. He considered it a validation of his parental superiority and was rewarding the girl with gifts, special privileges, and the attention he had never before bestowed. Now she was refusing to see her mother at all.

I asked the woman if she hoped to have the judge order her daughter returned to her primary custody. She told me she knew her daughter's preference at age 16 would be given great weight, and was glad her ex-husband was finally acting like a father. She wanted her daughter to have the opportunity to continue experiencing that new relationship, but she didn't want to be excluded from her daughter's life.

I asked her what she would think about a proposal that she be given shared legal custody and partial physical custody of her daughter, detailing the liberal custodial schedule such a proposal could include.

The woman began crying. "That would be so wonderful! But my ex-husband will never agree to any of that, and neither will my daughter. She's so mad at me. I just pray that I'll at least be allowed to see her at Christmas time."

"That won't do," I said. I told the woman that I was sure her daughter loved her, because it was obvious how very much she loved her daughter. Maybe tough love had turned out not to be the best approach with a child who was going through enough tough times of her own, but when the two of them had a chance to talk things over, I was quite sure it would all work out.

"Let's see what I can do," I said, as I marched over to her ex's attorney.

The lawyer was in no mood to negotiate with a blue-jean-clad interloper claiming to be a lawyer. He spoke to me begrudgingly and his demeanor was dismissive. "Her daughter hates her. She's sixteen years old.

Judge Biester isn't going to order her to spend time with her unstable mother. There will be no deal." He had nothing more to say. I sensed he expected me to vanish when the recess ended, like an annoying apparition that was just pretending to be there.

The tipstaff, a court official, appeared shortly thereafter, asking whether an agreement was likely. I explained that I was from Legal Aid, taking a day off, and just happened to be in the courtroom. I told him we had tried without success to resolve the matter, whereupon the tipstaff informed us that court was reconvening.

When Judge Biester returned to the bench, he addressed me directly. "I hear you offered to assist the respondent, but no agreement has been reached. Is that correct?"

"Yes, Your Honor," I replied.

"Let's try conferencing the matter," Judge Biester said, and he ushered me and the other attorney into his chambers. I began to apologize for my conspicuously inappropriate attire, but the judge cut me off. "I'm just grateful that you volunteered. Cases are always easier to handle with a lawyer on both sides."

Judge Biester gave each of us five minutes to argue the issues and delineate what we thought his order should be. I assumed he would then tell us his thoughts on the matter, enabling us to negotiate again within that framework, but instead, when our time was up, he abruptly announced: "Okay, then, let's have our hearing!"

I cannot adequately describe how those words hit my brain and my body. But there was no time to think and no safe place to faint. Trailing Judge Biester and the husband's attorney back to the courtroom, I motioned to the woman to sit by my side at the defense table. "We're having a hearing, and you will be testifying," I whispered to her. "All you need to do is answer the questions truthfully. The judge is a nice man. Don't be afraid." I have no idea how I managed to speak, because I am quite sure that I wasn't breathing, but I could hear my voice sounding calm and reassuring.

"I'm not afraid, now that you are here," the woman said. She was no longer trembling and looked utterly serene. I resolved at that moment that my own rising panic would stay banished from view. As we sat side by side at the defense table, I whispered to her once again, "I'm sorry, but I neglected to ask: what is your *name*?"

I do not recall much about that hearing. I remember that the ex-husband testified, and that I cross-examined him at length, his angry eyes focused on me as he squirmed in his seat. I remember that the woman who had become my client took the stand, and that her sweetness suffused her testimony. I remember that closing arguments were made by the man's attorney and by me, and that I advocated forcefully for the custody schedule I was seeking for my client. But the details of that hearing are a haze, except for Judge Biester's final decision. I have, to this day, a crystal-clear memory of the custody order he issued, because it was identical in every respect to the one I had requested.

My client was ecstatic, thanking God, once again, for sending me to her. It wasn't the forum for a religious debate, so I didn't argue the point. Besides, I must admit, it felt rather nice to be someone's guardian angel.

Altogether, it was a joyous occasion, the first of many to come in that courthouse.

As soon as I could get to the payphones in the hallway (it was 1984, after all), I called David Tilove to update him on how my day off had worked out. I could tell he was pleased, not only with me but also with himself. "So you jumped into the water and it turns out you can swim," he said, just a bit smugly.

But that was not the lesson I learned that day. I have never stopped believing in the importance of painstaking preparation before every court hearing, because people are not widgets. And I didn't learn that everyone who comes to court deserves a lawyer by their side, because I already knew that. No, the lesson I learned that day was that I really *was* a lawyer—and a good one—whether I looked like one or not.

2. "You Might As Well Be a Lawyer"

I never expected to be a lawyer.

After graduating from high school, I swore off any more schooling. I thought graduating from high school was accomplishment enough when it came to formal education, and given how many classes I had cut, it really *was* an accomplishment. The following year, I married Jim Groff, the older brother of my two best friends. And the year after that, our daughter Ruth was born. It was the start of the legendary Sixties, and Jim and I looked and lived like hippies. We moved around a bit, but ended up residing in a little rented house at the top of a steep hill in the backwoods of Pennsylvania. Surrounded by trees and berry bushes, we happily eschewed modern conveniences like electricity and running water, and rid ourselves of extraneous material possessions in favor of what we called "the good life."

Then, as now, Jim was multitalented—a carpenter, electrician, mechanic, landscaper, and fine craftsman in leather and wood. He could make or fix almost anything. But Jim was picky. Regardless of how much the job might pay, he refused to be hired to make or fix anything that wouldn't end up being beautiful or functional. He thought there was already too much ugliness and dysfunction in the world without any contributions from him.

My efforts to bolster our household income through gainful employment were even less successful, but for a different reason: I had no marketable skills. As a result, I gradually constructed a résumé of short-lived, low-paying jobs for which I failed to show even a glimmer of ability. My incompetence as a waitress, for example, had earned me a small measure of renown at more than one restaurant. Not that I was sullen or inattentive. Just that I could never remember who ordered what, didn't know one salad dressing from another, and could easily trip over a smudge on the floor.

Once, when we lived in an up-and-coming slum in Philadelphia, I tried to be a taxicab driver. The plan was doomed from the start because it was years before the advent of GPS and I am directionally dyslexic. I lasted on the job for two harrowing days, both of which I spent getting hopelessly lost trying to deliver my passengers to their desired destinations. I still recall my last passenger, who sat patiently in the back seat as I drove down one street after another, searching in vain for a sign that would tell me where in the world we were. When he finally escaped from the cab, he gently suggested that I had not yet found my niche.

But nothing was as catastrophic as my brief stint at the local sock factory, where I managed to get the lower front of my cotton shirt swallowed by a mammoth sock-making machine, leading to a disruption of sock production unmatched in the factory's half-century history.

It was the sock factory incident that changed the direction of my life.

My mother happened to call me a few hours after I fled shirtless from that traumatic scene, and, as she was wont to do, she bugged me about going to college. "If you don't get a higher education," she said, "you'll be working in sock factories all your life."

Suspecting such employment might no longer be available to me, I bowed to her bugging and enrolled in college. I didn't realize it at the time, but it was the first step on my way to becoming a lawyer.

☙   ☙   ☙

I couldn't afford to go to college full-time. The first semester, I took two courses instead of four. Our daughter Ruth, just five years old, became very sick, very suddenly, during the onset of juvenile diabetes, and I had to reduce my attendance from two courses a semester to one. At that rate, I feared I'd never finish being a freshman. But I kept taking classes and slowly, very slowly, I accumulated college credits.

Several years passed. Then I heard about Goddard's Adult Degree Program, which finally enabled me to speed up the process, largely through independent study, and earn my degree. I had taken many psychology courses, all of which were fascinating, and I thought I wanted to become a psychologist. But that thought shifted in a different direction one night, at about three a.m., when I woke to the sounds of frantic knocking on our front door.

I opened the door to the sight of a tear-stained young woman, barefoot, dressed only in a nightgown, with disheveled locks of long, blond hair partly shrouding her pretty face. I had never seen her before.

"Please help me!" she begged, before weeping overcame her. Her legs buckled, and she would have fallen if I hadn't caught her. I held her upright in my arms and began guiding her inside.

"What's *happening*?" I asked anxiously as I cradled her. "Are you *okay*?" She was so slight and delicate, she felt almost weightless in my arms. Like a tattered linen doll.

Through gasping sobs she told me, "He took Tad."

"*Who* took Tad?" I asked, wondering *Who is Tad?*

She tried to answer but couldn't stop weeping long enough to form words. I half-carried her to the couch, sat her down beside me, and began reciting meaningless platitudes meant to comfort. "Everything will be all right," I told her, when there was no reason to think that everything would be. The hem of her nightgown rested just above her knees, and below it dark red bruises were blossoming on both legs. When her sobs subsided sufficiently for her to speak, her words poured out in a torrent.

Her name was Lily. She had fled from her boyfriend Bobby two days before, making her escape when he left their apartment after dinner to go to the gym, as he always did on Monday evenings. With the help of her best friend Alison, she had planned the escape for weeks. She couldn't stay at Alison's, because Bobby would know to look for her there. Instead, Alison's brother Abe, who had a car, arrived at the prearranged time to drive her, with her five-week-old infant, the sixty miles to the home of his friends, John and Chrissy Anderson, who had offered them sanctuary. Lily fled with a few changes of clothes for herself and Tad, all the diapers she owned, and some baby supplies.

The plan had gone well. The Andersons were out of state on vacation when Abe called to inform them that Lily and Tad were on their way, and Lily got to speak to them during the call. "Make yourself at home," they said. "You can stay as long as you need to."

The Andersons knew a lot about domestic violence. Chrissy's sister, her only sibling, had been murdered by her boyfriend years before, when both sisters were in high school. John's father had been a classic abuser. They were glad to give aid to a victim in need.

Abe had stopped at a supermarket on their way, where he paid for the groceries Lily might need until the Andersons returned in a week from their vacation. When they got there, Abe gave Lily his key to the house and showed her the guest bedroom that was waiting for her, with a makeshift bassinet nestled next to the double bed. Abe had a night-shift job, so he couldn't stay long, but before departing he gave Lily five 20-dollar bills and kissed her on the forehead. Through new tears, Lily told me how safe and loved she had felt then, for the first time she could re-member. That night, after breastfeeding Tad and laying him in his new bed, she had slept like a baby.

But somehow—Lily didn't know how—Bobby found out where she was hiding. And the next night—*this* night, less than an hour before—he had driven up the Andersons' long driveway, with his car's headlights turned off. Lily was sure of this, because headlights shining through the bedroom window would have wakened her. She was awakened instead by his menacing shouts: "Open the fucking door, bitch!"

Lily told me she was shaking uncontrollably as she hugged Tad to her chest and peeked out the window. She could see Bobby in the dark-ness, with what looked like a hatchet in his hands. Within seconds, he was plunging that hatchet into the front door.

She grabbed the phone and dialed 911. "He's breaking the door down with a hatchet!" she screamed. "I'm all alone with my baby!"

"We'll send help right away!" the officer on the line told her. "What's your address?"

But before Lily could answer, he asked another question, "Do you recognize the man?"

"Yes! He's my ex-boyfriend!"

"Oh," the officer said then (Lily said his voice suddenly sounded very 'official'). "Why didn't you say that initially? We don't get involved in domestic disputes."

"But he's breaking the door down with a hatchet!" Lily screamed again.

The officer responded: "Sorry, lady. It's policy. We don't do domestics."

Lily kept pleading. "Please help me! Please! He's breaking down the door!"

"Well, it's *his* door, too," the officer said, then mouthed a brisk "Sorry" before hanging up.

The door was half hacked to pieces when Bobby kicked in a splintered panel next to the frame. Lily watched as his hand reached in and seized hold of the inside latch. "I'll kill you, you fucking bitch!" he was shouting.

Tad started bawling. Lily ran to hide in a closet, but there was no way to lock it. She just huddled there behind the clothes rack, quaking, unable to breathe, holding Tad tightly as his cries grew to piercing wails.

It took only seconds, Lily told me, for Bobby to fling open the closet door and rip Tad from her arms. Then he kicked her repeatedly in her stomach, legs, and back as she lay screaming, fetal-position, on the closet floor. And then he bolted from the house to his car, Tad pinned under one arm, and sped back down the driveway. He was already at his car before Lily could climb past the shattered front door.

Through it all, Tad never stopped wailing.

In pain and hysterical, Lily called Alison, who instructed her to run to the nearest neighbors for help. Abe worked from midnight to nine a.m. and couldn't leave mid-shift. He wouldn't be able to get her until the next day. "Go *now*!" Alison had told her. So Lily ran the equivalent of a city block, to the Andersons' nearest neighbors—to Jim and me, and our daughter, who was sleeping peacefully in her bed.

Lily was cold. She had stumbled through the chill autumn air in the dark, shoeless, in a flimsy nightgown, and although our coal stove was working and Jim built a blazing fire in the fireplace, she couldn't get warm. I gave her a pair of socks and a sweater so big for her that it fit more like a coat, and Jim brought out warm blankets that I wrapped around her twice. But Lily couldn't get warm. I made her coffee and toast and tried but failed to soothe her distress. Throughout the telling of her story, she kept interjecting, "I'm *breastfeeding* Tad," crumpling back into sobs each time she said it. By the end, I was sobbing, too. Because Lily had been breastfeeding her baby, and a dangerous abuser had broken into her hideaway, had beaten her frail body, and had snatched her baby away.

Although Lily was obviously telling the truth, I wondered about her understanding of the 911 officer's response. Surely there must have been some sort of miscommunication.

Lily was exhausted. When she finally fell asleep on our couch, I called the police to report the crime and find out what steps they would be taking to find Tad and arrest Bobby. But this was two years before the first Protection from Abuse Act was passed anywhere in the United States, and the officer's response was exactly as Lily had reported. They didn't "involve themselves" in domestic disputes.

"It wasn't a 'dispute,' " I said angrily.

"Well, that's what we call it."

"What about the fact that he was trespassing on our neighbor's property?"

"The owners of the residence can file a complaint within twenty days of the incident," the officer replied, enunciating each word with exaggerated care, as if talking to someone who had difficulty grasping simple concepts.

"He kidnapped a nursing infant!" I yelled.

The officer had an answer ready for that. It was an answer I would someday become very accustomed to hearing. "It's *his* kid, too, so it's not illegal."

When daylight arrived, I looked in the phone book for a lawyer, calling the first one listed under Attorneys: Criminal. He told me Lily could try to convince the police to charge Bobby with assault, but she'd have to know where Bobby went (which she didn't) so he could be served with a copy of the paperwork. What's more, since the case was "a domestic," assault charges would be extremely hard to prove. As for absconding with a breastfeeding baby, well, it was Bobby's kid, too.

"She could get a family law attorney to file for custody, which she may or may not win," the lawyer added, "but it sounds like she has no money and lawyers aren't cheap. Let's face it. She messed up. She should have gotten further away. Fled Pennsylvania. That's the only real solution in these kinds of cases."

Lily stayed at our house overnight. Even in her sleep, she was crying. The next day, Abe came to take her to Alison's. We stayed in touch, and rejoiced with Lily when Bobby, whose whereabouts had been unknown, finally resurfaced and gave Tad back. A friend of his convinced him to do it, and anyway he had grown tired of being stuck with a traumatized baby. Bobby kept him for five weeks, which was half of Tad's little lifetime. He was still wailing the day he was returned.

Lily's experience was my first exposure to the realities of domestic violence. It caused me to reconsider the idea of becoming a psychologist. If I ever managed to graduate from college and had a chance to continue my education, I wanted to be a lawyer. A lawyer that women like Lily could afford.

But I was 37 years old when I finally earned my college degree, and the realization came over me that law school would take another three years to complete. Even if I could go full-time, I'd be 40 years old by the time I was done. Reluctantly, I concluded that law school was a pipe dream. And I told myself I was too old to be indulging in pipe dreams.

My mother listened attentively as I explained the reason I decided not to apply to law school. When I got done talking, she said: "You're right. You're 37 years old, and in three years you'll be 40." She paused, just long enough for me to think she agreed with my decision. But then she added, slyly, almost as an afterthought, "Of course. . . in three years you'll be 40, one way or the other . . . You might as well be a lawyer."

My mother was like that, full of wit and wisdom. So I mailed my application to Temple University's School of Law, and when the acceptance letter came, I had no lingering misgivings about going to law school. Because the logic was irrefutable: I might as well be a lawyer.

3. Law Is Not About Justice

I felt like a misplaced person during my first semester at law school, and the thought of quitting crossed my mind many times. But I had taken out a five-thousand-dollar student loan to pay for that first semester, and if I dropped out of school the loan would come due. I didn't have any way to come up with that kind of money. My income for the entire year before law school had been substantially less than five thousand dollars, an accurate reflection of my earning capacity. So there was no way out. I had to stay in law school.

Because Temple University's School of Law was in Philadelphia, three counties away from our rustic abode in the boondocks of Pennsylvania, Jim and I agreed that it would not be feasible for me to commute daily. So, with money from my student loan, I rented an apartment in Philly and returned home to my husband and my real life only on weekends and school breaks. By then, my brilliant daughter Ruth was living on campus at Swarthmore College, where she'd been admitted after basically skipping high school. Just like that, we were all in different locations.

For the first few months, I was desperately lonely. Jim and I had lived together forever, and suddenly we were living apart and alone. Weekends came slowly, and sometimes even that time together was stolen from us by a work-study obligation or a too-heavy snowstorm that kept me stuck in Philadelphia.

But even worse was the problem I discovered on my very first day of law school, when the entire class—the class of 1983—was herded into a large auditorium for our orientation. The dean was speaking from the stage and everyone seemed to know exactly what he was talking about. Everyone, that is, except me. His speech was packed with legal terms, words I had never heard before, and the crowd in the auditorium was nodding knowingly, laughing at appropriate intervals, listening along. As I sat there, comprehending almost nothing, I had a mounting sense that I had gotten myself into the wrong place.

At one point, the dean asked for a show of hands: "How many of you have a parent who is a lawyer?"

I looked out over the large assembly of strangers who were now my classmates and saw almost every hand shoot up, waving proudly.

"How many of you have another close family member who is a lawyer?" he asked.

Now every hand was up and waving. Every hand, that is, except mine.

Yes, all of my classmates were the offspring, siblings, or relatives of lawyers. Quite a few of them had worked as paralegals. They had been around lawyers all or most of their lives, and they all knew the jargon. By contrast, there were no lawyers lurking anywhere in my extended family or in the families of anyone I knew. The law, with its peculiar terminology, was a foreign language to me, which I was now discovering that everyone around me spoke. I needed a translator, but there were no volunteers in sight.

Thankfully, help did arrive. I was assigned to work-study at the law school's Legal Aid Clinic, where I had been given a handful of cases to handle under the supervision of a professor who helped run the program. When he took me aside, early on, to praise me for the quality he saw in my work, I felt compelled to disclose my deep feelings of incompetence. "I really don't think I have what it takes to be a lawyer," I confessed.

"Tell me which one of your classmates you think is better qualified than you," he said.

"I think all of them are," I answered.

He looked at me steadily. "Name one."

I picked Jonathan, who always knew "the answer" and how to say it in perfect legalese.

"Do you know what I think?" the professor responded. "I think Jonathan's a pompous parrot who has memorized the right things to say. I predict he'll flunk out by the end of the year, if not sooner."

I was shocked. It's true that Jonathan did strike me as a little pretentious, but I'd attributed that assessment to my own inadequacies. Not having the money to pay back my law school loan might have kept me from quitting that first semester, but it was this unexpected, supportive exchange with my supervisor at Temple's Legal Aid Clinic that helped cure my crisis of confidence. By the time I returned to law school after the summer break to begin my second year of studies, I was not at all surprised to learn that Jonathan, along with many others, had not been invited back.

By my second year, Jim and I had become reasonably adjusted to our new circumstances, and I began to acclimate to law school. Constitutional Law, Criminal Law, and Civil Liberties & Civil Rights were fascinating to me, but my favorite course was Family Law. Family Law was all about the intricate and intriguing psychology of people. I read the cases the same way I read short stories, for the characters and for the plot. But over time, as the cases accumulated and the plots kept unfolding, the biases of the law and the courts began unveiling themselves to me. The stories did not always have the happy endings I wanted them to have, and I found myself becoming ever more resolved to do my part to change those endings when I became a lawyer.

I was interested in law because I was interested in justice, but it did not take long for me to figure out that law school—even a law school as progressive as Temple—was largely designed to teach us that justice was not the point. "Law" was composed of legislation and the precedents established by legal rulings; the role of attorneys was to represent their clients zealously within that narrowly confined framework. Justice was a whole different concept, not to be confused with the law. If I had any doubt about this, it was settled one day when I was called on in class to dissect a case from our textbook, and I expressed my belief that the court's ruling in the case was unjust.

"None of you should be wasting your time looking for justice in the law," the professor said in response, addressing the entire class while looking straight at me. "We're all *grown-ups* here."

Later that same day, one of my classmates at the Legal Aid Clinic began complaining about a client. The client was a young woman, a single parent with a very sick infant, who had been fired from her job for missing too many days of work to take care of her baby. She was being evicted from her apartment for nonpayment of rent.

"My client is so stupid," my classmate said, her tone a blend of irritation and contempt. "She actually thought she couldn't be evicted because her baby is sick and she has nowhere else to go. I told her the Landlord Tenant Act doesn't include an exception for sick babies, but she's too dumb to understand it."

"Is that what *law school* is teaching you?" I yelled at her. "That it's perfectly understandable that the law doesn't care about sick babies when those babies are poor? And anyone who has trouble accepting that fact is stupid?"

In effect, that *was* what law school was teaching us, but I was determined not to learn it. And I found some professors who were sympathetic and encouraging to my way of thinking, believing many of our laws were in urgent need of changing and that lawyers could and should be agents of that change.

I ended up doing well in law school, and in some small ways I left a mark. I was the only person who looked like a hippie in the class of 1983, so I stood out. When we were told we needed to wear a suit for our Moot Court presentation, I objected. I wasn't trying to be difficult. I just didn't own a suit and couldn't afford to buy one. I argued that wearing a suit was not a requirement listed anywhere in my letter of acceptance or on the syllabus for the course. If Temple University's School of Law was intent on my wearing a suit, Temple University's School of Law was going to have to buy one for me. My professor, faced with a mutiny he had never faced before, was stumped. He reported the situation to the dean, who called me to his office for a chat.

The dean was both loved and hated. He was a master fundraiser, so the board of directors adored him and kept increasing his salary to ensure his continued contentment with his job. But many faculty members and other school employees had grievances with actions he had taken, and he was often accused of being more of a dictator than a dean. I didn't know anything about the politics of it all. And I had no idea how he would respond—either as a dean or as a dictator—to the unique problem I was causing.

Our chat went well. The dean listened politely as I argued my case, then told me, with a big smile, that because the law school did not allocate funds for student clothing, I would have to give my Moot Court presentation wearing whatever I felt like wearing. I felt like wearing blue jeans and a plaid flannel shirt, and so I did.

4. The Only Job I Wanted

I n May 1982, at the end of my second year of law school, a Girl Scout camp in Bucks County, Pennsylvania, advertised for a camp ranger. It was a position so tailor-made for Jim that he was hired midway through his interview. Camp Tohikanee consisted of 237 acres of woodland dotted with primitive campsites. Located in the rural outer reaches of Quakertown, at the uppermost corner of Bucks County, it served as a full-time overnight camp in the summer, with a camp director, camp counselors, and a slew of little girls on-site. In the spring and fall, girl scouts and their troop leaders came for weekend campouts. The rest of the time, it was the ranger's private abode.

There were a million things for Jim to do. The many buildings and structures on the property (including the ranger's house, a wonderful perk of the position) needed to be tended to; all kinds of equipment and machinery had to be kept in good working order; the camp's large pool had to remain spotless and chlorinated to code throughout the summer; and miles of dirt roads winding through the woods needed to be maintained. There were old building projects to finish and new building projects to begin. When things broke, they needed to be fixed, and when things got dirty, they needed to be cleaned. Jim was responsible for it all.

We got to live in a large, charming house that we would never have been able to afford, surrounded by acres and acres of magnificent woods, and Jim was free to do the work the way it should be done, making the camp more functional and beautiful than it had ever been before. What's more, the camp was an entire county closer to law school than was our previous residence, reducing my 2½ hour commute each way to almost half that time. To us, it was a dream come true.

Countering this good fortune was a major occurrence that did not bode well for my career plans. In November 1980, two months after I entered law school, Ronald Reagan was elected president of the United States. His election threatened to negatively impact my future as a lawyer because I'd gone to law school with the goal of becoming a Legal Aid attorney, to help every Lily I possibly could—and Ronald Reagan despised Legal Aid.

The Legal Services Corporation—the organization that oversees the offices of what is usually called Legal Aid—had come into being as a result of President Lyndon Johnson's endeavor in 1964-1965 to eradicate poverty in America. Johnson envisioned the creation of a Great Society in which "no child will go unfed, and no youngster will go unschooled." Many initiatives were put into place in furtherance of the Great Society, such as Medicare and Medicaid (providing health care for the elderly, the disabled, and the poor); increased Social Security benefits and coverage (protecting the elderly and the disabled from becoming destitute); food stamps (helping keep poor families with children from going hungry); Head Start (enabling the children of low-income families to share in the benefits of preschool education); college grants (enabling college-eligible students from low- and middle-income families to attend college); and subsidized housing vouchers (shielding the poor from homelessness).

Legal Aid was part of this array of programs. It was designed to give low-income people access to the legal system by providing them with free legal services in noncriminal cases. The Constitution of the United States guarantees free legal representation to low-income people in *criminal* cases, where a person is facing the possibility of imprisonment, but there is no similar right to representation in noncriminal cases. While all lawyers are urged to do some *pro bono* work (a Latin phrase, meaning "for the good," used to describe legal work performed free of charge), sporadic voluntary acts of charity by individual attorneys could never provide low-income people with more than the faintest hint of access to the legal system. Legal Aid attempted to fill this gap.

In practice, funding for Legal Aid was always tight and a strict setting of priorities was always necessary, so only a small percentage of low-income people in need of legal representation could actually obtain services. But Legal Aid attorneys gained a reputation for their tireless commitment to their clients and their resolute efforts to challenge laws and practices that caused the poor to be treated unjustly. All of the work done by Legal Aid was "for the good."

It was those challenges to unjust laws that caused the battle lines to be drawn between Ronald Reagan and the Legal Services Corporation.

When Ronald Reagan was governor of California, Legal Aid attorneys in that state went to court many times to challenge the draconian cuts to social programs that Reagan had enacted, and they were remarkably successful in proving his actions to be unconstitutional or unjustified. In their representation of farm workers, Legal Aid attorneys won a number of crucial cases against powerful agricultural interests in California, interests that Reagan counted upon as allies in his political campaigns.

These Legal Aid victories on behalf of the poor made it clear that, if one's objective was to deny legal protections to laborers and cut services that assist low-income people, the first program that needed to be eliminated was Legal Aid.

Governor Reagan tried to get rid of Legal Aid in California by blocking all of its funding from the state, but he lacked the power to close it down entirely because the bulk of Legal Aid's funding came from the federal government. But now, Ronald Reagan was president of the United States.

I was right to be concerned. One of Reagan's first presidential acts was to call for the complete defunding of the Legal Services Corporation and the closing of every Legal Aid office in America.

Fortunately for Legal Aid, the American Bar Association came to its defense, and a majority in Congress refused to comply with President Reagan's "zero funding" proposal. Nonetheless, he was able, by 1982, to slash funding for the Legal Services Corporation by 25 percent. He also removed all of the corporation's board members, replacing them with people who supported his plan to dismantle it. The loss of such a large portion of its funding forced the closing of many Legal Aid offices across the country and the wholesale layoff of their attorneys and support staff.

In the midst of this devastation, Reagan continued to pressure forcefully for a 100 percent cut in federal funding.

I was one year away from graduating law school when this was happening. Providing free legal services to people who needed them most was the work I wanted to do, and all around me I could see the desperate need for it. In fact, the need was growing rapidly. But my goal of being a Legal Aid attorney was looking like a grim fantasy.

Reagan's cuts to Legal Aid were a natural part of his broader approach to government. He was a proponent of supply-side economics, an approach that is popularly referred to as the trickle-down theory of economics. Rather than putting programs in place to help the poor and middle class, the trickle-down theory asserts that what society actually needs are massive tax cuts for the wealthy. The reasoning is as follows: tax cuts make the wealthy even wealthier, giving them more money to spend and invest, and the benefits from their increased spending and investments will automatically trickle-down to the rest of the population.

In line with this theory—which has never worked but remains popular in certain circles to this day—President Reagan sought an immediate 30 percent federal income tax cut, the bulk of it benefiting those at the highest income levels. Again he fell a bit short of his objective, the richest having to settle for a tax cut of only 25 percent. At the same time, Reagan vastly increased the military budget. The huge costs of these two actions were supposed to be offset by the economic growth promised by the trickle-down theory as well as by the elimination or severe reduction of funding for government programs designed to help the non-rich.

Things didn't work out according to theory. The sudden tremendous loss of tax revenue, combined with the huge expansion in military spending, created soaring federal deficits. The national debt tripled during the Reagan presidency. As the Great Society programs were eviscerated, poverty rates rocketed. For the first time since the Great Depression of the 1930s, impoverished people sleeping on the streets became a common sight in America's cities. (When asked about the steep upsurge in homelessness, Reagan famously placed the blame where he thought it belonged, saying: "People who are sleeping on grates . . . the homeless . . . are homeless, you might say, by choice.") As more and more people fell into poverty, the number of low-income people needing free legal services rose substantially. At the same time, Legal Aid agencies throughout the country were shutting down offices and laying-off lawyers and staff.

Legal Aid salaries had always been modest. Snaring a high-paying job after graduation was a common goal for many law students, but I had gotten to know a fellow classmate who shared my desire to be a Legal Aid attorney. It was she who told me, during my last year of school, about the Reginald Heber Smith Community Lawyer Fellowship Program.

Born in 1889, Reginald Heber Smith, was an attorney who wrote a renowned book titled *Justice and the Poor*, wherein he promoted the concept of free legal assistance for poor people. "Without equal access to the law," he wrote, "the system not only robs the poor of their only protection, but places in the hands of their oppressors the most powerful and ruthless weapon ever invented." Smith's book led to the American Bar Association's advocacy of the importance of *pro bono* work, and its later vigorous support of Legal Aid.

After Smith's death, the Reginald Heber Smith Community Lawyer Fellowship Program was founded in his honor. Its mission was to encourage young lawyers to devote their efforts to representing low-income people who would otherwise have no representation. In furtherance of this mission, every year the fellowship program sponsored two law school graduates from each state in the nation to be Legal Aid attorneys. Recipients had to demonstrate "high-caliber legal talent" and a genuine concern for the concept of "justice for all." The winners, nicknamed Reggies, were paid a salary and sent to Legal Aids that had made their own successful grant applications, requesting that a Reggie be placed in their office. If the Reggie did a good job the first year, his or her fellowship would be renewed for a second year. The salary was not large, but it was larger than the salaries that Legal Aid attorneys were receiving. There was one additional requirement: one-fourth of each Reggie's time had to be devoted to a project to help the community in which the Reggie had been placed.

As soon as I learned about the existence of this fellowship program, I applied for it. I also contacted the Legal Aid in Bucks County, asking them to apply for a Reggie placement. The odds of winning were against me, I knew, because only two law school graduates would be chosen from the entire Commonwealth of Pennsylvania. But the possibility gave me hope.

On the grant application, I was required to list three places to which I would be willing to be sent if I won. The form specifically advised that, to avoid limiting my chances to be chosen, my third choice should be "anywhere in the United States." My first choice was the Bucks County Legal Aid Society. My second choice was "anywhere in Pennsylvania" and my third choice was "anywhere in the United States except the South."

I had seen the South. When I was eight years old, my family had driven from Pennsylvania through the South on our way to Mexico City for a six-month stay. It was the 1950s, and we were aghast to see White Only signs prominently displayed everywhere in every southern state we passed through. When we stopped once at a restaurant in Mississippi, my sister Diane and I defiantly chose to use the restroom designated Colored. Lit by one dim overhanging bulb, the room was filthy, with no toilet paper in the single stall and a broken-down sink in the middle of the room. There was no soap or towel dispenser. Finding the facility unusable, we went to the White Only restroom, which, in stark contrast, was very clean and well-stocked, with multiple stalls and sinks. Seeing such blatantly cruel discrimination made a lasting impression on my young mind, causing me to care deeply, forever after, about the establishment and protection of equality for all people. And it made me want never to return to the South.

I was interviewed for the fellowship program by three male attorneys from its board of directors. The interview did not start off well.

I was asked, almost immediately, about why my third choice excluded all the southern states, so I told them about my childhood experience travelling through Mississippi. One of the interviewers then asked pointedly, "So you're not willing to live in the belly of the beast?"

I was familiar with that expression from the Sixties. It meant (stated tactfully) trying to create change from inside a powerful country or institution that resists change.

"I don't mind living in the belly of the beast," I answered. "I just don't want to live in its bowels."

"*I'm* from Mississippi," one of the interviewers responded, sounding offended.

"But I see you aren't there now," I said without thinking. I'm an outspoken person, and my sense of humor can sometimes lean towards flippancy.

As soon as I said it, I regretted it. An interview to win a chance to have the career I desperately wanted was not the time or place to be flippant. The interviewer chuckled, and his two companions laughed, but I wasn't sure if they all really thought it was funny. I apologized. "I admit I'm prejudiced against the South," I said, "but I know free attorneys are needed everywhere in America, and I know many things have changed since my childhood. So the truth is, I'd go anywhere to be a Legal Aid attorney."

Three weeks later I got the call telling me that I was one of the two recipients they had chosen that year from Pennsylvania. Further, the Bucks County Legal Aid Society had applied for a Reggie, so I would be getting my first choice of assignment.

I was beyond elated. I finally had to go out and buy that suit—along with pantyhose, and a pair of flats because I could tell my moccasins didn't match the suit. But even that didn't dampen my spirits. Truly, for Jim and me, every dream we could imagine had come true.

Or so it seemed. I hadn't really thought about what I would do if I won the fellowship but was sent far away. Now the question appeared to be moot. I had made sure that the Legal Aid in Bucks County applied for a Reggie, and they had been granted one. Since I lived in Bucks County, why would the Fellowship Program send someone else to Bucks County and choose to send me far away?

Ten days before graduation, I got the answer to that rhetorical question.

I got a call from the fellowship program informing me of a change in plans. The other Reggie from Pennsylvania, a Black woman from Pittsburgh, had been assigned to a Legal Aid office in Lewistown, Mifflin County, which is a very rural area in the middle of Pennsylvania. She had visited the site and discovered the town had very few Black people. She didn't feel comfortable having to live there. And the folks in charge of the fellowship program understood her feelings, as did I. So *she* would be going to the Legal Aid in Bucks County, and I would be going to the one in Mifflin County, a three-and-a-half-hour drive from the camp.

The decision was final; there was nothing I could do about it. Jim and I had already weathered three years of being physically separated much of the time. Now we would just have to keep doing it for a while longer. It was the only job I had, and, more important, it was the job I desperately wanted.

Now I had to rent an apartment in a town I had never seen. I called the Legal Aid office there to see if someone could help, and learned that my secretary-to-be owned a number of furnished apartments next door to the office (which she also owned), one of which happened to be vacant. I promptly rented a small two-room apartment, sight unseen. If I had to live in Lewistown, it was certainly in the perfect location, just a short path from the entrance to my new place of employment.

I graduated law school ten days later, in late May. In August, Jim and I packed some of my belongings into the back of his truck and headed to Lewistown. It took us five hours to get there because we got lost along the way. When we arrived at the apartment, we unloaded the truck together and put my things inside. Jim hung a few pictures on the walls, fixed a broken latch on a cabinet door, tightened a loose leg on the kitchen table, and plugged in our TV. He had a long return trip, and our two dogs at home needed to be tended to, so he couldn't stay very long. I held back tears as he kissed me goodbye at the door, and watched him leave, wishing I could go with him.

I remember how lonely and anxious I felt, all alone in a strange place, about to begin a job I wasn't sure I knew how to do. I turned on the television to keep me company, but there was only a static haze emanating from the screen. I learned the next day that Lewistown has no reception without a cable connection because it is surrounded by mountains, but I had no idea, that evening, why my trusty TV had chosen that moment to go on the blink. It seemed as if my entire future was engulfed in fog.

5. Protection from Abuse

I slept fitfully that first night in Lewistown, waking up the next morning hours before my alarm clock signaled the official start of a new day. It was, of course, much more than a new day. Everything was new.

At 8:25 a.m., I left my apartment and walked to the Mifflin County branch office of Keystone Legal Services, counting the steps (exactly 18) from my new home to my new workplace. It amused me that the yellow brick road to Oz could be so short. I paused at the door to Legal Aid and took a slow, deep breath. "Good luck," I told myself, and opened the door.

The door opened to a waiting room that had a lived-in feel, with comfortable stuffed chairs, a bit frayed, lining the wall on the left side and shelves and filing cabinets on the right. A large oak desk was situated a few feet in front of the back wall, facing the entrance. At the desk sat a silver-haired, matronly woman in her mid-sixties, who quickly leaped up from her chair to greet me. "So you're our new lawyer!" she exclaimed heartily. "Welcome!"

Arlene Shehan was the perfect person to greet everyone who came into the Lewistown office. She had a kindly but no-nonsense, take-charge manner that made people feel instantly comfortable. You knew you were in capable hands. Arlene was not only the secretary and receptionist at Legal Aid. She owned the whole building, so she was our landlady. And she owned the apartment building where I was lodged, so she was *my* landlady, too.

Arlene called out to Leo and Lois, who both emerged from their respective back rooms to greet me warmly. Leo Vasmanis was the senior attorney. He was about fifteen years younger than me, tall, trim, and handsome, with strawberry-blond hair and green eyes. I thought he could have been a model instead of a lawyer. On the day I first met him, he had already been a lawyer for one full year, which was one full year longer than I had been one.

It turned out we complemented each other well. Leo was low-key and meticulous. He liked doing legal research, and actually enjoyed poring over the dense pages of *The Commonwealth of Pennsylvania Court Rules,* which dictated every legally necessary procedural step. He strongly preferred those areas of the law where cases inched slowly and methodically through the legal system. He wasn't fond of excitement. Given the choice, he would pick tedious paperwork over courtroom drama every time.

My arrival gave Leo the luxury to always make that choice, because I was his polar opposite. Back in those days before the internet and legal software, I dreaded doing legal research. I had no talent for it, and my final results always felt too hit or miss to be safely relied upon. As for the arcane *Commonwealth of Pennsylvania Court Rules*, they were practically impenetrable to me. They were written in a dialect of legalese so obtuse that I frequently could only shake my head in disbelief that any human being—or committee of human beings—had composed them. When I wanted to know what a rule was trying to say, I asked Leo. What I loved was family law, where the cases at Legal Aid were, more likely than not, *emergency* in nature; where there was no minute to spare, where everything needed to have been done yesterday, because people's very lives might depend on the outcome.

It turned out that Leo was also one of Arlene's tenants. It could easily have been an awkward arrangement in that small office, with too many interacting points of contact, but it wasn't. We were simply all in it together. We were family.

Lois Knepp was the office paralegal. She handled all the administrative law cases, involving issues like bankruptcy, welfare, and social security disability, at every stage from inception to negotiated settlement or administrative hearing. Lois couldn't represent clients whose cases ended up in the Court of Common Pleas, but that was only because she didn't have a law degree. Over the years, I've met a great many lawyers who could not come close to matching Lois Knepp's advocacy skills. In her mid-thirties, Lois had an engaging smile and was one of those vivacious people who always appear to be in motion even when they're sitting still. Like Arlene, Lois had been born and raised in Lewistown, and she seemed to know everything there was to know about everybody who lived there. That breadth of knowledge, which could only be acquired in a small town, came in handy for me in my cases.

The Lewistown branch of Keystone Legal Services was bare-bones, functioning with no real oversight from the executive director at the main office an hour away in Centre County. Just a secretary/ receptionist, two inexperienced attorneys, and a single paralegal, tasked with providing high-quality legal services to every low-income person in Mifflin County (and neighboring Juniata County) who had a legal problem that met our priority guidelines. It could have felt overwhelming, but that first day, meeting my new officemates, I knew without a doubt that I had hit it lucky. I had been greeted by a coterie of good, hardworking people who warmly welcomed me to join them in their honorable endeavors. I would learn from them. They would learn from me. Long before that first day ended, my initial anxiety had been replaced with pure excitement.

This was the work I was meant to do.

ભ   ભ   ભ

I spent the first few hours of Tuesday, my second day at Legal Aid, setting up my new office. The room was so small, with a desk and two chairs so large, that the project required a fair amount of ingenuity. There was barely enough space between the wall and the right side of the desk for me to squeeze through to get behind it. And it was practically impossible for me to get behind the desk from the left side of the room, because a tall, legal-sized file cabinet almost completely blocked the remaining space. The layout wasn't conducive to a quick escape.

The miniature dimensions of the room, and the massive pieces of furniture that needed to stay within it, cramped my ambitions for inte-

rior design. But I didn't have the luxury of choosing more suitable fur-
nishings because neither Legal Aid nor I could afford replacements for
what they had on hand.

I did my best to make the room feel cozy. Removing a bare overhead
bulb, I hung a multi-colored stained glass lamp from the ceiling above
the desk, which cast a soft, muted light across the room. On one wall, I
taped a colorful poster from the American Civil Liberties Union that
cheerfully illustrated the ten great freedoms preserved in our Bill of
Rights. Next to the poster, I placed my law and college degrees. Jim had
beautifully framed my law degree, the wide mat a gorgeous cobalt blue,
the wood a luminous black. With his magic touch, a traditional document
had been transformed into a work of art. On the facing wall, I suspended
a large corkboard adorned with my favorite *New Yorker* cartoons, and
with slips of colored paper printed with quotations that inspired me,
about liberty, justice, and human rights. At the center was this poignant
reflection from Anne Frank, which I re-read every morning to remind
myself anew: "How wonderful it is that nobody need wait a single moment before starting to improve the world."

I might not have had much to work with, but when I was done dec-
orating my room I was happy with the result. I was an antiquated hippie
with a law degree and a passion for justice, and my eclectic little office
conveyed that spirit.

I had just finished arranging things and was taking a minute to ad-
mire the results when Arlene informed me that my first client was on her
way. She was a victim of domestic violence who needed a protection from
abuse order, and I would be the person to get it for her.

I quickly pulled off my trusty bandana and changed into my new
suit and shoes. Then I rushed to our "law library" (a shelf of books in
Leo's room) to locate Volume 23 of *Purdon's Pennsylvania Consolidated
Statutes Annotated*. At the time, every family law in the Commonwealth
was contained in that one volume. (Over the years, Volume 23 has gradually grown in size and now fills three separate books.) I needed to read
the Protection from Abuse Act.

I had taken the family law courses in law school, but the Protection
from Abuse Act had not warranted more than a passing reference. I knew
that a domestic violence statute had been passed in Pennsylvania, but

the professor had not taught us anything about it. So I was going to have to teach myself. I felt a little queasy. Today was the day I needed to learn that law.

I read the act studiously, trying to imprint its provisions into memory. I was struck by its many limitations. Someday, I knew, I would have to do by part to improve it.

The Protection from Abuse Act had been enacted in 1976, making Pennsylvania the first state in the nation at the time to have such a law. It offered certain protections from domestic violence for a limited category of persons who were related to the abuser by either blood or marriage. Common-law marriage was legally recognized in Pennsylvania when the law was passed (it no longer is), so the act also covered "people who lived together *as if married*." However, since common-law marriage was rare and difficult to legally verify, this category offered protection to very few people. Victims of domestic violence whose abusers were not spouses or members of their family were ineligible for protection. "Living together as if married" did not include engaged couples, or boyfriend/girlfriend relationships (or ex-boyfriend/ex-girlfriend relationships), whether the parties lived together or not. Homosexuals were not allowed to marry then, so the Protection from Abuse Act offered no protection from domestic violence to any gay person whose partner was abusive (unless she or he was married, despite being a homosexual, to an abuser of the opposite sex).

Another onerous limitation of the act was that the abuser had to have "legal access" to the victim's residence. The effect of this provision was that victims who fled from the marital or family home and secured their own place to live ceased to be eligible for protection, because the abuser no longer had "legal access" to their residence. It didn't matter if the abuser continued to stalk the victim, continued to call and threaten the victim, and/or broke into the victim's new residence and attacked her. If there was no "legal access," there was no legal remedy.

Theoretically, victims who were not covered by the Protection from Abuse Act could seek protection through criminal statutes, like the laws against assaulting people, or those against stalking or making terroristic threats. But, in reality, the police did not arrest "domestic" abusers for any of those crimes. For the police and the district attorneys across Pennsylvania (and, indeed, across the entire United States), only homicide seemed to qualify as an actual crime in domestic violence cases. Short of murder, domestic violence was rarely perceived to be a criminal act. It was semi-officially described as a "dispute" between two people.

"Disputes" are not crimes.

Before protection from abuse statutes were enacted in America, there were *no* legal protections for adult victims of domestic violence. If the police responded to a call for help (which they did not always bother to do, since no crime was being committed), they would tell the abuser to "take a walk around the block to cool off," or tell the victim to find another place to stay for the night, or suggest that the victim go to the hospital to get treatment for her injuries. After which, the police would go their merry way, leaving the victim to deal, alone, with an abuser who was now enraged that his victim had had the audacity to call the police. Victims were often badly beaten and sometimes murdered shortly after the police departed.

It can take a long time for new laws to change a culture. That has proven true with protection from abuse statutes. For years after their enactment, the police continued to respond to domestic violence cases as if the laws did not exist. Police actions (if not attitudes) began to begrudgingly budge (ever so slightly) in Pennsylvania in 1990, when the Probable Cause Statute was passed, mandating that the police arrest an abuser when they have "probable cause" to believe a domestic violence incident has occurred. This is not a mandate in every state, and even in states that have this mandate, victims cannot routinely rely on its enforcement. The police can still find reasons not to respond to a call for help; not to arrive in time to apprehend the abuser; not to make the subjective assessment that there is, in fact, "probable cause" to arrest; or to announce that they'll have to arrest both parties because they just can't tell who the abuser might be (this last approach invariably makes the victim plead for no arrest to be made). So mandate or no mandate, arrests remain disgracefully rare to this day.

But this was 1983. There was only one thing that could make the police come to the aid of a victim of domestic violence, and that was if she had a protection from abuse (PFA) order. Because when an abuser violated the terms of a PFA order, he was disobeying a *judge's orders*. And since disobeying a judge's orders is against the law, it was the job of the police to arrest the perpetrator rather than suggesting he take a walk around the block. PFA orders put abusers on notice that they could no longer commit acts of violence or intimidation against their victims without risk of punishment. So getting a PFA order was (and still is to this day) a crucial first step in protecting victims.

It was now my job to get those orders for clients who were covered by the law. It was my job to help keep those victims safe.

When my first client arrived, I could hear her in the reception room speaking with Arlene. I could tell how frightened she was by the quaver in her voice.

The system was that Arlene first opened a Legal Aid file for clients before they were directed to Leo, Lois, or me. There was a two-page form in each file that had to be filled out, providing basic information about the client and the opposing party. With Arlene's assistance, it usually took about ten minutes for clients to complete the form.

I'm a fairly quick study, but I was thankful for that extra ten minutes. Between the time I was told that the client was coming and the moment that Arlene escorted her into my office, I had been able to read and reread the Protection from Abuse Act four times. I had also been able to find, in the dread *Pennsylvania Rules of Civil Procedure*, the official format for the petition that I would need to file on my client's behalf if she wished to seek a PFA order from the Mifflin County Court of Common Pleas.

"Meg, this is Tina Merrick," Arlene said, handing me the file as she brought the client into my office. Then, as she was leaving, Arlene said to Tina, "You're in good hands." Statements like that can raise my blood pressure, because I feel duty-bound to live up to them, but on this important occasion it hit me especially hard. I needed to be somebody's very competent lawyer.

I exchanged pleasantries with the client as I opened the file. The two-page form was inside, filled out in Arlene's clear script and stapled securely to the left-hand side of the file. On the right-hand side, a petition form was neatly paper-clipped. Also inside was a small handwritten note from Arlene, which said: "When you finish writing the petition, call

Judge Searer's chambers to see how soon he can give you an ex parte hearing." She included the judge's phone number.

I realized that, in my preoccupation with trying to memorize the Protection from Abuse Act, I had completely forgotten to ascertain the local procedure for actually *obtaining* a protection from abuse order. I read Arlene's instructions with relief and gratitude. If anyone was in good hands, it was me.

Tina Merrick had heard about someone getting a protection order, and she had come to Legal Aid to find out if she could get one, too. She was very young, having married two years earlier when she was only 17. Her husband, who was ten years older, had insisted that she drop out of school and would not allow her to get a job. She was hesitant, at first, to talk to me about the abusive treatment she had been enduring, about the many times her husband had hit her and the names he constantly called her. Her voice was halting at first, and tinged with shame. But the more she talked about it, the faster her words poured out and the stronger her voice became. Initially, she expressed some misgivings about going to court, worried about what her husband might do after she left him and what she would do without him. Friends and family had repeatedly warned her that she needed to do something to protect herself from her husband's escalating violence. But how could she, when he had so much power?

Yet little by little, as I talked to her about all of it—including the authority of the law that was on her side and the precious life opportunities that awaited her—I saw her lingering self-doubts getting washed away. It wasn't just her protecting herself anymore. *I* was going to protect her, too. With all the power invested in me by my law degree, I was going to help harness the powers of the court to protect Tina Merrick. So the balance of power had shifted. It was headed straight towards justice.

Tina was my first domestic violence client, and by the end of the interview I was almost overcome with empathy and anger. I did not know then that I was destined to do thousands of such interviews, and that almost every one of them would have the same effect on me. But I did understand, from the very beginning, how profound a privilege it was to have a chance to change someone's world for the better.

Mifflin County had exactly one county judge in 1983, the Honorable Francis Searer. I called his chambers after the petition was written, and his secretary said, "Come over right now." So off I went, Tina Merrick in tow, to the small courthouse in the town's center square four blocks away, to represent my first client at my first court hearing.

It was an ex parte hearing (*ex parte* being a Latin term for "on one side only"). The Protection from Abuse Act provides that a temporary order may be granted to a plaintiff at an ex parte hearing if, based on the allegations of abuse in the petition, a judge deems it necessary to protect the plaintiff and/or minor children from immediate and present danger of further abuse. An ex parte order remains in effect only until a full hearing, which is required in a Pennsylvania PFA case to be held within ten days of the initial filing of the petition.

The Mifflin County courthouse had only one courtroom and only one judge's chambers, so even for a person like me, who has no sense of direction, there was no possible way to get lost. This was fortunate, because I didn't want my client to have any reason to suspect that I had never stepped foot in the courthouse before. She had enough things to worry about.

Judge Searer's secretary took us into his chambers, and the judge stood to greet us, looking very tall in his black robe. "So you're the new Legal Aid lawyer," he said, cordially. News travels fast in a small town. "Welcome to Lewistown!"

After reading my petition, Judge Searer asked my client a few questions about the incidents of violence that she had alleged, and I chimed in here and there when her timid answers needed a bit of bolstering. Then the judge granted the temporary order we were requesting, ordering Tina's husband not to abuse, threaten, or harass her, and to have no contact with her at any location, including by telephone. He also granted Tina temporary exclusive possession of the parties' apartment. He scheduled a full hearing for the following Monday.

My client was so happy she seemed almost to be levitating. So was I.

I had thanked Judge Searer for his graciousness in welcoming me to Lewistown, and I had told him I was glad to be here. And I realized that it was all absolutely true. I *was* glad to be here, in Lewistown, even though my heart was aching for my real home, so many miles away.

6. My First Hearing

T ina Merrick and I spent time together preparing for her full hearing, scheduled for Monday morning. I learned there had been no witnesses to any of her husband's assaults, but a number of times Tina had taken photographs of her visible injuries. For use as evidence in court, the photos were highly problematic. She had taken close-up shots of the bruises—some red, some a dark purple/blue, some large, some the size of fingerprints—but it was not possible to tell whose body the bruises belonged to. In some of the photos, it was not even possible to tell exactly *where* on the unidentifiable body the bruises were located. And there was no indication as to *when* any of the photos had been taken. I was to learn that taking pictures like these is a common mistake that victims make. But on this first occasion, I found myself wondering, "What was she *thinking?*"

What she had been thinking, of course, was that the husband she loved had hit her, grabbed her, punched her . . . that she was alone, afraid, and had no one to turn to. She didn't know anything about the admissibility of evidence. She just wanted to take pictures of her injuries to keep for herself. Maybe, someday, those images might give her the strength to leave.

I decided that the photos were flawed, but they were photos nonetheless. And if a picture is worth a thousand words, a flawed picture should be worth at least a hundred.

We arrived at the courthouse early. The moment we entered the lobby, Tina whispered: "That's him." She said it without motioning in any way. I quickly scanned the room and saw only one other person. I would have thought it was a woman. The person was dressed in a gender-neutral manner, wearing blue jeans and a loose cotton shirt, with a slight frame and longish curly hair. The overall effect struck me as effeminate.

"That's your husband?" I asked, nodding in his direction. Tina had previously described her husband as looking like a "tough guy."

"Yes. That's him," Tina said.

"Do you think he looks a little . . . *girlish?*" I asked, gingerly.

Tina looked at me quizzically. "No," she said. "Do you?"

"I guess it really doesn't matter," I responded. "I'm going to go speak to him, to see if he'll agree to the entry of a final order."

So off I went, to talk to the only other person I saw in the room.

"I'm your wife's attorney," I began, by way of introduction.

Simultaneously, the person's mouth and eyes opened wide. "What the hell are you talking about?" she yelled. "Do you think I have a *wife?*"

There was no question about it. The effeminate person was definitely a woman—a heterosexual, extremely offended woman. It was not a perfect start to my day.

I returned sheepishly to my client. "Who were you talking to?" she asked innocently. "I thought you were going to talk to Tom."

I evaded her question. "Where *is* Tom?" I asked.

"Over there," she said, without motioning.

I looked across the room once again, seeing no one but the extremely offended woman, who scowled at me as my glance passed over her.

I was starting to feel desperate. "You need to point him out to me," I said.

Nervously, Tina pointed towards a hallway, at a far corner of the room, where I finally glimpsed the figure of a man. I hadn't noticed him loitering about halfway down that hallway, leaning against a wall. Muscled arms bulging from his tee shirt, he did indeed look like a "tough guy." Relieved, I walked over to talk to him.

He had come without an attorney. I told him that if I won the hearing—which I said that I fully intended to do—the judge would find him guilty of abuse before entering the order, but if he instead agreed to the order, it would be entered without a "finding of fault" on his part. I explained that the order would have the same provisions as the temporary order and would stay in place for one year.

The whole time I spoke to him, he was shuffling his feet. When he finally stopped shuffling, he mumbled, "Okay."

"We need to go into the courtroom to put our agreement on the record," I said, managing a matter-of-fact tone, as if this was something I did every day. "But remember. You can't talk to Tina ever again, starting *now*."

Tina looked anxious as I walked back to her with her husband trailing behind me.

"We have an agreement," I told her. "Let's go into the courtroom to let the judge know."

It all went very smoothly. I informed the tipstaff that an agreement had been reached; he summoned the judge; the parties swore on a Bible to tell the whole truth and nothing but the truth; and my client, the defendant and I stood before Judge Searer as I stated the terms of the agreement. After which, the judge announced that the protection from abuse order was granted and that copies of the transcript would be sent to Legal Aid, both parties, and the police.

That was it. I could hardly believe how easy it had all been. Tina was smiling. She no longer looked anxious. "You saved my life," she said.

As Tina and I left the courtroom together, we were greeted by her two sisters, who had come to escort her back to her apartment. They praised me profusely, and in that moment, surrounded by an appreciative trio of siblings, I felt quite accomplished. But then I caught a glimpse of the effeminate person who was definitely a woman, who was still in the lobby and still obviously miffed about her recent encounter with a mentally defective lawyer. She began walking in my direction.

"It was truly a pleasure to represent you," I said, hurriedly, to Tina. "But right now I've got to run." And without further ado, I made a dash for the courthouse door.

Later, back at my office, I reflected on my overall performance that day. There was no denying there was room for improvement.

7. No More Apologies

M ifflin County was almost as rural as you could get in Pennsylvania in the early 1980s, scarcely meriting its single county judge. The two neighboring counties, with even smaller populations, didn't rate that privilege; they shared a judge on alternating weeks. I don't recall the exact number of lawyers who practiced in Mifflin County, but it was so few that the Attorneys section in the local phone book took up less than one-third of a small page. For our convenience, Arlene made a copy of that part of the page and taped it inside the book's front cover.

My arrival in Lewistown instantly doubled the number of women lawyers in the county. I soon learned that my counterpart was not thrilled about this. If I recall correctly, her ad in the phone book called her "Mifflin County's only female attorney." My very existence had messed with her message.

As fate would have it, Mifflin County's former only-female-attorney became the second lawyer (after Leo) with whom I had contact. Our introductions occurred when she called my office, demanding to speak to me. As Arlene transferred the call, she forewarned me, "It's Vivian Hoffmaster. She says she's Tom Merrick's lawyer, and she sounds mad as hell."

I was forty years old, and an officially inducted member of the Pennsylvania Bar. Someone being "mad as hell" at me shouldn't have shaken me up. But it did. And it didn't help that I didn't know what Vivian Hoffmaster was mad about.

I greeted her cheerfully. "I've been looking forward to meeting you. Maybe we could have lunch some time." It seemed best to be friendly. After all, we had a gender in common.

"I'm Tom Merrick's attorney," she said, icily, making it clear that she had no desire for lunch. "What's your excuse for not informing me about the protection from abuse hearing?"

I was taken aback by her question. I had no legal or ethical obligation to notify anyone other than the defendant about the hearing date, as I'd had no way of knowing that Vivian Hoffmaster was Tom Merrick's attorney. We'd had no prior dealings. When asked at the courthouse if he had an attorney, Tom Merrick had said, "No." He'd had a week's prior notice of the hearing, giving him plenty of time to contact Vivian Hoffmaster if he had wanted her to represent him. He had obviously not chosen to do so.

So I actually had many "excuses" for not informing Ms. Hoffmaster about the hearing, the paramount one being that no excuse was needed. But instead of just saying that, I began to apologize. I was very sorry, I said, for not having known that she was Mr. Merrick's attorney. I assured her, contritely, that it would not happen again. But Ms. Hoffmaster was not appeased, yelling at me instead: "Shame on you! Your actions were *inexcusable*!"

I was in the midst of reiterating my apologies when Vivian Hoffmaster abruptly hung up the phone.

My first response to this unexpected occurrence was a feeling of anxiety. In the past, I had never been able to endure having anyone angry or upset with me. It didn't matter if I was right or wrong, I felt culpable either way, since I considered myself the one responsible for the other person's agitation. I felt obligated to apologize, and I wouldn't feel okay until my apology was accepted. But as I sat there at my desk, listening to that dial tone, I began to reflect on this attitude in relation to my new job.

I had thought I already knew the many qualities required to become the kind of lawyer I wanted to be: the ability to think analytically and deduce intuitively; the capacity to listen and learn from one's clients; an aptitude for understanding the complexities of law and psychology; a knack for weaving relevant facts into compelling true stories; a willingness to work beyond fatigue.

Sitting there at my desk, listening to that dial tone, I had an epiphany. To be the kind of lawyer I wanted to be, I also had to stop apologizing when I was in the right. How could I be an advocate for others if I was incapable of standing up for myself against unjustified attacks? My intention was to be an agent of change, which was likely to make some people rather angry at me. Under no circumstances could I let their anger deter me. Nor could I validate their anger with undeserved apologies.

I didn't know then how very many bruising battles I would have to wage over the years to win justice for the abused and impoverished people whom I was entrusted to serve, but I was starting to get an inkling. Much of the time, the fight for justice really *is* a fight, and I had to be a fearless combatant.

8. Everybody Knows Chuck

"**A** custody case is on her way!" Arlene announced cheerfully.

I had to laugh. I remembered a job I'd had as a coat-check girl at a gay bar when I was in my twenties. Whenever a throng of people showed up at the same time, the bar's bouncer, who sat on a chair by the entrance near where I was stationed, would call out to me: "Here come the coats!" It's a common insider habit, I suppose, to momentarily earmark people by the job you do for them, but both the bouncer and I knew that the bar's patrons were not material objects. A "custody case" was on her way, for sure, but no one at Keystone Legal Services would ever think of a client as merely a "case."

Cindy Brownstone was, of course, much more than a custody case. She was a good mother and a kind person, left without financial resources when her husband suddenly abandoned her for a younger woman. Now, eight months later, she was on her way to Legal Aid because he was suing her for custody of the children he had left behind.

Over the years, I would come to see a familiar pattern: men would leave marriages with little or no warning when their romantic affairs became serious enough to let them switch partners without much personal disruption. Most men, I learned, left their wives when they had another woman securely lined up to replace the original. It was different, usually, for women. Women left when they simply couldn't take it anymore.

Everything about Chuck Brownstone's actions fit the classic pattern. During the marriage, he'd spent little time with his three children, now ages seven, six, and four. He liked to roughhouse for ten minutes or so every once in a while with his son—as roughly as he could get away with under the guise of playing a game, ostensibly to help teach the little boy to "be a man." As for his daughters, he had shown no discernable interest in either of them beyond demanding that they stay clean, pretty, and quiet at all times.

In the eight months since his abrupt departure, he had asked to see his children on only two occasions. The first time, he had kept them for approximately five hours. The second time, he had called Cindy after less than three, insisting she come get them right away. Yet now here she was, sitting in my office in tears, showing me the copy of the custody petition she had been served early that morning by the constable her husband had hired.

A custody petition can be deceptive. In Pennsylvania, it's titled "Complaint for Custody," which can cause a layperson to think that primary custody is being sought, even though sometimes the petitioner is really only seeking partial custody. Reading through the petition's legal language to the last paragraph, I ascertained that Mr. Brownstone was not requesting primary custody of the children. My client began weeping in relief when I informed her of this fact—one that her husband could easily have told her, prior to filing and having her served with the petition.

I comforted her as she cried, bringing out the box of tissues that I had been advised to keep ever ready behind my desk. Arlene, who was super-alert to the sound of crying, hurried into my room with a tall glass of water. "This is for you, dear," she said to Cindy, and hurried out again.

Cindy kept crying. A dam of pent-up grief had somehow broken, and eight long months of anguish were pouring out.

"He doesn't want primary custody," I repeated, hoping that this would help comfort her. Then I added, emphatically: "And from now on, he's not the only one who has an attorney!" I thought a little detail like that might also be consoling.

Gradually my client's sobbing subsided. She wiped her eyes and tear-stained face, and said: "I'm sorry. I don't know what came over me."

"There's nothing to be sorry about," I told her. "If anyone's going to be sorry when this is over, it'll be your sorry excuse for a husband."

A beautiful smile came over her face. "Do you think so?"

I smiled back at her. "I *know* so."

I don't know how I knew it. This was my very first custody case, so I clearly didn't have a reservoir of experience to back it up. But somehow I wasn't bluffing.

There was an order page attached to the petition, setting a conference date in two weeks' time with the Honorable Judge Searer.

With my client calm, I was able to discover that she wasn't opposed to her husband having partial custody of the children. She was also sure he was aware of that, so she wondered why he had felt the need to file a custody petition. But as I learned more, the explanation as to why custody litigation had been initiated—and who was probably paying for it— became quite clear.

Cindy had heard from a number of people that her in-laws were angry at their son for so quickly (and openly) carousing with another woman after leaving his wife. They thought it looked bad. They also thought his lack of contact with his children looked bad. Yet learning that their son had secretly kept a mistress during his marriage had not fazed them. (According to Cindy, until his recent heart attack, her husband's father had never been without a mistress of his own.) Nor had it mattered to them that he'd never had a real relationship with his children.

Obviously, shameful facts that stayed hidden from view did not bother Chuck Brownstone's parents. They cared about appearances. And now their son's actions were on display in Lewistown, threatening to reflect poorly on *them*. Last and least, his conduct was cutting them off from contact with their grandchildren. According to Cindy, her assurances to them that they were always welcome to spend time with the children had not helped matters. They found it distasteful to have to interact with her, even briefly, for that purpose, so they chose not to. For them, I could see, litigation was the better route. Filing for partial custody made it look like their son had to fight to see his children.

I spent half the morning with Cindy, interviewing her in preparation for the upcoming custody conference. Together we developed a partial custody schedule that she felt comfortable with, which we agreed I would propose to her husband's lawyer prior to the conference date. Possibly the matter could be settled without the necessity of a hearing, now that she had an attorney.

Cindy Brownstone left my office looking like a different person than the one who had entered it earlier that day. She was smiling and standing tall, her head literally held high, and I noticed for the first time how very pretty she was. I promised to call her as soon as I made contact with opposing counsel.

Alone in my office, I looked again at the custody petition on my desk, searching for the name of the attorney who had filed it and was representing Cindy's husband. Finally I saw it: William Searer, Esquire.

The judge's name was Francis Searer. It was an interesting coincidence. I wondered if the surname "Searer" was common to the region.

I went next door to Leo's room, where he was engrossed in a law book, and interrupted his concentration. "What do you know about William Searer?"

Leo responded in his usual laid-back fashion. "He seems to be a nice guy. I've never had him for a case, though, so I can't say for sure."

"He's not any relation to Judge Searer, is he?"

Leo laughed. "Sort of . . . He's the judge's brother."

Leo laughed again when he saw my expression: open-mouthed yet speechless. The words I couldn't form in that moment hardly needed to be spoken: how could the judge's brother represent a client in a case being litigated in his brother's court?

The rules of professional conduct for lawyers and judges are stringent. One of the foremost rules is that a conflict of interest—or even the *appearance* of one—must be scrupulously avoided. Unless a formal waiver is signed by the client, an attorney is not permitted to undertake representation of a client if the attorney currently has, or has previously had, a relationship of any sort with the opposing party, or with a witness, or with any prior client or third party whose interests are at variance with that client's interests. The same rules applied to judges. There was no way that Judge Searer would not have, at the very least, the *appearance* of a conflict of interest if he presided over a case where his brother was the lawyer for one of the parties.

"We only have one judge in Mifflin County," Leo reminded me. "It so happens that our judge has a brother who's a trial attorney. In fact, the two of them were in practice together—Searer & Searer—until Francis Searer was elected to the bench. What's his brother supposed to do, leave town or change his profession?"

The strange reality of this state of affairs started to sink in. The only judge in the county was hardly in a position to disqualify himself on the basis of his personal relationship with one of the participants, because no other judge was available to replace him. Finally finding my voice, I began fussing loudly about the absurdity of the situation when Lois popped into Leo's room. "Meg, this is *Lewistown*," she declared. "It's a *small* town. In one way or another, *everybody* has a relationship with *everybody*. Get over it!"

So I got over it. The opposing counsel in my first custody case would be the judge's brother, and there was nothing that anyone could do about it. And who knows? Maybe they were steeped in sibling rivalry. (I had the right to hope.)

A few minutes later, I called William Searer's office and identified myself to his secretary as Cindy Brownstone's attorney. He came to the phone right away. "I *heard* there was a new lawyer at Legal Aid. Welcome to Lewistown!" he said jovially.

There was no doubt about it. I was living in a *small* town.

Leo was right. William Searer was a nice guy. He was not only amenable to negotiating an agreement prior to the custody conference, he thought my client's offer was eminently fair.

"Let me talk to Chuck about it, and I'll get back to you," he said. "I can tell you now that I'm going to urge him to accept the offer."

"Can you bring him into your office when you talk to him about it?" I asked. I wanted to separate Mr. Brownstone from his parents when decisions about custody were being made.

"That's precisely what I plan to do right now," said the judge's brother.

Before the day was over, we had an agreement.

I proceeded to draft a custody stipulation, which Arlene quickly typed and delivered to William Searer's office a few blocks away. Shortly thereafter, his secretary returned it to us, signed by her boss and his client. Cindy had already come back to Legal Aid, and we officially cemented the agreement with our signatures. I was intent on finalizing the matter as swiftly as possible, to ensure that Chuck Brownstone's parents would have no opportunity to intervene.

Cindy was extremely pleased with the almost instant result. "I have the best lawyer in America!" she proclaimed with great sincerity, as she raised both arms and waved the stipulation in the air victoriously. Her exuberant assertion obviously had no basis in fact, but that didn't detract from how good it felt to hear it.

Custody stipulation in hand, Arlene rushed to the courthouse to get it filed minutes before court closed for the day. The filing caused an immediate cancellation of the custody conference. The case was settled.

Dealing with the judge's brother had been a very pleasant experience, and when I ran into him after work a few days later at the local supermarket, I made a point to tell him so.

"Hey, it was a fair offer," he said, "and you know Chuck. You gave him exactly the right amount of time to take care of three little kids."

I was momentarily surprised by that statement, because I perceived it to be a revealing comment about his client's parenting capabilities. But then one key phrase of it rebounded with crystal clarity: "You know Chuck."

There it was, again, that strange reality that I was starting to grow fond of. In a small town, it's a small world. *Everybody* knows Chuck.

9. Escaping Howard Long

Howard Long was a true believer in the theory that the best way to hold onto a woman was to keep her barefoot and pregnant. He added frequent beatings to the mix, to quash any danger of the woman forgetting who was boss. During his nine-year marriage, his wife Margaret had given birth to four children and had suffered four miscarriages. When she suddenly ran off with the children in the dead of night while he was sleeping, Howard was left with nothing to hold onto but his rage.

Margaret had fled with the children before fully recovering from her most recent miscarriage, taking almost nothing with her, and Howard had no idea where she had gone. Prior to her escape, he had gotten it into his mind that his wife had secretly had her fallopian tubes tied while she was in the hospital. That must have been the reason, he concluded, that it was taking her longer than usual to recover from her last miscarriage. It couldn't have had anything to do with the almost daily beatings he had been administrating, to discipline her for her recent laxness in cleaning their house to the level of his expectations.

Howard had also gotten it into his mind that the lawyers at Legal Aid, in collusion with Margaret's doctor, must have convinced her to do it.

We first became aware of Howard Long and what was in his mind when he placed a midnight call to Leo, whose home number was listed in the phone book, in order to inform Leo that he was going to exact "the ultimate punishment" on the "scheming vermin lawyers" at Legal Aid for what we had done to him. He followed this up with a series of menacing phone calls to our office, demanding to be told where we were hiding his wife and children and advising us that we were going to pay the price for our villainous acts.

Neither Leo nor I had ever had the occasion to meet Margaret Long, a fact we thought relevant and tried to convey to him each time he called, but he did not believe our claims of innocence. Arlene contacted the police, who told her to give them a call back if and when Mr. Long came into Legal Aid without our permission and "took steps" to do us harm. I wondered what steps he would have to take before it triggered our right to request a policeman's help. During a conversation with a neighbor of Howard's, who told us all about Howard's abuse of his wife, we also learned that he was a gun fancier and possessed a huge arsenal. Naturally, this piece of information added to our anxiety. When I told Jim about it, he insisted I purchase a gun of my own and learn how to use it. But I couldn't imagine shooting at anyone. Instead, I tried to deal with the situation by joking about it.

Everyone at the office had a shiny, gold-colored nameplate displayed at the front of their desk. Arlene had ceremoniously presented me with mine on my first day at work. My big joke was to tell Arlene that I had decided to give my nameplate to her as a gift and hoped she would place it prominently on her desk in the reception room. All I asked in return was that she give me *her* nameplate in exchange, as a token of her appreciation. As humor goes, it wasn't up to my standards, but we were stressed enough to consider it funny.

Leo responded to the situation more stoically. Basically, he ignored it all and went about his business as if a crazed abuser was not threatening to kill us.

Leo and I suspected that the entire sterilization story, not just our complicity in it, was a figment of Howard's disturbed imagination, but we knew it was useless to try to convey that thought to him, no matter how carefully it could be worded. A friend of Arlene's, who wanted to be helpful, suggested that the smartest thing for us to do would be to commiserate with Howard.

"Tell him you're as outraged as he is about his wife's immoral behavior," her friend advised.

But that was not an approach we were willing to consider. Any external validation of the legitimacy of Howard's anger might put his wife in greater danger. It may sound odd, but one has to be able to live with oneself, whether one lives or dies.

Along with Leo's safety and mine, I was worried for the safety of Margaret Long. I thought there were ways I could aid her and her children, but, like Howard, I had no idea where she was. Lewistown didn't have a battered women's shelter. In fact, there was no shelter of that kind in all of Mifflin County or in any of the adjacent counties. However, I had heard whisperings about a sort of Underground Railroad that existed in the mountainous landscape outside of town, a sparse network of safe houses that might offer temporary sanctuary to victims of domestic violence. Maybe Margaret and her children were hiding in one of those secret places. But how could I locate her to offer my services?

I searched the small Human Resources section at the front of the local phone book, looking for a helping agency besides Legal Aid that Margaret Long might have turned to for assistance. There weren't many, but one stood out: Planned Parenthood. I decided to go to their office in person, since the information I needed was not of a nature to casually solicit over the phone. Like every establishment in Lewistown, it was only a few blocks away.

The Lewistown branch of Planned Parenthood turned out to be just a small outreach office, a one-room storefront manned by a part-time employee named Tommi Solms, who bore the title of assistant to the director. She was in the office when I arrived. After introducing myself as the new Legal Aid lawyer, I first asked her to educate me about her agency. She was happy to oblige, explaining that Planned Parenthood offered a broad spectrum of women's healthcare services, priced on a sliding scale that enabled the poor to receive medical treatment free of charge. Tommi performed counseling sessions at the outreach office, but for other services she could only refer them to the fully functioning Planned Parenthood clinic in Centre County, an hour or so away.

I told Tommi about Legal Aid's current dealings with Howard Long and my concern for the safety of his wife, and asked her if she had any knowledge about the existence of local safe houses. She did have some knowledge, she said, and was a person to contact if I had an abused client who needed to flee, but she had "a feeling" that Margaret Long was not presently at a safe house. She had "a feeling" that Margaret and her children were indeed at a safe location, but that it might be far from the Commonwealth of Pennsylvania.

I got "a feeling" that Tommi's feelings were accurate. The news was a great relief.

At the time, abuse victims in Pennsylvania could lawfully flee with their children if no custody order was in place. Pennsylvania's law has since changed. Now, even when there is no custody order, a victim of domestic violence is not allowed to leave the jurisdiction with her children without the written consent of the other parent or the issuance of a court order.

Tommi told me that the few safe houses outside of town were no match for the need, and that their proximity to town often made their residents vulnerable. It wasn't the only life-saving aid that couldn't be gotten in Lewistown. Tommi sometimes worked with rape victims, and she spoke of the many supportive services they needed to help them overcome the traumas they had endured. They needed a trained advocate to help them interact with the police. They needed someone knowledgeable and compassionate to accompany them to court proceedings if criminal charges were filed. They needed individual and/or group counseling. They needed assistance with relocating, or with applying for financial aid. They needed helping hands for all the injured aspects of their lives. But what they needed first and foremost was a safe place to live during their recovery.

Tommi told me she had long envisioned the opening of a rape crisis center in Lewistown for residents of Mifflin County, with shelter facilities and comprehensive services. I loved the idea but offered one modification, to which Tommi quickly agreed: "Mifflin County should have a place like that for *all* abused women."

So it was settled: Mifflin County needed an *abuse center*, located in Lewistown. Now we just had to do something about it.

I was happy as I walked the short distance back to Legal Aid. Margaret Long and her children were evidently safe and free. And Tommi and I had made a date to meet again in three days, to begin strategizing about the steps to come.

The good news continued when I got to the office. It was the end of the workday, and no one had heard from Howard Long. We didn't know it then, but in fact we would never hear from Howard again. How or why we dodged that bullet remains a mystery. We wrote it off as luck, and, following Leo's lead, we went about our business.

10. Change of Plans

The office hours at Keystone Legal Services were strictly regimented. We opened at 8:30 a.m. sharp, closed for lunch at noon, reopened at precisely one p.m., and closed for the day at 5:30. I don't know how it was decided that everyone should take a one-hour lunch break at the exact same time, but the policy was firmly in place when I arrived. Early on, I successfully negotiated a personal deviation from that rigid schedule, the result being that every other weekend I was permitted to leave the office at noon on Friday (if I didn't have a hearing), and not to return until one p.m. on Monday (if I didn't have a hearing). In exchange, I agreed to make up the time by working every remaining weekday until 6:30 p.m. The extra time off every other weekend enabled me to spend those weekends with Jim, and to make the approximately three-and-a-half-hour drive to and from Bucks County during daylight hours. As for the agreement that an hour of work be added to all the other weekdays, it didn't really change anything for me. Like Leo, it had already been customary for me to remain working at the office long after the doors had officially closed.

Meanwhile, Tommi and I began meeting to lay out an action plan for the founding of an abuse center in Lewistown. We wanted to define our mission carefully before we began the process of gathering together a group of volunteers willing to dedicate their time and energy to the endeavor. We knew the array of services we wanted the center to offer to clients throughout Mifflin County, but we also knew we were unlikely to amass sufficient funds quickly enough to be able to offer all those services from the start. To prioritize the most pressing needs, we had to be able to make an informed assessment. We had to educate ourselves on how nonprofit organizations are established and how to find the right people to serve on the board of directors. Finally, we had to identify funding sources and develop fundraising strategies.

Having only been in town for three months, I was far too much of a newcomer to know the best local people, organizations, and political leaders to turn to, while Tommi was a Lewistown local, so she knew everybody. We decided that after we had gained a clear sense of all the steps that needed to be taken, Tommi would put out a call for volunteers to join in the work.

It happened that the Reggie Fellowship that paid my salary actually had a built-in provision for one-quarter of my work time to be spent away from the office, working for the betterment of the community. The Fellowship didn't issue any guidelines about what particular kinds of community efforts we Reggies were supposed to devote a quarter of our time to. I knew I wasn't the only Reggie, fresh out of law school, to be suddenly deposited into the middle of what was, in some ways for us, a foreign land, so I had wondered how this rule about extracurricular activities could be applied. It had seemed enough of an achievement to start learning how to be a lawyer, a set of skills that law school does not teach its students. Not only that, but no one at Keystone Legal Services, either at the Lewistown branch or at the main office in Centre County, had shown any inclination to view me as anything less than their 100 percent, full-time Legal Aid attorney.

When I originally spoke to the second in command in Centre County about the fact that I was supposed to spend only three-quarters of my time working directly for Legal Aid, she said the Reggie Fellowship didn't strictly enforce that provision. I was a little uncomfortable with her casual dismissal of the issue, but part of me was relieved. Finding a way to spend ten hours of my week on an undefined community activity in a community I barely knew had felt like an insurmountable task. But now I had stumbled upon a quintessential project for the betterment of the lives of my neighbors. Helping to create an abuse center for Lewistown was a project to which I was more than willing to devote every spare minute of my time.

I didn't want to clash with my bosses at Legal Aid. I understood their desire not to have my time be diverted, because the Lewistown office certainly needed no less than two full-time attorneys. But Lewistown also needed an abuse center, and the Reggie Fellowship expected me to spend a quarter of my time on just such a project. The dilemma seemed unsolvable until an obvious fact struck me: there are many more than 40 hours in a week. I could spend 25 percent of my time on a community project without impinging for a minute on my schedule at Legal Aid. All I had to do was add the 25 percent, not subtract it. My job officially ended at 6:30 p.m. on weekdays, but I rarely went to bed before midnight, and I stayed in Lewistown every other weekend. So the matter was settled to everyone's satisfaction. I would work for Keystone Legal Services full-time and still faithfully honor all of my Fellowship obligations.

My caseload was quite manageable. There were a number of custody and child dependency cases, which so far I'd been able to resolve to the benefit of my clients without having to go to court. And there was a steady flow of protection from abuse cases, which I loved handling. The Protection from Abuse Act mandated an expedited legal process, making it possible to change people's lives—and sometimes to *save* people's lives—very quickly. For me, there was nothing more rewarding than having the opportunity to assist with that process.

It was easy to litigate PFA cases before the Honorable Judge Searer. He seemed genuinely sympathetic to the plight of victims of domestic violence. He always made himself available for ex parte hearings, and he had granted a final order for protection to every one of my abused clients. Because the population of Mifflin County was small, each case was heard in its own special time slot. In court, there was never a "calling of the list" because there was never a list of cases scheduled. At the time, I had nothing to compare the system to, so I did not fully appreciate how relatively stress-free it all was. But I knew I liked it.

I also liked the town itself. I liked that everything was within walking distance, that the people were so friendly. Except for instances of domestic abuse—which, tragically, occur everywhere—crime was practically nonexistent in Lewistown (perhaps because, in such a small town, it would be hard for a perpetrator to escape identification). Lewistown was also a picturesque, peaceful village, lying alongside a graceful river, nestled amid majestic mountain ranges. If it weren't for the fact that my husband lived 158 miles away, with our two beloved dogs that pined for me, I would have been glad to live in Lewistown forever.

But my husband *did* live 158 miles away, so leaving Bucks County on a Monday morning was always very hard. Once back in Lewistown, I was too busy during the day to think about Jim, but late at night I missed him terribly. We spoke every evening by telephone—usually briefly, because gabbing on the phone does not come naturally to either of us—but there was no denying the physical distance between us. I feared that, eventually, it might begin to distance us in other ways.

But then, in February 1984, seven months after my arrival in Lewistown, I got a call from David Tilove, the executive director of the Bucks County Legal Aid Society.

I had met with David on one occasion, near the end of my last year in law school, to discuss the fact that I was going to be applying for a Reginald Heber Smith Community Lawyer Fellowship and wanted him to make an application for Bucks County to be a Legal Aid program recipient. We had an instant rapport. I talked to him about my burning desire to be a Legal Aid lawyer and about the fears I had that President Reagan's continuing efforts to eradicate the Legal Services Corporation nationwide would eventually be successful. David expressed optimism that Legal Aid would prevail, and assured me that a compelling application for a Reggie placement would be completed by him that very day. When I got the great news that I had been selected and would be sent to the Bucks County Legal Aid Society, David was the first person I called. And when I learned that plans had been changed and I was being sent to a different program, he was again the first person I called. "If we are ever in a financial position to hire another attorney, you'll be the one," he said. But I knew there was little likelihood that they'd ever be in such a position.

Now Arlene was informing me that David Tilove was on the phone. I knew it wasn't possible that more funding had become available. So I told myself that it was just a friendly call from a very nice guy. But I could hear the rapid beat of my heart as I picked up the phone.

David had surprising news: the other 1983 Reggie from Pennsylvania had just been hired by a law firm in Philadelphia. In two weeks' time, the spot that was supposed to have been filled by me would be available. Did I still want the job?

What wonderful luck!

Except that I was instantly gripped by nuggets of doubt. Did I really want to leave Lewistown so soon? Did I really want to leave everyone and everything behind—my colleagues, my clients, Tommi, our shelter plans? But really, did I have a choice? What other opportunity would I have to return to the family I'd been forced to leave behind and still be a Legal Aid lawyer? It was now or maybe never.

I told David, "Of course I still want the job."

David advised me to quickly contact the coordinator at the Reginald Heber Smith Fellowship, the person who had called me at the beginning to tell me that I'd been chosen and who later had had to inform me that I would be working in Mifflin County rather than Bucks County. He had been apologetic then. But now he was caught off guard and seemed irked by my call. "How did you find out about this?" he asked, as if it had been misconduct on the messenger's part to have informed me. It was apparent that he'd had no intention of telling me about the vacancy.

His question made me angry. "I *should* have found out about it from *you.* I've been separated from my home and my husband since my placement in Bucks County was taken away from me. I understood, and accepted, being demoted to second in line for that placement, but now it's become available. Don't you think *justice* demands that it be offered to me?"

It took a moment for the coordinator to respond. "You're right," he said finally, his voice softening. "You can transfer to the Legal Aid in Bucks County if that's what you want to do."

"I'll give a month's notice," I said.

Management at the main office in Centre County were displeased when notified of my impending departure, but my coworkers in Lewistown responded perfectly: sad that I was leaving but glad that I was happy. Leo, who had grown up in Bucks County in the house his parents still lived in, asked me to put in a good word for him if the Bucks County

Legal Aid Society ever had another opening for a lawyer. (Years later, I would have the opportunity to do so.)

I felt terribly guilty about leaving. But Leo assured me that he could take over my caseload, which hadn't grown very large. And Tommi had already been gathering other folks to join our mission, so I knew the work would proceed perfectly well without me. I felt confident that my clients would be well served, and that, someday soon, Mifflin County would have an abuse center in Lewistown.

The day in March that Jim arrived to help pack up my belongings and load them into his truck for the trip back to the camp was bittersweet. As Jim finished packing the last of my things into the back of his truck and asked, "Are you ready to leave?" I was filled with mixed emotions. Looking out at the town and the scenic mountains surrounding it, I realized that somehow, in a brief period of time, the place that had seemed like the middle of nowhere had begun to feel like home.

Jim and I left Lewistown together, in our separate vehicles, driving the three-plus hours to Quakertown without a stop. The vast expanse of lawn at the camp's entrance was glistening with vestiges of the last snowfall, clinging to the roofs of the house and the four outbuildings that dotted the land surrounding it—the old barn, the arts and crafts building, the rustic trading post, and the one-room staff house where camp counselors would gather each summer to gossip and eat pizza and popcorn on their nights off.

As we pulled into the long driveway, I saw our darling dogs, Tigger and Bambi, standing at the top of the lane, as they always did when I returned, wagging their tails furiously. Every other weekend they had been there, two little dogs eagerly awaiting my arrival. I had often wondered aloud about how they possibly knew when I would be coming, and Jim's only answer had always been, "It's a mystery." But now he confessed that our dogs had waited there for me at the top of the lane, for hours and hours, every single day that I was gone.

Tigger's entire body was wagging and Bambi was jumping up and down as I got out of the car to greet them. I plopped onto the ground, laughing, as they leaped on top of me and lathered my face with kisses. Jim drove slowly past us to the front of the house and began unloading my things from his truck.

It felt so strange and wonderful to leave home and arrive home in different counties, all in the same day. But it was official now. This is the place where I live.

11. "This Has to Change!"

T here wasn't much time to settle in. We got back from Lewistown at about four p.m. on a Saturday and my new job was to start at nine a.m. on Monday. Although I didn't feel the level of apprehension I had experienced before my first day of work in Lewistown, I was definitely nervous about meeting all the staff at the Bucks County Legal Aid Society. It was a much bigger agency than the little Lewistown branch of Keystone Legal Services. And although people often don't realize it, I am shy.

The camp was in Quakertown at the far upper edge of Bucks County, while the Bucks County Legal Aid Society was in Bristol at the far lower edge. The trip between the two took about an hour and a half each way, two hours or more during rush hour. It was going to be a big change from my days at Keystone Legal Services, where my trip to work took less than a minute, measured in mere steps. But the long commute was a small price to pay to be reunited with my family.

I had heard a lot about Bristol. It bordered on the Delaware River and had once been a thriving industrial hub, home to bustling factories and shipyards. But those factories had emitted millions of pounds of toxic chemicals and industrial wastes, making the river a bit akin to an open sewer. Bristol's industrial heyday was long over by the early 1980s, but Rohm & Hass and the Du Pont Chemical Company were still dumping lethal chemicals into the river, and I was told that the fumes rising from it could still make vulnerable people sick.

Bucks County is known for its charming towns, but Bristol then was not yet one of them. However, it was one of the few places in Bucks County where poor people could afford to live, so it was the right place for Legal Aid to be.

Because I have no sense of direction and am compulsive about never being late, I left for work at six a. m. that Monday morning to be sure to get to work by nine. I had gone to the Bucks County Legal Aid Society one time in the past, to ask that they apply for a Reggie, and had managed to get lost both coming and going. One prior visit was not nearly enough to keep that from happening again. True to form, I got lost on the way to *find* Bristol and lost again when I was *in* Bristol, searching blindly for One Pond Street.

When I finally pulled into Legal Aid's parking lot, I still had thirty minutes to spare, which gave me plenty of time to sit and peer at the structure that housed my new workplace. It was a many-storied rectangular box, drab and poorly maintained, and lacking the slightest hint of architectural style. Despite its considerable size, the first floor had no windows. An old-time gas station/car repair shop was on one end of the building and a new-and-used tire store was on the other, with the Bucks County Legal Aid Society ensconced in the middle. It wasn't very good-looking. But looks aren't everything.

When I walked into Legal Aid's waiting room, I was struck by how grungy it was and by the number of people waiting inside it. Aged metal chairs filled with clients lined the room. Children were everywhere, squirming in their mothers' laps or running around the room, crying and laughing and fussing and shrieking, while a parent or two chased them and other people yelled at them to stop. The linoleum floor was covered with cracks and scuff marks, and the walls (a fading color best described as "Old Caucasian Flesh") had dark stains in random places.

Looks aren't everything, I reminded myself.

David Tilove came out to greet me and took me on a tour of the office. He led me down a long, circular hallway, with small rooms on each side, stopping briefly at each room to introduce me to its inhabitant. Counting David and me, there were six attorneys, one a volunteer, as well as three paralegals, five secretaries, one administrative assistant, one receptionist, and two file clerks. I don't easily remember names or faces, so all these short introductions were mostly a blur. I got a friendly Hello from everybody, but everyone was too busy working to have time for chit-chat.

"This is *your* office," David finally said. My eyes were instantly drawn to three stacks of files, each about three feet high, teetering precariously against a wall. "Those are for you," he said breezily. They were the active cases left behind by the departed Reggie.

As quickly as that, I too had no time for chit-chat.

ઝ ઝ ઝ

I had been devastated when the representative from the Reginald Heber Smith Fellowship had called to inform me that I would be going to Keystone Legal Services instead of the Bucks County Legal Aid Society. But now I realized how incredibly fortunate that turn of events had been. At the Lewistown office, I had been part of a supportive team, and the guidance and nurturing I received there had made me brave.

At the Bristol office, I was pretty much on my own.

Eight months before, I don't know if I could have managed being on my own. But going to Lewistown had provided me with the confidence and know-how I needed. Isn't it interesting how often a seemingly bad thing turns out to be a good thing in the end?

My experience at Lewistown was also invaluable in other ways. It gave me the perspective to question how family law cases were being handled at Bucks County Legal Aid, and the conviction to insist that certain policies and practices be changed.

What most needed changing was the approach to protection from abuse cases. At Lewistown, I'd become accustomed to meeting with victims of domestic violence on the same day they contacted our office. In fact, unless I was in court on another matter, our policy at Keystone Legal Services had been to meet with all such clients as soon as they could physically get to our office. I assumed abuse cases were handled that way at every Legal Aid office. Now I learned otherwise.

I was walking by the waiting room when a young woman, disheveled and distraught, rushed in from outside and told Rosemarie, the receptionist, that she'd been beaten by her boyfriend. Half-crying, she asked to see a lawyer.

"I'm very sorry,' Rosemarie said, "we don't take walk-ins."

I could hardly believe my ears. I could tell from the soft tone of her voice and the caring look on her face that Rosemarie felt sorry saying it, but she had said it nonetheless.

As the young woman started to cry, Rosemarie quickly added: "I can schedule an appointment for you. There's an opening next Friday afternoon at three p.m. Do you want to take that appointment?"

I rushed into the waiting room and spoke to the young woman the way Arlene would have spoken to her. "I can meet with you right now, dear. Come with me."

Rosemarie looked startled. "I thought you needed to go through the rest of your new case files today," she said.

I spoke calmly, although my insides were churning. "My files aren't in danger. I can deal with them tonight."

At the end of the day, Rosemarie came to my office to talk to me. She said, "I'm sorry I didn't check with you first this morning. It's just that . . . it's against our policy to take walk-ins. I'm supposed to enforce that rule. Walk-ins disrupt our scheduling."

Again I spoke calmly. "We need to change that policy. When people are in crisis, we need to help them. Delay in these cases is dangerous."

Rosemarie stared at me. I braced myself for what she was going to say.

"I'm really glad you're here," she said.

I exhaled, unbracing. "I'm glad, too," I said.

Rosemarie told me that victims of domestic violence who called for help typically had to wait as long as two weeks for an appointment. Those who came without an appointment, like the young woman that morning, were told they needed to schedule one, and were turned away.

This was shocking to me. Victims of domestic violence are almost always at imminent risk of further abuse. They should never be made to wait in line for potentially life-saving intervention. It is common for victims to reach out to Legal Aid for help within hours of being badly assaulted or threatened with serious injury or death. They typically call at the peak of their physical and emotional desperation to find a way to escape from their abuser. If help can't come quickly, they often lose their courage and resolve. The little faith they might have had that any real help could possibly be out there for them fades quickly when no help is forthcoming. The longer the wait to see a lawyer, the greater the drop-out rate. In Bristol, when the waits were at least a week, more than half of the callers would be no-shows.

One of the secretaries overheard our conversation and came over to join it. "Abuse victims are fickle, in my opinion" she commented. "First they demand instant attention, and then you can't rely on them to even show up for their appointments."

I didn't want to alienate a new coworker during my first week on the job, but opinions like hers needed to be refuted.

"If someone were drowning, crying out desperately to be saved, and a lifeguard responded, 'Be patient. I'll get to you in a week or so,' who would you say can't be *relied upon*—the victim or the lifeguard?"

The secretary chuckled. "Well, I guess I see your point."

Why, I asked, did Bucks County Legal Aid have these harmful policies?

The secretary had an answer. "We never have more than one lawyer and one paralegal who know PFA law and how to draft that kind of petition. So, really, it's the best we can do."

It was infuriating how casually she said it. For a second, I wanted to yell at her. But it wasn't really her fault. It was a cover story she may have heard many times before adopting it as her own. This wasn't a small office in a little place like Lewistown, where secretaries had a say in setting polices.

"Actually, it *isn't* the best we can do," I said firmly.

And Rosemarie, sweet Rosemarie, repeated: "I'm really glad you're here."

As if the usual reasons to act quickly in these cases were not reasons enough, Rosemarie informed me that Judge Link, whose seniority gave him great authority over family court, had a little rule he'd made up about the granting of PFA orders. He insisted that the most recent incident of abuse had to have occurred within two weeks of the filing date of the petition. If more than two weeks had elapsed, the petition would be denied. The delays experienced by victims waiting to speak to a lawyer at Legal Aid automatically deprived many of them of the crucial protection the law was meant to provide.

Apparently no attorney in the entire county had dared to challenge Judge Link's fabricated rule, even though no trace of it existed in the Protection from Abuse Act. Further, no one at the Bucks County Legal Aid Society was taking his rule into consideration when scheduling appointments for victims of abuse.

As bad as all this was, there was more. Rosemarie told me Legal Aid never requested a temporary protection order prior to a final PFA hearing. According to her, Bucks County lawyers never did.

In Lewistown, besides seeing abuse victims right away, we *always* sought temporary protection orders for our clients. Leaving an abuser can be life endangering. A victim trying to escape should have immediate protection.

"For God's sake, why would temporary protection orders not be requested?" I asked. It was almost beyond comprehension.

Again it was the secretary who answered. "Our judges don't give temporary orders in protection from abuse cases. Judge Link is opposed to them, so it's a waste of time to try to get one."

When I asked who at Legal Aid had advanced that "waste of time" notion, I was told that the attorney who had handled the family law caseload for many years in the past—now retired—had had a firm policy of never doing anything that might irritate a judge. The other Reggie had inherited this policy when she arrived. Now that she was gone, there was no one to stop me from changing things. And if anyone had tried to stop me, they would have had a fight on their hands.

My contact with the executive director David Tilove had been limited. But now I needed to talk to him again. I was going to change things drastically, and it seemed prudent to warn my boss of my intentions.

The door to David's office was always open. He was always sitting at his desk, his back to the door, engrossed in thought or paperwork, typing away on his computer, or talking on the phone. He was forever busy. But as I soon learned, David always managed to make time for anyone who needed it. When I appeared in his doorway the next morning, he turned in his seat and asked, "What's up?"

I considered this an invitation to vent, and I did—at length. David didn't interrupt me. I gradually saw from David's facial expression that he'd been unaware of the issues involved. He had left scheduling decisions to the attorneys, and, although his knowledge of the law was extensive, family law was not an area of his expertise.

"This has to change!" I said adamantly.

David rose from his seat. "I agree with you completely. Thank you for bringing all this to my attention. Do you have a plan?"

I did have a plan. It involved me teaching the Protection from Abuse Act to every lawyer and paralegal in the office, training them on how to interview victims of domestic violence, and coaching them on how to draft a compelling petition. Including David, we had six lawyers and three paralegals. Surely that was enough people to allow us to always be able to meet with abuse victims on the same day they called, or, if they came to Legal Aid without calling, to meet with them the minute they walked in the door. I would review the petitions before they were filed, provide ongoing supervision, and take the cases to court. Victims would be helped so promptly that Judge Link's phony two-week rule would never be applicable due to our failings. But if he or any other judge dismissed a PFA petition because a client of ours had chosen to seek a protection order more than two weeks after the last time she was abused, Legal Aid would file an appeal, which I was confident we would win. And prior to representing our clients at final PFA hearings, I would seek temporary protection orders for every one of them.

By the time I finished expounding on my plans, David was nodding his head enthusiastically. It turned out my new boss appreciated zealotry. "Your plans sound great," he said. "Put them into effect any way you see fit."

I got started that very day, and the impact was immediate. Domestic violence victims no longer drifted away in droves. Instead they *came* in droves, and all of us were permanently on call to assist them promptly. It created a lot more work for everyone, and some colleagues were initially resistant. They already had plenty of work to do and, at Legal Aid, more work didn't translate to more income. But I cajoled and lectured and got mad and waxed eloquent, and gradually the pockets of grousing ended and everyone came fully around.

We could all see that we were working together to save lives. Who wouldn't want to be a part of that?

12. A Breakthrough

T he first time I filed a protection from abuse petition in Bucks County, I included a request for a temporary protection order. The prothonotary of family court, which is what the head clerk is called at the office where family court documents are filed (and also, as a short-cut, what people call the office itself), took note of it, saying, "I've never seen one of *these* requests before."

"You'll be seeing them from now on," I told her.

The assigned judge for the case was the Honorable Michael J. Kane, who would become one of my favorite judges. He had a razor-sharp intelligence that slashed through the obfuscating webs that some lawyers were adept at weaving to keep the truth from showing. He had the ability, in a flash, to size up attorneys, parties, and witnesses with uncanny accuracy. For me, who was constantly battling for the truth to be seen and so often had to deal with opponents who were skillful liars and judges who at best lacked discernment, Judge Kane was a gift.

Many other attorneys disliked Judge Kane, either because of his penetrating brilliance or because he had a mercurial temper and little patience for displays of mediocrity. He expected attorneys to come prepared, to know what they were talking about when they opened their mouths, and to do a good job, and he could get very angry if any of that didn't happen. He had been known to announce a ten-minute recess by suddenly storming out of his courtroom in an exasperated huff.

I would never come to court unprepared, and I always thought I knew what I was talking about, but doing a good job to Judge Kane's demanding standard added a higher level of stress to a day in court. Yet it was an important stress, because doing a good job for my clients and for the advancement of the causes I held dear was the reason I was there. So I was always glad when Judge Kane was presiding in a custody or abuse case of mine. In fact, whenever possible, I would finagle in every way I could to get him assigned to be my judge.

But when that first ex parte hearing was scheduled on my request for a temporary protection order for my client, the Honorable Michael J. Kane was an unknown entity to me. Judge Kane sat only in family court, so the other lawyers at Legal Aid, who represented clients in the other areas of law that Legal Aid handled (such as landlord/tenant, Social Security, welfare, bankruptcy, child dependency, and unemployment compensation cases) hadn't had occasion to make his acquaintance. In Lewistown, either Arlene or Lois knew everything about everyone in court. But the snug cocoon of Lewistown was far behind me now. Surrounded by many more coworkers, I was nonetheless on my own.

So I was nervous, sitting with my client outside Judge Kane's chambers, waiting to meet him for the first time. Waiting to try to get a temporary protection order for the first time in Bucks County, as far as I'd been told.

After a few minutes, Judge Kane's secretary poked her head into the half-opened door to his chambers, spoke briefly with him, and then told us, "Judge Kane will see you now."

I put my arm around my client and whispered gently, "Don't be nervous." I was saying it to myself as much as to her.

Judge Kane was standing behind his desk when we entered. He was tall and slender, like Mifflin County's Judge Searer, but younger. He looked to be about my age, which I found comforting. We're peers, really, I told myself. He was also rather good-looking, I quickly noticed, a humanizing detail that added to my growing sense of calm. He was a good-looking guy my age, whose signature I happened to need. It was as simple as that.

And it *was* as simple as that, almost. After Judge Kane reviewed the petition, taking his time as he read my graphic descriptions of the many incidents of abuse my client had suffered at the hands of her husband, he addressed her with a voice full of sympathy, "Is everything that is written here true?"

My client lowered her head, her voice a whisper. "Yes. All of it."

Judge Kane looked over the statutory list of temporary protective relief provisions that I had requested for his approval. They included the provisions that the defendant be prohibited from abusing, threatening, or harassing the plaintiff; that he be prohibited from having any contact with her at any location; and that he, as well as any third party on his behalf, be prohibited from contacting her by telephone or any other means. My client didn't want to return to the marital residence, and the parties had no children, so I didn't have to broach the potentially more contentious issues of whether or not a defendant should be temporarily evicted from his home or deprived of the full array of his custodial rights by way of an ex parte proceeding.

Judge Kane lifted a pen from the top of his desk, and I watched and counted, with my breath held, as his hand moved quickly down the proposed order page, placing a check mark beside each requested provision. Then, with a grand flourish, he signed the temporary protection order and handed it back to me. My breath expelled, like a sigh.

"Thank you, Your Honor," I said, in an entirely professional tone, when what I really wanted to do was shout out, "Hallelujah!"

Judge Kane responded with a slight nod, after which he stated, "Take this back down to the prothonotary. You can get as many certified copies as you may need there. I'm sure you know that after the defendant is served with a copy, you'll need to file proof of that service."

I had the feeling that Judge Kane was not at all sure if I *did* know that proof of service had to be filed. Since it was not the practice in Bucks County to request temporary protection orders, he clearly had good reason to think that it was the first such order I had ever been granted. So it was a kindness for him to pretend he was certain I needed no educating.

I hadn't mentioned to my client that my effort to get a temporary protection order was a first for the Bucks County Legal Aid Society and possibly for the entire county. It didn't seem like information that was necessary or helpful for her to know. I did warn her that we might not be successful in obtaining an order at this stage in the litigation, and that if we didn't succeed it would have no bearing on the strength of her case at the final hearing.

Because my client had no idea how historic the occasion was, I had to muzzle any expressions of euphoria. She was pleased and relieved when the temporary order was signed, and we shared a happy hug when we left the courthouse. But my excitement would have to wait until I got back to the office and I could begin celebrating in an appropriate manner. For me, not being a drinker, this was a two-chocolate-bar event.

Sometimes systemic change is not as difficult to achieve as one might expect. It did not take long for news of this event to spread, and surprisingly soon requests for temporary orders became the norm in Bucks County.

13. Custody Class

The Legal Aid building at One Pond Street in Bristol probably should have been condemned by the health department. The heating and air conditioning systems were defective; the landlord (who no one had ever seen) never thought it necessary to change the air filters in the improperly installed exhaust pipes; and there was a worrisome concentration of formaldehyde from an unknown source. A partial cinder block wall had been erected between Legal Aid and the gas station/car repair shop to which it was connected, but the wall did not extend all the way to the ceiling, so gaseous fumes from the shop floated in. There was no exhaust fan or dehumidifier, and, as I've mentioned, there were no windows, so there was no way for the slightest whiff of fresh air to dissipate the recycling mixture of vapors.

David Tilove had the good fortune of being oblivious to the prevailing odors, but he was the only one. Periodically, a member of Legal Aid's staff experienced headaches or bouts of nausea, dizziness, burning throat, tight chest, or irritated eyes. On one memorable occasion, when the toxicity in the atmosphere reached a high point and the temperature inside the building rose to 80 degrees, there was a mass one-day walkout to protest our unsafe working conditions. But on the whole, we were an extraordinarily tolerant group of workers. We were just too busy to find the time to complain.

From my first day of work, I was brimming with energy for the tasks ahead, driven by a mission, impossible though it was, to help every low-income person in Bucks County who needed a family law attorney.

Except when I had a full-day hearing at the courthouse in Doylestown, the county seat about thirty minutes from the camp, my commute to and from work was long. I put the commuting time to good use by propping a small tape recorder on the passenger seat and spending the entire trip recording petitions, opening statements and closing arguments, tidbits of strategic thoughts I wanted to be sure to remember, and itemized lists of more things I needed to do.

Admittedly, I was (and continue to be) a fanatic for the cause of equal justice for all. Really, there is no choice but to be a fanatic, when the need is so obvious and overwhelming, and the resources so woefully lacking. It makes a hard job harder, to know that you can't allow yourself to tire, but it was a job I truly loved. The hours and days flew by, with never one instant of boredom. On the contrary, I wished the time could go more slowly, so I could get more done. The earlier I could start work and the later I could stay each day, the better I felt. Every additional hour was another hour when I was gaining on my goal.

Gilbert Winner, who is Jim's best friend, liked to claim that he was working on inventing a "time-stretcher" for me, and I desperately wanted to have one. There was just not enough time in a day, in a week, in a year, to get ahead of the need.

One glaring problem in our office was the lack of an effective system for dealing with the burgeoning custody caseload. Every week, fifteen to twenty prospective clients would call Legal Aid seeking information about custody law. Each caller was given an appointment as soon as an opening was available. As there was usually only one lawyer who handled custody cases, there was already a waiting list many pages long when I first arrived, and the list kept growing. At first I tried to shrink it through the sheer number of client appointments I scheduled every day, including evening hours and weekends. But no matter how long my days extended, they were not long enough to keep pace with the daily deluge of new clients.

The idea of a "custody class" was suggested to me by Ayn Crawley, a brilliant paralegal at Legal Aid who shared my passion and became a good friend. I quickly fashioned a class to my liking, which I held every two weeks in our large conference room. Usually about twenty-five people signed up. I would explain the basics of custody law, its legal terminology and procedural steps, discuss the pros and cons of filing a custody petition, and provide both generic and individually tailored advice. By design, the class was casual and fun, making it a comfortable setting for attendees to ask questions about their own particular circumstances. I discovered it was helpful for the crowd to hear my answers to other people's questions, not only because people often had similar questions, but also because it encouraged everyone to feel comfortable about speaking out.

A common misconception that clients shared about custody law was the unfounded belief that all parents need to have a custody order. Very often, especially for Legal Aid clients, getting thrust into the judicial system for the purpose of seeking an unnecessary custody order was the last thing they should be doing.

The majority of Legal Aid's clients are women, because the majority of poor people are women and children. Typically, they were the primary caretakers of their children. All too frequently, they were the children's sole caretakers, because the fathers of the children were not around.

In the case of absentee fathers, going to court necessitated that they be located in order to notify them of the date and time of the custody conference that would be scheduled as a result of the filing. The notice the fathers would receive, in the form of an Order to Attend, informed them that they could be arrested if they did not attend the conference. It wasn't true, but that's what the notice said. So they *would* attend, thinking they had to do so to avoid arrest, but they'd be angry about it.

Custody conferences were presided over by one of the four conference officers employed by the court, whose job it was to see if an agreement could be reached or to schedule a hearing date if it couldn't. The conference officer would tell these absentee fathers they had custody rights equal to those of the other parent. And very often the conference officer would blame the other parent for the father's lack of involvement in his children's lives. This confluence of events had the effect of handing a weapon to fathers who had no actual ability or interest in being real fathers: they had *rights*, and they would exercise their rights as they saw fit!

I explained all these facts to the attendees of custody class, helping them understand that they did not automatically need a custody order to parent their children. They also learned who to call if changed circumstances later caused them to need one. Typically, there would be three or four clients in each class who, for one reason or another, *did* need to obtain a custody order. After the class ended, I would assist those clients in filling out a *pro se* custody petition (*pro se* being Latin for "on one's own behalf"), which I would file at the courthouse the next morning. Filling out the petition was the only *pro se* step in the process. From the moment the petitions were filed, clients received full legal representation. Usually, they received this representation from me, but occasionally a volunteer attorney was available. (Through the Bucks County Bar Association, we actively solicited attorneys to either give a monetary donation to Legal Aid or to donate their time and expertise by volunteering to handle one or more Legal Aid cases a year.)

An initial consultation with a client concerning custody frequently took two hours or more. By contrast, in a custody class typically lasting less than four hours, I could provide that service to about twenty-five people at the same time. Plus our clients really enjoyed the class. It was common to see them making friends with their fellow classmates. One client told me it had felt like being on *The Oprah Winfrey Show* (a remark I continue to brag about shamelessly).

There were always a few clients each week who needed immediate individual appointments with me because the other party had already filed against them or because their cases involved emergency situations. I was able to begin representing these clients without delay, thanks to the custody class. After it was initiated, I still had a huge custody caseload, but the long waiting list became a thing of the past.

14. The Burned Baby

T he call to Legal Aid came from a distraught grandfather, Frank
O'Neil. His daughter's baby—his little granddaughter, Josie—was
in the hospital after having suffered second and third degree burns in his
home. And the Bucks County Children & Youth Social Services Agency,
the county's child protection bureau (which we called simply CYS) had
just informed him and his daughter that the baby would not be returned
to them the following week when she was scheduled to be released from
the hospital. Instead, CYS intended to put the baby in foster care.

The call was transferred to me. Rita Andover, the attorney at Legal
Aid who specialized in CYS cases, was not in the office that day when the
call came in. Representing parents in these matters was one of my duties,
but I was only the back-up person in that area of the law. Seasoned and
tough, Rita seemed to enjoy the combat involved in CYS cases. I, to the
contrary, disliked CYS cases—and would soon grow to hate them.

At Keystone Legal Services, I had made it clear from the onset that
I wasn't willing to represent a parent who had abused a child. When it
came to abuse, I would represent only the victims. But I had no problem
taking the neglect cases, because I quickly gleaned that in the twisted
parlance of Mifflin County's CYS workers, "neglect" was just another way
of saying "poverty-stricken."

While in Lewistown, I had handled only three minor neglect cases,
all of which were quickly resolved when I was able to obtain permanent

housing and other assistance for my clients. So my contact with Mifflin County's CYS workers had been thankfully brief and limited. Still, in the short time that I'd dealt with them, I had developed a strong distaste for the way the agency's workers treated the people they were supposed to be helping.

However, Bucks County was not Mifflin County, so from the start I decided to remain open-minded and not form any negative preconceptions about Bucks County CYS.

David Tilove had suggested that Rita could be my mentor as I began to take on some of Legal Aid's CYS caseload. "Maybe you could give Meg some practice tips and observe her first few CYS cases," David had said to Rita, in my presence, and I had responded, "That would be great." Rita, however, said nothing. Later, I overheard her telling her secretary, "I just don't have time to be a babysitter."

I would have to manage without a mentor.

Now I was being handed my first CYS case in Bucks County, and it certainly sounded like an abuse case. A baby had suffered burns bad enough to require hospitalization for almost two weeks, and CYS was intervening to remove the baby from its mother. It sounded like the kind of case that I was going to have to refuse to take—the kind of case that needed to go to Rita. I would take the same stand with David that I had taken at Keystone Legal Services: under no circumstances would I represent an abusive parent.

However, I did take the call, because there was no one else available to take it. I figured I would get the necessary preliminary information from the grandfather, talk to David, and then refer the matter to Rita Andover.

But after speaking for almost an hour with the grandfather, my plans changed. I wanted to keep the case.

I learned from Mr. O'Neil that his granddaughter, who was four months old, had been severely injured when her teenaged father, enraged at her crying, had flung the contents of a cup of boiling hot coffee at her. In that instant, many areas of Josie's infant skin were burned to the second and third degree.

Mr. O'Neil told me that Josie had been fast asleep in her crib when his daughter Missy—Josie's mother, who had just turned eighteen—left the room for half an hour one morning to take a shower. It only took that time for Josie to wake up, crying heartily as babies often do upon awakening, and for her father (her mother's boyfriend) to act out his frustration at his inability to console her.

Perhaps the young man's frustration went deeper than that. Perhaps he was frustrated with suddenly being a father when he didn't want to be one, when he was only eighteen years old and had other things that he wanted to be or do. Either way, it was likely he had not intended to injure the baby when he committed that stupid, impulsive, reckless act.

Mr. O'Neil, who had been in the kitchen on the first floor when the incident occurred, raced up the stairs and into the nursery when his granddaughter's crying changed to piercing screams. Missy, who had leapt from her shower dripping wet, came running into the room wrapped only in a towel at the same time he did. When Missy saw her baby's flaring injuries, she began screaming hysterically and collapsed onto the floor. Her boyfriend, frightened and in shock, was shouting over and over again: "I'm sorry! I'm sorry! I'm sorry!"

Mr. O'Neil told me that he immediately called 911. An ambulance took the baby to the hospital while the police took the boyfriend into custody. Mr. O'Neil and his daughter were not permitted in the ambulance with Josie, so they went to the emergency room together in his car. Once there, they waited for hours in a state of extreme distress before a doctor finally came out to speak to them. Because of the nature of Josie's injuries, they were told, she would need to stay in the hospital, probably for a week or more, but visiting hours were every day from early morning until early evening.

Missy was so distraught that it was a struggle for her to stand upright without assistance, causing a nurse to suggest that she wait until an attendant could bring a wheelchair to help her traverse the distance to the children's unit. But Missy didn't want to wait for the wheelchair. She was too anxious to be with her baby, so she leaned unsteadily against her father as they made their way up elevators and down long hallways. Josie, who had been given a heavy dose of pain medication, was in a deep sleep when they entered her room. Mr. O'Neil was relieved to see Josie looking so peaceful, but at the sight of all the bandages that encased her tiny daughter, Missy burst into tears and could not stop weeping.

Mr. O'Neil told me that he said to Missy, "Let me take you home, so you can rest. Then I'll come back and stay with Josie."

That was what they did. The next morning, Missy tried again to visit with her baby. But when a nurse came to put new dressings on Josie's burned skin, Missy became overcome with anxiety, running to the bathroom crying, barely reaching the toilet before vomiting. Mr. O'Neil again drove his daughter home to rest, and returned to stay with Josie. After that, they agreed that Missy should not try coming to the hospital again. She couldn't bear to see Josie's injuries, let alone endure the sight of her baby in pain. So it was the grandfather, Mr. O'Neil, who spent every minute of every day, from eight a.m. until eight p.m., by Josie's side at the hospital. He told me he would have stayed overnight if he'd been permitted to.

It was obvious to me that Mr. O'Neil loved his grandchild just as much as he loved his daughter. I learned that he was a single parent, devoted to his family: his wife had died of cancer when Missy was very young and he had never remarried. When Missy got pregnant at age seventeen, he was unstintingly supportive. He told me that *his* parents had disowned his sister when she became pregnant out of wedlock, citing the Bible as justification. But Frank O'Neil read the Bible differently. He was a religious man, but the religion he honored was devoid of punishing judgments and retribution. So when the parents of Missy's then-seventeen-year-old boyfriend threw their son out of their home, he took him in.

"It was the right thing to do, in my opinion," Mr. O'Neil explained. "Missy thought she was in love with the boy, and they were going to have a baby together."

A worker from CYS had interviewed Mr. O'Neil and Missy, individually and extensively, the day after Josie was hurt. It was clear that neither of them had ever abused the baby, and both said they were willing to abide by CYS's instruction that they have no further contact with the baby's father. So they had every reason to expect to bring Josie back home with them from the hospital.

But CYS had other plans.

A CYS worker had come to Josie's hospital room, where Mr. O'Neil was sitting by the side of his granddaughter's bed, singing her a lullaby, to inform him that the agency had filed a petition seeking legal and physical custody of Josie. A dependency hearing was scheduled in two days' time, the CYS worker said, whereupon Josie would be transferred directly from the hospital into foster care. She made it sound like there was nothing Mr. O'Neil or his daughter could do to stop them. Josie was going to be designated a "dependent child," and CYS was going to put her in foster care. The CYS worker handed Mr. O'Neil a copy of the petition before exiting the room, turning to say, "Your daughter can attend the hearing if she wants to, but she doesn't have to come."

From my experience, this was classic CYS behavior. Portray the agency as a stand-in for God and mislead the low-income parents (and grandparents) into believing that they had no rights.

I had kept my promise to myself not to form any negative preconceptions about the Bucks County CYS. Now I could judge them by their actions. And my judgment, untainted by preconceptions, was not difficult to reach: they were bastards.

There was no time to dally. The hearing was in only two days. And it couldn't be delayed, because the morning after that Josie was going to be released from the hospital. The rest of my day was already packed with client appointments, so I arranged to meet with Mr. O'Neil and his daughter at their home that evening to talk for the first time to Missy, who would be my client, and to officially open a Legal Aid file.

At about eight that night, I pulled my car into the driveway of the small row house that Mr. O'Neil and his wife had purchased two decades earlier in the rural town of Sellersville. He opened the door for me before I got to it, greeted me warmly, and led me into his home. It had a tidy look: the calico sofa and chairs, well-worn, were cushiony and comfortable, there were flowering plants on the windowsills, and the wall behind the sofa was adorned with framed photographs of smiling loved ones. It felt like the kind of home that people would feel lucky to live in.

Mr. O'Neil thanked me profusely for coming and gestured for me to take a seat. A moment later, his daughter emerged from the kitchen carrying a plate of cookies, which she placed on the coffee table beside me. "I made these for you," she said shyly.

Missy looked a lot like her father. Both were slim and slight in stature, with strawberry-colored hair and strikingly blue eyes. Missy's face was festooned with freckles, as was her father's, although his were more subdued. Having red hair myself, with my own residue of freckles from my youth, I immediately identified with both of them. Red-headed people tend to have an instant affinity, I've noticed, borne of our shared anomaly. I imagine that greatly outnumbered members of any minority group might feel the same way.

"Does Josie have red hair, too?" I asked.

Missy smiled. "Yes. It's exactly the same color as mine and my dad's." Missy was still smiling as her eyes brimmed with tears. "Can you help us get her back?"

"I'm going to try, with all my might, to do just that," I said.

It was all I could say. I was painfully aware of my lack of experience and of the enormous power wielded by CYS. The situation didn't warrant any bravado on my part.

It was quite late when I finally finished interviewing Missy and her father. I had learned everything I could think to ask about them, building my case while trying to anticipate every cross-examination question that could possibly be thrown their way. I took some pictures of Josie's room, which was decorated sweetly, and of the empty crib with the mobile of little white lambs hanging above it awaiting her return.

"I'll call tomorrow to go over the specific questions I'll be asking each of you at the hearing," I told them, as I put on my coat to leave. Missy scooped her remaining home-made cookies into a bag, insisting that I take them with me.

Driving home, bone-tired, I kept rehashing in my mind all the positive information I had obtained and wracking my brain for an answer to the one overriding question I had: why did CYS want to wrench this baby from her loving family and put her in foster care?

It was past midnight when I pulled my car into the driveway to the camp. I opened the front door to the house as quietly as I could, trying my best not to wake up Jim, but the dogs barking excitedly at my arrival made that a futile effort.

"How'd it go?" Jim asked, standing in the doorway to our bedroom, looking more asleep than awake. I told him it went well. He nodded drowsily. "That's good. Are you coming to bed now?"

I was much too riled up to go to bed. Besides, I had studying to do before CYS opened for business the next day. It was already too late to get up early enough to do it in the morning. So I sat at the kitchen table with a cup of diet cola, reading and rereading the Juvenile Act, which was the statute that CYS needed to rely upon to seize legal and physical custody of Josie O'Neil, and began carefully analyzing the accompanying case law. Nowhere in the act, or in the case law stemming from it, could I find any justification for CYS's claim that Josie was a dependent child who needed foster care placement for her protection.

The next morning, I called Janet Hicks, the CYS worker in charge of the case who had conveyed the idea to Mr. O'Neil that Missy could attend the hearing "if she wanted to" but she really didn't have to bother. I introduced myself to Ms. Hicks, giving her the bad news that Missy had a lawyer. So, yes, Missy *would* be attending the dependency hearing, and so would I. And then I asked: "On what possible basis is CYS claiming that Josie is a dependent child who needs to be removed from her mother?"

"Missy O'Neil is utterly incapable of providing proper care for that child," Ms. Hicks said, in a voice so cold it sent a chill through my body.

"Do you really think that *your agency* would be providing proper care for that baby by snatching her from her family and sticking her in a foster home?" I responded, my voice as cold as hers.

"Foster placement is just the *first* thing we intend to do. Our end goal is the termination of your client's parental rights."

I was speechless for a moment, long enough for Janet Hicks to add, "We will see you at the hearing."

That was the end of our conversation.

I had heard from Rita that healthy White babies available for adoption were a hot commodity in wealthy Bucks County—one that money can sometimes buy. Rita had told me it was the outspoken conviction of more than one worker at CYS that poor people should not be *allowed* to have children, and that, absent the right of the state to sterilize them, any children they did have should be taken away and given to those more deserving. I had assumed that Rita was being facetious.

Josie O'Neil was a healthy White baby, the child of a vulnerable teenager from a working-class family, and that baby, teenager, and family had only me to protect them from what I saw to be the immense power and malevolence of Janet Hicks and her agency. A sudden realization of the fearsome burden of the task sent another chill through my body. Had it been thoughtless of me, a lawyer for little more than a year at that point, to believe that I could do this case justice? Should I have turned it over from the start to Rita Andover, a combat-ready veteran in this area of the law? Maybe it wasn't too late.

I called Rita to ask if she could possibly represent a young mother at a crucial Dependency Hearing the following day, apologizing effusively for the lateness of my request. "I'm beginning to think I'm not experienced enough to handle it," I explained, "but I've put together all the information you would need."

"I've got a conference to attend tomorrow morning that's been scheduled for weeks," Rita responded. "I'm really sorry, but you'll have to get your experience on the job. Good luck!"

So I was on my own. I needed to shed my self-doubts and gather my strengths, because I was about to do battle with an Evil Empire. And really, I was ready. I knew every provision of the Juvenile Act, which outlined ten separate circumstances (or "grounds") under which a child can be deemed "dependent" and therefore transferrable to the custody of CYS or to some other entity. Nine of those grounds had no conceivable applicability to this case. That left only one—the first one listed—which states, in a nutshell, that a child is dependent if she is without the proper parental or custodial care necessary for her physical, mental, or emotional health. A determination that such proper parental or custodial care is lacking may be based on evidence of conduct that places the health, safety, or welfare of the child at risk.

A lack of proper parental care or control was the ground that CYS was alleging in its petition, the one they were relying upon to obtain legal and physical custody of Josie in order to put her in foster care. That was the ground I would need to disprove.

I had the ammunition I needed. I had learned that from the moment of Josie's birth, Missy O'Neil, despite her young age, had always been an able and loving mother. She had breastfed Josie for three months. She had stayed awake rocking her throughout many colicky nights. She had taken Josie almost everywhere she went, peacefully nestled in a cloth carrier that rested against her chest. She had never left her baby without custodial supervision. Missy and her father delighted in Josie and had never hurt her in any way. When Josie did get hurt, through no fault of theirs, they immediately got her the care she needed. They dutifully obeyed the edict from CYS to have no further contact with Josie's father. They never abused alcohol or any controlled substance.

The only thing Missy O'Neil had done wrong was becoming over-whelmed by the sight of her injured daughter in the hospital. It had taken such a toll that her father had stepped in and taken over, to facilitate the recovery of both of "his girls" during that two-week period of time.

While in the hospital, Josie's physical, mental, and emotional health had never gone unattended. And there was no reason to believe that any of it would go unattended when she got back home. But Janet Hicks' heartless statement continued to echo ominously in my brain: "Foster placement is just the first thing we intend to do. Our end goal is the ter-mination of your client's parental rights."

I remained shaken by that statement. The fact that Ms. Hicks felt no need to disguise her callous goal was a stark reminder of the enormous power and authority she held as an agent of CYS. I tried to calm myself with the thought that I had a greater power on my side: I had morality and the law. And I told myself that I didn't need to be more experienced, because the case was not complicated. I simply needed to show the judge that Josie O'Neil did not in any way fit the Juvenile Act's description of a dependent child, and that Missy and her father were good parents and good people.

I prepared direct examination questions for Missy and Mr. O'Neil, which, I hoped, would place them in the sympathetic light they deserved. I went over each question with them to make sure their answers were straightforward, clear, and persuasive. I explained that my prepared questions weren't exactly a script, and I didn't want them to memorize their answers, but they needed to understand that every question and answer had an important part to play in telling our true story to the judge. I told them I might need to add some questions for them at the hearing, if CYS brought up any unanticipated issues that I felt we needed to respond to. I discussed the questions I thought CYS's solicitor might ask them on cross-examination, gave them some tips on the best ways to respond when being cross-examined, and alerted them to some of the tricks of the trade that CYS's solicitor might try to employ. Last, I assured them of my belief that the law was on our side.

Then I composed my first closing argument in a child dependency case.

A closing argument is a speech made to the judge (or to the jury, in a jury trial) at the end of certain legal proceedings, including a child dependency hearing. It is delivered after all the evidence has been entered and all the testimony has been heard from both sides. It provides an opportunity to pinpoint exactly how the evidence and testimony served to establish the legal merits of your case and/or how it demonstrated the other side's failure to establish the legal merits of *their* case, and to further persuade the judge (or jury) to render the decision that you are seeking.

I spent hours writing and rewriting that closing argument. I was trying to be clear and forceful, trying to best sum up the compelling testimony I expected to elicit from Missy and her dad, and to beseech the judge to return the proper ruling on my client's behalf.

The next day, I met with Missy and Mr. O'Neil at the courthouse a full hour before the scheduled hearing. From my first hearing to my last, it has always been my practice to meet early, to calm the nerves of my clients (and their witnesses) by acclimating them to the imposing courthouse environment, answering any last-minute questions, receiving any last-minute information, and reinforcing their confidence that they have a lawyer who cares about them and will always be by their side.

Dependency hearings in Bucks County were held in conference rooms instead of courtrooms. Our hearing was scheduled for ten a.m. in conference room 5. When we entered at 9:50 a.m., the judge and the court reporter were already sitting at the head of a long table, and the tipstaff motioned for us to take seats. CYS's solicitor arrived with Caseworker Hicks a few minutes later, and they took seats on the opposite side of the table, directly across from us. Between the sizable table and the extra chairs parked against the walls behind us in the narrow room, there was no space to maneuver as we sat there facing each other, me and the O'Neils on one side, the representatives of CYS on the other. The layout felt claustrophobic.

Conference room settings are less formal than those of a courtroom, designed to lessen tensions in the kinds of cases where tensions run high and where children are often called upon to testify. But in our case the effect was exactly the reverse. The last people in the world I wanted to be hemmed in with that day, sitting eyeball to eyeball, were CYS's solicitor and Janet Hicks.

It was CYS's petition, making them the plaintiffs, so they had the initial burden of proof to establish that Josie O'Neil was a dependent child. CYS's first witness was a nurse from the hospital. She testified about the extended visiting hours the hospital provided for the children's wing because of how important it was for hospitalized children to have the comfort of being with their parents; about the mere two times that Missy O'Neil had "deigned" to visit her daughter in a two-week period; how short those mere two visits had been; and how unhelpful Ms. O'Neil had been during each of them. She testified about the agonizing pain that the baby was forced to experience, not only from the burns she suffered but also from the medical treatments necessary to heal them.

Then the nurse authenticated, one by one, a series of photographs that had been taken of Josie, each of which graphically displayed her terrible injuries. Some of the photos had been taken in the ambulance on the way to the hospital; others showed a little red-headed baby pitifully encased in bandages. The solicitor for CYS handed each photograph to me, briefly, for my review, before marking them as exhibits and passing them to the nurse. Neither Missy nor I had seen those heart-wrenching pictures before they were presented at the hearing. Looking at them together, our eyes simultaneously flooded with tears. Missy began to weep.

I was about to ask the judge if we could have a short recess, but the photographs were already in his hands and I watched as a look of sheer horror came over his face and swiftly turned to fury. When he looked up from those devastating pictures, he glared at Missy with blazing contempt.

There is no question about it. A picture is worth a thousand words.

"I don't need to hear anything more," the judge said to CYS's solicitor.

Having basically been told that he had already won the case, the solicitor dispensed with his plan to put Caseworker Hicks on the stand. Instead, he announced, "In that case, Your Honor, I have no further witnesses."

I didn't have time to think about how to respond to what had just
happened. The judge had just said aloud that he didn't need to hear anything more. It was over. He had made up his mind. He had heard
enough from CYS, and it was crushingly clear that he had no desire to
hear a word from *my* witnesses. Having them attempt to testify would
only have further enraged him. But I had to act instantly, in some unique
way, because CYS had already won. Impulsively, driven by a desperate
instinct, I stood up and launched into my closing argument.

I spoke quickly, to prevent interruption, and no one tried to stop
me. I spoke passionately, about a sweet and loving family, besieged by a
sudden tragedy not of their doing, who were anxiously awaiting the return of their dearly loved child. I talked about the steadfast devotion of
Josie's grandfather, sitting by her bedside at the hospital hour after hour,
day after day, and about how he would be there for Josie in exactly the
same way when she returned home. I said he was more a *father* than a
grandfather to Josie, the only true father-figure she had ever known. I
acknowledged the temporary failings of my young client, for not being
strong enough to recover sooner from the trauma of seeing her child's
injuries—injuries that Missy had obviously experienced as intensely as if
they had been her own. But I reminded the judge of how very difficult it
was, for each of us, to even view *pictures* of those wounds on that precious child. And I reminded the judge of what the nurse had said, about
how important it is for children to be with their loved ones during times
of stress and recovery, using that testimony to argue how important it
was for Josie to be home with her family, to be in the comforting arms of
her grandfather, and her mother, as she continued to convalesce. Think
of the terrible fear and confusion that this baby will be condemned to
suffer, I said, if she is taken from the hospital to be left alone with
strangers in a strange house.

When I finished talking, everything felt very still. The only sound I
heard was Missy crying softly. Out of the corner of my eye, I spotted Rita,

sitting silently by the door. I hadn't noticed her entering the room. I had no idea how long she'd been there.

I sat down quietly, waiting tensely for the silence to be broken. And then the judge spoke. "I'm sending this baby home," he said, "into the legal and physical custody of her grandfather, Francis O'Neil."

The judge said more after that, about how the mother's contact with the child was to be supervised by the grandfather, and how the natural father of the child was prohibited from having contact with the child or any member of the O'Neil family. He ordered that Missy participate in parenting classes through an approved county agency, and stated that after those classes had been successfully completed, her attorney could file for a review hearing to vacate the order concerning her supervision.

I must have heard everything the judge said, because my legal pad had notes on it—in my handwriting—concerning each provision. But the only part I really remembered hearing was his first five words: "I'm sending this baby home."

That quickly, the hearing was over. Janet Hicks, scowling, left the room with CYS's solicitor. Missy hugged me. Her father hugged me. The judge walked over to Mr. O'Neil and shook his hand. "Take care of that baby," he said.

Mr. O'Neil responded emotionally: "We will, sir! I *promise* you we will!"

I looked towards Rita, who beckoned with her finger for me to come over to her. Feeling a flood of relief and, I admit, a touch of pride in the ingenuity I had exhibited, I was glad to share the triumphant moment with a colleague. But Rita had a different point of view about what had occurred.

"You can't just give a closing argument before putting on your case," she said, rolling her eyes in exasperation. "Didn't you learn anything in law school?"

15. A Woman's Place

About once or twice a week, occasionally more often depending on the need, the commute from Legal Aid back to the camp took a bit longer than usual. Those were the evenings when I made a detour on my way home to go to A Woman's Place, Bucks County's shelter for battered women. Its undisclosed location wasn't too far off-track from my normal route.

A Woman's Place (AWP) is the kind of abuse center that I had envisioned for Lewistown. Opened in 1976, the year that the Protection from Abuse Act was passed in Pennsylvania, the agency had already been a sanctuary for domestic violence victims for eight years by the time I began working at Bucks County's Legal Aid. It had already helped thousands of victims become survivors.

AWP provides safety and services for women and their children who are fleeing from domestic violence. At that time, the shelter was only large enough to house about four families at a time (increased now to seven). The stay-time is expected to be only a month or two. Other forms of help offered are not time-limited, however. AWP staff and volunteers work hard to try to ensure that every family remains safe and continues to have access to services after their brief residency period comes to an end. One of those services, before AWP was able to add attorneys to its staff, was a referral to the Bucks County Legal Aid Society for free legal advice and possible representation in court.

Public transportation was (and still is) almost non-existent in Bucks County. Legal Aid's Bristol office was a long distance by car from AWP, and many of the women staying there didn't have a car, so it made sense for me to travel to the shelter residents rather than the other way around. Car or no car, when families first arrived at the shelter they were overwhelmed and sometimes immobilized by despair and trepidation. Many had good reason to fear for their lives. I understood how frightening and difficult it could be for them to leave the shelter and travel a long distance in order to consult with a lawyer,

The executive director of AWP was Beth Taylor, a dynamic advocate for social justice and a fierce defender of victims of domestic violence. Beth was constantly calling Legal Aid on behalf of her residents, which is how I first got to know her. When she found out I'd changed Legal Aid's procedures, making same-day appointments available to everyone who needed a protection from abuse order, she pronounced us friends for life.

AWP is much more than a safe place to stay. It also provides much-needed emotional support, individual and group counseling, and expansive advocacy to help clients get aid and services from government agencies and other nonprofit organizations. Free clothing is made available to families who come with little more than the clothes on their backs. AWP also operates a 24-hour hotline and a number of outreach programs to educate the community about the dangers and dynamics of domestic violence.

I spent a lot of time at AWP, meeting with individual shelter residents, providing initial consultations, and offering ongoing legal representation. New families were always arriving as others departed, so the supply of potential clients never ended.

Almost every new resident wanted and needed a protection from abuse order, so my first meeting with a client at the shelter usually included getting the information I needed to draft a strong PFA petition. I would then type the petition at home that evening; read it over the phone to my client early the next morning, for her approval before a final edit; meet her at the courthouse at eight a.m., or, if she didn't have a car, drive to the shelter to pick her up; go with her to the prothonotary to file the petition; represent her at an ex parte hearing to seek a temporary protection order; accompany her to her car or drive her back to the shelter; and, finally, either drive to Legal Aid in Bristol to begin my workday, or, if I had a hearing or conference that morning with another client, stay at (or return to) the courthouse in Doylestown. Occasionally, I would have more than one PFA client going through this process with me on any given morning.

It sounds more complicated on paper than it was in real life. I got it all down to a system that worked well. After news of Legal Aid's requests for temporary protection orders spread through the legal community, ex parte PFA hearings became the norm in Bucks County, and one judge would be on call each day for that purpose.

Besides Beth Taylor, the other superhero at AWP was Amy Gendall. Beth, Amy, and I interacted frequently. One of my favorite books when I was growing up was Louisa May Alcott's *Little Women*, about four sisters whose names were Meg, Beth, Amy and Jo, so it always made me laugh whenever our names were bandied back and forth in close succession. "All we're missing is Jo!" I quipped once, and Beth and Amy knew exactly what I was talking about.

I prized every minute I spent at AWP. Seeing how deeply Beth and Amy cared about the welfare of domestic violence victims, and how good they were at turning their concerns into action, constantly inspired me. Over the years, I have never stopped having a close affiliation with AWP, in one or more capacities. I've witnessed countless examples of the courage and compassion displayed by AWP staff and volunteers, and I've listened to hundreds of touching testimonials from current and former residents, describing how their contact with the agency saved their lives and changed them forever for the better.

Every county needs a place of hope and refuge like A Woman's Place. How wonderful to know that Lewistown has now had such a place for many years. It is called the Abuse Network, Inc. of Mifflin and Juniata County and, as first envisioned, it provides emergency shelter and other crucial services to victims of domestic violence and sexual assault.

16. Blessed in a Blighted World

Annette Jefferson was one of my favorite clients. I told her so many times. I said it was because she looked a little like Tina Turner, and I loved Tina Turner, but really it was because she was so full of grace and optimism that it was a joy to be around her. Annette was a single parent of four little girls, working full-time at a low-paying job and forced to deal with an abusive husband whom she feared, yet her disposition was always sunny and her plans for the future always bright.

I admired Annette's parenting skills. Her daughters were adorable, well-mannered, and engaging. She was firm and loving with them, somehow managing to treat each one as if she were an only child, encouraging and valuing them as unique individuals. She was a wonderful mother. Many of my clients inspired me, but Annette shone brightly at the top of the list.

She had left her abusive husband with only a temporary shelter to run to, fleeing with no belongings beyond the clothes she and her daughters were wearing. Lloyd Jefferson had treated his family like pieces of worthless property and Annette was determined to divorce him. But still she prayed for him every day, hoping that someday he would conquer his anger at the world and transform his life. Annette believed in redemption.

A colleague of mine from Legal Aid represented Annette at her protection from abuse hearing, and got her a one-year PFA order, the longest
term available at that time. Thanks to the Bucks County Opportunity
Council, a nonprofit agency that helped pay Annette's security deposit
and first month's rent, she was able to lease a small condo for her family.
Through it all, Annette's indomitable spirit remained unscathed.

Within weeks of the PFA hearing, Lloyd filed a petition seeking primary custody of the children. This is a favorite tactic of abusers. Victims
of domestic violence often stay because of the abuser's threats to get custody of the children if they leave. When victims do leave, abusers usually
try to make good on those threats. If they can get custody of the children,
they know their victim may come back.

Contrary to popular belief, mothers do not always win custody of
their children. Studies show that, when custody is contested in court, fathers nationwide often have an advantage over mothers. Bucks County is
no exception. Often, fathers can afford lawyers while mothers are unrepresented. Often, too, mothers do not have what is considered a stable living arrangement at the time of the hearing, since they are staying at shelters or with family or friends. The fact that the mother had to flee for her
life from the father's allegedly stable home is commonly discounted by
judges in custody cases. They rationalize: maybe he was abusive to her,
but unless there is irrefutable proof that he was also abusive to the children, isn't it better for the children to be in the primary custody of the
parent whose financial situation is more secure?

So although Annette was an exemplary parent, I still had reasons to
be concerned when I got notice that Lloyd had filed for custody. Tension
builds up in contested custody cases like this one, where the stakes are
so high and the insidious aspects of domestic violence are so easily overlooked or misunderstood.

The custody hearing was presided over by Judge Kane, thanks to
some surreptitious maneuvering on my part. He had an incredibly sharp
mind and was a shrewd judge of character. When Lloyd Jefferson testified that he had a spacious four-bedroom house for the children, com-
pared to the tiny two-bedroom condo that Annette was renting, Judge
Kane interrupted him. "Didn't your wife depart from that four-bedroom
house because you were *beating* her?" When I heard Judge Kane ask that

perfect question, I could have hugged him (if it were possible to do in a professional manner).

When Judge Kane entered his order granting Annette primary custody of the children, Lloyd turned and glowered at her, his eyes like black daggers, and a sneer flashed across his face. Now he was two-down legally: there was a protection order against him, which ordered him not to abuse, threaten, or stalk his wife or to have contact with her at any location, and there was a custody order in his wife's favor, dashing his plans to wrest the children away from her.

Annette would have wanted to formalize her separation from Lloyd by seeking a divorce and child support payments, but this wasn't feasible. Legal Aid did not have the resources to handle divorce or support cases, and, obviously suspecting that I would do so for Annette, David Tilove had specifically reiterated to me that Legal Aid was not contractually permitted to handle those matters. Annette would have to save up to hire a private attorney to represent her in the divorce, which meant it wasn't going to get started any time soon. At least the court system was set up to enable primary caretakers to file for child support relatively easily without an attorney, but Annette decided (and I agreed) that child support was too dangerous for her to pursue. Having failed to win custody, Lloyd would have been enraged if forced to give Annette one cent in support for their children. Foregoing child support is a hardship that many victims of domestic violence are compelled to accept in exchange for their safety.

But Lloyd Jefferson was already enraged.

Nine months after the custody hearing, he broke into Annette's home late one evening. The little one was asleep in her crib, and the other three girls were in the queen-sized bed in the master bedroom. Annette was already in her nightgown. Once inside, Lloyd beat, raped, and sodomized her. It was his usual mode of operation. Except that, this time, he beat her to death.

When Lloyd realized that Annette was dying, he decided it would be a good idea to take her upstairs and put her in a bed. It's hard to imagine that he thought it would look as if she had just died of natural causes in her sleep. Just thirty-two years old, she had been beaten so badly that multiple bones were broken and she had fatal internal injuries. The reasoning behind Lloyd's plan is unfathomable, but in furtherance of it he forced two of his daughters, who had run downstairs after being awakened by Annette's last screams, to help him drag their dying mother up the stairs to the second floor.

As the children, ten and eight years old at the time, later described the scene in court, their mother was unconscious, but they heard one low, gurgling sound come from her throat as they and their father pulled her body up the stairs. They were too scared and traumatized to say a word as they followed their father's commands.

"Get back to bed and wait until morning," he had told them, before he left their home. "If you tell anyone what happened, I'll go to jail, and it will be your fault."

Afraid to disobey their father, the two girls huddled together in their bed, crying through the long night.

When morning finally came, they fed their two little sisters cereal and changed the littlest one's diaper. They tried to keep the four-year-old occupied when she kept asking, "What's wrong with Mommy?" But finally the eldest called their aunt Bernadette and told her what their daddy had done. The child knew it would be her fault if her father went to jail, but her mother had taught her and her sisters to always tell the truth.

We didn't know whether Lloyd intended to beat Annette to death that night or if he only meant to show her that no court order could stop him from brutalizing her whenever he wanted to. But what difference did it make?

Lloyd Jefferson was convicted at trial and sentenced to twenty years of imprisonment. I thought the guilty verdict would bring me solace, but it did not.

Annette and I had had many conversations in the months before she was murdered. One thing she always said, smiling her lovely smile, was, "I'm so fortunate." I asked her once, out of curiosity, "In what way are you so fortunate?" Someone who didn't know Annette might have asked that question out of disbelief, but I was looking for enlightenment. How does one come to feel so blessed in a blighted world?

She told me, "In too many ways to count. I've got my beautiful children, my faith, my freedom, my job, my home . . . and my wonderful free lawyer!"

After she died, I realized that Annette had taught me a lot about how to count *my* blessings. One of them had been her.

GR   GS   GR

A few years later, a letter arrived at Legal Aid, addressed to the executive director, the return address being a maximum-security prison located about 200 miles away. David Tilove handed the letter to me.

It was from Lloyd Jefferson. He wrote that he had read Pennsylvania's custody statute, knew his rights, and wanted visitation with his children. He thought their aunt should be court-ordered to drive them, at least twice a month, back and forth from Bucks County to the distant penitentiary where he was incarcerated, so he could enjoy "family visits." He wanted the Bucks County Legal Aid Society to represent him.

"I'll leave this up to you," David said.

The unthinkable brazenness of Lloyd's letter enraged me. But even more unthinkable, even more enraging, was the fact that he was not mistaken. As far as the law was concerned at that time, murdering the mother of one's children was not reason enough to automatically deprive a father of his custodial rights to those children.

I promptly composed the following response:

Dear Mr. Jefferson:

Legal Aid will never represent you. Our client will always be Annette Jefferson, the wonderful woman you brutally murdered.

Sincerely,
Meg Groff, Attorney at Law

I contacted Annette's sister Bernadette, to inform her of Lloyd's letter and to offer my *pro bono* services if he decided to file a petition for custody despite Legal Aid's refusal to assist him.

Thankfully, neither of us ever heard from Lloyd Jefferson again.

17. A Sense of Smell

A ll the phone calls to Legal Aid in Bristol went first to Rosemarie, our receptionist. It was her responsibility to ascertain the nature of each call and then transfer the caller to the appropriate person to handle the matter. Much of the time, no transfer was necessary because the appropriate person to handle the matter was Rosemarie.

People called Legal Aid for all sorts of reasons—to cancel or reschedule appointments, to sign up for my custody class, to ask about the services available from other non-profit agencies. And, of course, by the thousands, they called looking for a lawyer to represent them. To become a Legal Aid client, the callers had to undergo an initial screening by Rosemarie. To meet the guidelines for eligibility set for us by the federal government, our primary funder, a person had to be an American citizen and a Bucks County resident, had to have a very low income, earning no more than 125 percent of the federal poverty-level, and have a legal matter in Bucks County that fit within Legal Aid's authorized priorities. Those priorities were cases involving custody; landlord-tenant disputes; public housing; elder law; child dependency; termination of parental rights; unemployment compensation; bankruptcy; consumer fraud; eligibility for Medicaid/Social Security Disability/Welfare Aid; and domestic violence requiring a protection from abuse order. (Separate funding from the Commonwealth of Pennsylvania provided a special exception to the income guidelines, allowing Legal Aid to represent all victims of domestic violence in protection from abuse cases in Bucks County, regardless of the victim's income.)

With each screening, Rosemarie also had to thoroughly check Legal Aid's client list to make sure the caller was not a "conflict" for us, which would be the case if Legal Aid was representing the opposing party or had done so in the past.

Almost everyone who called Legal Aid was an American citizen and a Bucks County resident. But many people called seeking an attorney for a legal problem that was in an area of the law that Legal Aid was not authorized to accept, and it was Rosemarie who had to give them that bad news. If it was a criminal case, people who couldn't afford an attorney were sent to the Public Defenders' Office, but for other legal problems that Legal Aid didn't handle, people who couldn't afford an attorney were out of luck.

As far as I was concerned, Rosemarie had the most demanding job at Legal Aid. She was the gatekeeper, the enforcer of restrictions that we wished we didn't have. The phone lines at her desk never stopped ringing, the callers were often emotionally distressed, and it wasn't always possible to provide them with the help they needed. On top of that, her desk faced the waiting room, which was perpetually packed with anxious clients and rowdy children who were overdue for a nap. I don't know how long I could have handled her job, but Rosemarie never faltered.

I encouraged Rosemarie to look for ways to get around our funder-imposed client-eligibility limitations, bending the rules without breaking them. If it hadn't been for Rosemarie's skills in that direction, I might never have had the opportunity to become Lacey Berrington's attorney.

Rosemary buzzed me one morning to tell me about her. Lacey Berrington was an American citizen. She lived in Bucks County. She was poor. She had a custody case. She wasn't a "conflict." But there was one big, disqualifying factor: the custody litigation wasn't happening in Bucks County. It was happening in New Jersey.

"She just got served with a custody petition and she's crying hysterically," Rosemarie told me, sounding on the verge of tears herself. "She can't afford a lawyer. Seven months ago, her husband was sent to jail for sexually molesting her eleven-year-old daughter—his stepdaughter—and now his parents are trying to get custody of her other two children. I know you can't take a New Jersey case, but is there any way you can help her?"

Rosemarie knew I gave legal advice to non-eligible-clients whenever I got the chance (it was a secret we kept between us), but in this case there was a question I first needed to have answered. "You said she lives in Bucks County with her children. How *long* have the children been living in Bucks County?"

"I didn't ask her that," Rosemarie said, "but she told me her husband had been molesting her daughter in the basement of their home for a year before she found out and called the police, so it sounds like they've lived in Bucks County for at least that long."

That answer solved our problem, because except in special emergency circumstances, custody cases must be held in the state and county where the children have resided for the past six months or more. It's a rule that every state in America (except Massachusetts) has adopted. So it seemed it was Bucks County, Pennsylvania, that had jurisdiction in this custody case, not any county in New Jersey.

I explained the jurisdiction issue to Rosemarie and said, "Just give me Ms. Berrington's phone number. I'll call her right now."

Lacey was surprised to hear back from us so quickly. After she told me that her children had lived in Bucks County all their lives, I told her she was talking to her newly-retained attorney. She shouted with joy in response.

I asked her who'd given her the custody petition.

"It was a constable. He just knocked on my door and handed me a big envelope with an emergency petition, a letter from my in-law's attorney, and an order from a judge in New Jersey scheduling a custody hearing in three weeks."

As so often in custody cases, time was of the essence.

"Could you possibly come to my office today? There's a little paperwork for you to fill out so we can open a client file," I said. "I also need to review the legal documents you just got, and I have a lot of questions to ask you. It might take two or three hours to get everything done."

"I can come right now," she said.

Thirty minutes later, Lacey Berrington was sitting in my office. She was a tall woman, sturdily built, with shoulder-length, dark-brown hair and bright brown eyes. She had a friendly face and such a lovely voice that I had to ask if she was a singer. "In the shower," she answered, with a mischievous smile.

I learned the details of Lacey's case. Her husband had begun molesting her daughter Mary when she was ten years old, building towards his first rape on her eleventh birthday. He had threatened to kill the entire family if Mary told anyone, and she had believed him enough to keep silent for a year.

Mary was a pretty girl, who took pride in her appearance, always neatly dressed and well-groomed. When she started wearing ill-fitting clothes and neglecting to comb her hair, Lacey realized that something was seriously wrong. When questioned, Mary repeatedly denied that anything was amiss. But something clearly *was* amiss. Lacey sought the advice of the school's guidance counselor, who agreed to intercede. After a number of meetings with the counselor, Mary finally broke down and revealed what was happening to her, begging the counselor not to tell anyone. Lacey's husband was arrested that day.

Ronald (Ronald J. Berrington III, to be precise) never returned to the marital residence after that day. His wealthy parents paid his bail as soon as it was set, and he stayed with them in their palatial residence in New Jersey until the day of his trial. Ronald's grandfather had been a multimillionaire who died and left Ronald, Jr., his fortune. Somehow this sequence of events had confused Ronald, Jr. into believing that he and his wife were superior individuals. They acted accordingly. They had never considered Lacey to be good enough for their son. He was a college graduate from a "good" family, while she had only a high school education and parents who labored at menial jobs.

Pleading guilty at trial in exchange for a reduction of the charges against him, Ronald III was sent directly to prison to serve a five-to-eight-year sentence.

Lacey was sure that Ronald's parents hadn't known, before their son's arrest, that he had been sexually abusing his step-daughter, but they had long known that he'd been physically abusing his wife. They had seen Lacey many times with blackened eyes and purple bruises. The first time, her mother-in-law had asked how she'd gotten injured, and Lacey had told her. No questions were asked after that. When Ronald's parents came to Bucks County to visit their son and grandsons, they never commented on the growing number of holes the size of a large man's fist that marred the walls in every room of the house. Even after their son pled guilty, they refused to openly acknowledge his vile acts. No condolences were ever expressed to Mary or Lacey.

Under federal law, criminal incarceration renders a prisoner "involuntarily unemployed" (unless he somehow still has an attachable income), so Ronald was free of any legal obligation to pay child support for the duration of his sentence. Aware that Lacey and her three children had been plunged into poverty when their son was incarcerated, the Berringtons never offered any financial help.

Lacey had taken a part-time job as a check-out girl at a local big-box store when her youngest child had started kindergarten. She was able to get a small increase in her hours after Ronald was incarcerated, but full-time work wasn't available to her. Stores like that one preferred part-time workers, who weren't eligible for set hours and benefits like paid days off and time-and-a-half on holidays. Since Lacey wasn't earning enough to pay the monthly mortgage on the marital residence, she and the children were on their way to being homeless when a co-worker of Lacey's named John Mason stepped in to lend a hand. He had heard about the situation just as the lease on his apartment was coming due, and he asked Lacey if she had room for a renter.

The arrival of John Mason was a stroke of good fortune for Lacey and her children. It wasn't only the money he paid to live there, or the extra groceries he always brought home. It was also the fact that his personality and character were the absolute opposite of Ronald Berrington's. For Lacey and her children, John Mason was the proof they sorely needed that a man could be a good person.

Ronald's parents didn't approve of John Mason. As far as they were concerned, he didn't have a right to live in their son's house or to become a father-figure to their grandsons. Soon, the Berringtons decided that Lacey was not an appropriate caretaker for their grandchildren. They actually told her that any nanny they chose to hire would be more qualified for the job. What they didn't tell her was that they had decided to hire a top-notch attorney and file for primary custody. They had every reason to think that Lacey wouldn't have the resources to fight them. She hardly had enough money to survive.

The Berringtons' attorney undoubtedly advised them to find a way to get the children into their physical custody and then file in New Jersey. They could then spoil the children with lavish gifts and treats until the hearing, grooming them to be accustomed to living with their well-to-do grandparents instead of their indigent mother and sister. The right moment arrived when Lacey came down with the flu. Warning her that she was "contagious," they offered to keep the boys with them until she recovered. Their lack of concern about *Mary's* risk of contagion was consistent with their attitude towards Lacey's daughter, so it didn't raise any suspicions.

Three days later, when Lacey called to make arrangements for her younger children's return, she was told by her in-laws that they'd made plans to take the boys to a fancy amusement park the following day and to the zoo the day after that. "We'd like to keep them for a few more days," they said. It was a good ploy. Lacey wouldn't want to deprive her children of those special experiences.

On the day she was supposed to have gotten her sons back, she was wakened early in the morning by the constable with his manila envelope. As soon as she saw the emergency custody petition, her whole body began trembling uncontrollably. The constable had actually felt sorry for her. "Just get a good lawyer," he had advised.

Thinking she couldn't afford a lawyer, good or otherwise, Lacey called her in-laws. She told me her hands were shaking so badly she had trouble dialing their number. She tried to steady her breaking voice as she informed Ronald's mother that she was coming to retrieve her children. "But she told me not to bother trying to get them back, that they were going to live with her from now on. She said if I wanted to agree to a visitation schedule, I should call her attorney. Otherwise, she said, 'We'll see you in court.'"

I looked over the letter from the Berringtons' attorney. The heading showed she was a named partner in a large, prestigious New Jersey law firm—someone who likely earned about twenty times what I did.

I quickly read through the emergency custody petition to see what kind of story Ronald's parents were telling the New Jersey court. There had to be strong emergency circumstances for a court in New Jersey to hear this case, because the children hadn't resided in New Jersey for the required six months. To establish such an emergency, the Berringtons had to allege that the children had either been abandoned in New Jersey or needed emergency protection because they were being subjected to mistreatment or abuse in their home state.

Lacey had obviously not abandoned the children, and she had never mistreated or abused them. But the petition alleged that the conditions in their mother's home were so deficient that they amounted to mistreatment and neglect. The examples provided? The furnace was old and frequently broke down; their mother had been so delinquent in paying her bills that at one point the electricity had been turned off for three days; holes were smashed into the walls in every room; and the children's half-sister had been sexually abused in the house for an entire year before their mother had bothered to intervene.

I was outraged at the unscrupulous scheming behind the filing of the Berringtons' emergency custody petition and at the audacious hypocrisy of the allegations it contained. The effects of violence and poverty so disdainfully described by Loretta and Ronald J. Berrington Jr. had been caused by their own son. That they could attempt to divert blame onto Lacey was astounding.

Ronald's parents must have been advised by their attorney that their efforts to obtain New Jersey jurisdiction had little chance to withstand a legal challenge. But since they also knew that Lacey could not afford to hire an attorney, they had every reason to expect that no legal challenge would be forthcoming. It was gratifying to know that their expectations were about to be dashed.

My first step was to quickly draft a petition called Preliminary Objections to Jurisdiction, in which I refuted the Berringtons' assertions that New Jersey had statutory grounds to preside over the case. By law, I had twenty days from the date when my client was served the original petition before I needed to file these objections, but I didn't want to wait a single day to do it. I wanted to give the Berringtons and their attorney, Ms. Hot-Shot, fair notice that Lacey had the kind of lawyer on her side that they did *not* have—the kind of lawyer that money can't buy.

A paralegal at Legal Aid volunteered to drive to the New Jersey courthouse to file my preliminary objections, and Lacey decided to accompany her. They got to the prothonotary just before the doors closed for the day. When the paralegal called to let me know that she and Lacey were on their way back with time-stamped copies of the document, I called the Berringtons' attorney.

Ms. Hot-Shot sounded shocked to hear from me. Her firm handled only wealthy clientele; most of their family law cases were divorces involving the valuing of complex assets and the division of large estates. She'd never had a Legal Aid lawyer as opposing counsel. In fact, she claimed to have never heard of Legal Aid. After I explained to her about the work of the Legal Services Corporation, she waxed indignant. It wasn't fair, she said, that her clients had to pay for an attorney while my client got to get one for free.

I took a deep breath and responded calmly. It wasn't fair, I said, that her clients had a giant pile of money they never worked for, while my client had to labor every day for minimum wage.

After those pleasantries were exchanged, I told Ms. Hot-Shot that I had already filed Preliminary Objections to Jurisdiction, and that we both knew my objections would prevail. I was surprised by how quickly and matter-of-factly she conceded the point, saying, "I'll withdraw my clients' New Jersey petition and advise them they need to retain a Bucks County attorney to pursue their case."

So that solved the New Jersey issue. After we agreed to exchange our final filings, there was only one more thing I needed to say: "Your clients are illegally withholding my client's children. They must be returned to her immediately!"

Again Ms. Hot-Shot spoke matter-of-factly: "Yes. I'll inform them to do so."

When Lacey got back to our office, she couldn't stop thanking me. On her way out, she even hugged Rosemarie in the waiting room. Later, Rosemarie came to tell me that Lacey had declared triumphantly: "*My* lawyer is better than *their* lawyer! My lawyer is the *best!*" It's always nice to know that one's efforts are appreciated. But nothing can compare to the feeling I got when my Legal Aid clients, who weren't able to choose their lawyer, believed that the best lawyer had been chosen for them.

But the legal fight was only beginning. A week later, another custody petition arrived in the mail. This time, the Berringtons' attorney was James M. Whitley, Esquire, a partner in one of Bucks County's largest, most prestigious, and most powerful law firms. Two judges then on the bench had come directly from the firm, as had others in the past (and as would others in the future). The firm's attorneys charged exorbitant hourly fees, which has the intriguing effect of making many people think they are a cut above the rest—despite the fact that, in truth, some of the firm's attorneys were quite good, some were okay, and some were not very good at all—just like the varying skills of Legal Aid attorneys. The only difference was that those high-priced attorneys carried an aura of invincibility around with them, befitting their stature as members of That Firm.

I've never responded well to auras of invincibility. They're designed to intimidate, but they just piss me off. I knew I was going to have to take a number of deep breaths when interactions between me and Mr. Whitley began—because, I reminded myself, it is important to remain civil in all dealings with opposing counsel.

The new custody petition was unchanged from the original, except that the document was now signed by James M. Whitley rather than by Ms. Hot-Shot. A custody conference was scheduled to take place in twelve days.

Custody conferences are a required first step in Bucks County's custody litigation process. The parties and their attorneys (if any) are ordered to meet with a custody conference officer in a small conference room in the family master's office at the courthouse. During the conference, the custody conference officer collects basic information about the parties and their children. Then the party that filed states his or her reasons for filing and what kind of custody arrangement he or she is seeking, and the opposing party responds to any accusations made, makes his or her own accusations, and proposes a different result. After that sequence of events, negotiations are supposed to take place, and sometimes, when the disagreements are fairly minor, they actually do. If negotiations are successful, the conference officer types up the terms of the agreement, the parties (and their attorneys) sign the document, everyone gets a copy, and an order page arrives in the mail shortly thereafter, with a judge's signature, making the agreement an official order of the court.

Unfortunately, in contested custody cases, the disagreements between the parties are usually not minor. Arguments quickly flare and can just as quickly escalate. It was obvious that no agreement was going to be reached in this case, and I vowed to save my arguments for court. My goal was to get in and out of the conference as swiftly as we could, saying as little as possible.

The conference did give me a chance to meet the Berringtons and their lawyer. I was surprised to discover that James M. Whitley wasn't insufferable. In fact, he seemed like a decent guy. Courteous and reserved, he allowed his clients to hurl their accusations, but he didn't join in. I had a strong suspicion that the Berringtons were not the sort of people he would have elected to spend his time with in a nonprofessional capacity. As for the Berringtons, they were both exactly as I had imagined them to be: mean-looking, mean-spirited, arrogant, and condescending. Mr. Berrington spoke with a trace of a British accent, although Lacey told me after the conference that he was born in Iowa and had never been to Europe.

Custody conferences often turn out to be a waste of everyone's time, but occasionally information comes out that is helpful in preparing for a hearing. What came out at this conference was a previously undisclosed complaint about the living conditions at Lacey's home. According to the Berringtons, a noxious odor permeated the dwelling. This particular complaint concerned me. The judge assigned to hear our case, the Honorable Steven Palmer, might well be swayed in his deliberations by the image of a foul-smelling residence. It was something I needed to check out, especially because a worker from Bucks County Children & Youth Social Services Agency was scheduled to make a home inspection in response to a child neglect complaint lodged by the Berringtons. Depending on his or her overall findings, the CYS worker might be called as a witness at the custody hearing.

The custody conference had been held on a swelteringly hot Friday afternoon in August. The next day was even hotter—around 98 degrees and unbearably humid. It was Saturday, and I had planned to be sitting in an air-conditioned movie theater, watching a movie I really wanted to see. Instead, I was knocking on the door to Lacey's house, hoping to establish that a noxious odor did not really permeate the dwelling.

Lacey opened the door, with John Mason and the three children standing right behind her. The children smiled cheerfully when introduced. John Mason did, too. He was medium height, medium build, with medium-brown hair and medium-brown eyes. He looked like a thousand other guys. But it was quite apparent that he was a very special guy to Lacey and her children, and that they were very special to him.

I wasn't inside the house very long before I began detecting a musty smell. It wasn't overwhelming, it wasn't noxious, but it was noticeable. I suggested to Lacey that she spray a little lemon-scented air freshener around the house before the CYS worker came on Monday. There didn't seem to be much else she could do to alleviate the problem. Everything else that CYS was likely to care about seemed okay. The children looked happy, healthy, and well-groomed. The rooms were clean. There was no sign of mouse or roach infestation. The refrigerator was sufficiently stocked with food.

I glanced through the rooms on the first floor. "Where are all the holes in the walls?"

Lacey gestured towards John Mason. "He plastered and spackled and painted every room in the house."

I was impressed, and told him so. "The walls look wonderful!"

John Mason's labors meant a lot. I didn't believe for a minute that anyone besides the Berringtons would blame Lacey for the gaping holes that her husband had punched in the walls, but the fact that the unsightly imprints of those terrible times were now completely erased from the residence was an important milestone for a family on the road to recovery.

The house was hot. It didn't have air-conditioning in any of the rooms, or even a fan. Though all the windows were open, there wasn't a hint of a breeze. After an hour, sweat began pouring down my face faster than I could wipe it away. The combination of the heat and the lingering smell became a bit too much for me. I had planned to stay longer, but I couldn't. Later that day, I drove back to Lacey's house to donate a fan, but I didn't go inside.

I worried the rest of the weekend about the impending visit from CYS. It was scheduled for Monday morning, when I had to be in court for a contested hearing in another case. I tried never to leave my clients unguarded in the presence of a representative from CYS, but there was nothing I could do about it this time.

My hearing went on all day, finally ending victoriously for my client a little after six p.m. When I finally reached Lacey that evening, she could barely wait to blurt out the good news. "The visit went great! The man from CYS was really nice! He said he'd be glad to talk to you any time you want!"

It was a lovely way to end a long day, with a decisive courtroom win for one client and, for another, a rare successful encounter with CYS.

I phoned Jerry, the CYS worker, the next day. I was hoping he'd be willing to testify in the custody hearing.

I've always believed that it's best to start conversations with potential witnesses by first advocating for my clients, explaining the morality of their position and how much is at stake for them, before asking them to do my clients the great favor of coming to court to testify on their behalf. So before asking Jerry any questions, I told him how strongly I felt about the case. I described how Lacey's husband had physically abused her, sexually abused her daughter, and terrorized the family. And I told him how the husband's parents had never tried to intervene before their son went to jail, nor offered to help in any way afterwards. Now they were suing for custody, trying to take Lacey's boys away from her, so the positive testimony of a CYS worker would be invaluable.

Jerry said he'd be glad to testify for my client at the custody hearing. He had seen no signs that the children were being neglected; on the contrary, he had seen a warm and nurturing family. He'd been charmed by the cheerfulness of the two younger children, who had chatted guilelessly with him throughout his visit. When he asked them about their father, both children had told him they were glad he didn't live with them anymore. As for the residence, he had not observed any conditions there that raised a concern.

Jerry didn't say a word about the house's musty odor. Had that lemon-scented spray I'd recommended actually solved the problem? I wanted to leave well enough alone, but if Jerry was going to be a witness for us in court, I couldn't wait until he was being cross-examined to find out what he would say when asked about an odor.

"Old houses sometimes have a bit of a musty fragrance," I began casually, pausing to consider exactly how to phrase the question I needed to ask.

"That's probably true," Jerry interjected during the pause, "but fragrances are wasted on me. I don't have a sense of smell."

"What?" I wasn't sure I'd heard him correctly.

"I don't have a sense of smell," he repeated.

I almost burst out laughing.

Jerry explained that he had a medical condition called congenital anosmia, which rendered him completely unable to detect odors. Jerry's description of the condition, and its impact on him over the years, made clear how challenging it is to do without *any* of our five basic senses. It really wasn't a laughing matter.

I told Jerry that one of the reasons the Berringtons had given for why they should get primary custody of the younger children was their claim that Lacey's house had a noxious odor. I acknowledged that, while at the house on a stiflingly hot day, I had noticed a mustiness, which I said I associated with old houses. Then I posed the following question to him: "If, when you are testifying, you are asked if you detected a bad odor when you visited Lacey's home, would you feel comfortable simply answering 'No'?"

"I'd feel perfectly comfortable giving that true answer," Jerry responded. "Nothing would please me more than being able to be of assistance to this family."

At that precise moment, I could have sworn I smelled roses.

18. Poverty on Trial

A week before the Berrington custody hearing, I found out that Ronald III had hired an attorney to represent his so-called interests. Ronald himself was incarcerated more than halfway across the state and was not going to be permitted to attend the hearing, but he had arranged (undoubtedly with his parents' money) to have a lawyer there on his behalf. Predictably, Ronald's "interests" were that the children be taken away from their mother and sister and deposited into the primary custody of his parents. So I was going to have two high-priced lawyers opposing me instead of one.

Early on the morning of the hearing, I called Judge Palmer's chambers to ask his secretary how many cases besides ours were on the judge's court list, to get a sense of how likely it was that our case, or any portion of it, would actually be heard that day. A contested case with three lawyers was practically guaranteed to be more time-consuming than one with two, so the odds were that ours would be placed last on the list. The judge's secretary told me there were three other cases scheduled that day, one a minor matter but the other two probably entailing full hearings. If the status remained unchanged when the list was called at ten a.m., it seemed probable that our case would need to be rescheduled.

I was glad I had arranged for Jerry to be on call at his office at CYS, which was just a few miles from the courthouse. Being on call for the hearing meant that he had to be ready to come to court as soon as he received my call, but he wouldn't have to hang out there, potentially for

hours, waiting for our case to be heard. Keeping Jerry on call was a courtesy to him but it was also beneficial to me, because I didn't want the
Berringtons to know until the last possible minute that I had Jerry for a
witness. Now, if our case got continued to another day, the opposing
counsels would have no forewarning that I had somehow managed the
unimaginable: having CYS on my indigent client's side.

At the call of the list, Judge Palmer said he would take any agreements first. The minor matter had settled, but the rest of us were still
requesting full hearings. After the one agreement was placed on the record, Judge Palmer announced that he wanted to conference the Berrington matter. None of the lawyers had asked for a conference, so Judge
Palmer's sudden announcement was unexpected, but the unexpected
happens a lot in family court. All three of us attorneys dutifully trailed
the judge as he exited the courtroom through the door near his bench
and made his way to a small room behind the courtroom, an inner sanctum that was otherwise accessible only to judges and their staffs.

Ronald's attorney was Gina Mandrel, a solo practitioner whom I
had never previously had as opposing counsel. She was, in fact, a fairly
rare presence at the courthouse. I had been told that she was independently wealthy and liked to travel. She took cases only when the whim
struck her. I couldn't figure out what appealed to her about representing
Ronald Berrington III, but apparently the whim had struck.

Judge Palmer tended to be chatty at these backroom meetings. He
had practiced family law before becoming a judge, and the intimate details of family law cases still held his interest—especially when laced with
drama. So the odd and odious particulars of the Berrington case were
bound to intrigue him: child molestation with an overlay of incest, domestic violence, incarceration, and allegations of neglect.

As we all settled into chairs around a small conference table, Judge
Palmer addressed James Whitley, the attorney for Loretta and Ronald J.
Berrington Jr. "Your clients filed this petition, Jim, so you go first. Tell
me—briefly—why your clients should get primary custody of these children."

Whitley wisely distanced himself and his clients from Ronald J. Berrington III, referring to Ronald only as "Lacey's husband" or "the father
of the children," never as his clients' son. He concentrated on contrasting

the chaos and deprivation that the children had experienced in the custody of their parents with the privileged life that their affluent grandparents were able to provide for them. Describing the children as neglected,
he ended his argument with his best illustration, the final *coup de grâce*:
"While in their mother's custody, these poor children spent half the past
winter living in a house with a *broken furnace!*"

I watched Judge Palmer as he listened intently, appearing receptive
to Whitley's argument, while Gina Mandrel nodded solemnly in agreement. Apparently, Lacey's poverty was sufficient evidence of her inadequacies as a parent, and the Berringtons' great wealth was sufficient
proof of their parenting skills.

As was so often true in my cases, poverty was on trial. When it was
my turn to speak, I had to restrain myself from yelling at the whole pack
of them.

"Let's clear up the issue of who actually deserves our disdain," I said,
speaking as slowly and as calmly as I could. "These children spent half
the past winter in a house with a broken furnace because their mother
couldn't afford to buy a new one. She had to put aside money from her
low-paying job, week after week, until she could save enough to pay for
it. *That's* why these children had to spend half the winter in a cold house.
Their father, who's in jail where he belongs, doesn't pay any child support. What we should be asking is: what were the children's ultra-rich
grandparents doing while their daughter-in-law and her children were
huddled together in front of a kerosene heater? Did they purchase a new
furnace for the family, like any *loving* grandparents would do if they
could afford it? Like any *decent* grandparents would do, if they could afford it? No! Not the Berringtons. Despite their *inherited millions,* they
chose instead to add the broken furnace to their list of complaints. They
chose, instead, to hire an *expensive* lawyer, to assist them in their efforts
to separate these children from the mother and sister they love."

Some of the "calm" and the "slow" had departed from my speech by
the time I was done.

I expected James Whitley to come to his clients' defense as soon as
I finished speaking, but he said nothing. It was Gina Mandrel who
jumped into the fray. "Maybe the Berringtons should have bought a new
furnace. But it wouldn't have solved all the instances of neglect that the

children have had to experience while in the care of their mother. It's obvious that Mr. and Mrs. Berrington are in a far better position than your client to provide for the well-being of these children."

Before I could say anything in response, Judge Palmer chimed in: "Meg, you must admit that the Berringtons and your client live in two different worlds."

My last remaining efforts to stay even-tempered were blown away by that statement.

"I agree that the Berringtons and my client live in two different worlds!" I snapped. "The Berringtons live in the world that their son grew up in, the world that shaped Ronald-the-Third into the heartless pedophile and wife-beater that he is today. No other child should ever be forced to live in that world!"

The stunned look on Judge Palmer's face told me I had gotten through to him. I had disrupted the cherished myth that wealth and worth are intrinsically connected. But myths are hard to destroy. I didn't know for sure if I had done this one any lasting damage, or if I had just delivered a disorienting but fleeting blow.

Regaining his poker face, Judge Palmer told Whitley and me to go out and talk to our clients. "See if they'll settle for the children spending one weekend a month with their grandparents, maybe two weeks in the summer."

Suddenly it looked like the case might be won without a hearing, that the gilded Berringtons had indeed lost their sheen. As the three of us padded out of the conference room together, Judge Palmer called out to Ms. Mandrel: "Gina, if you can reach your client, tell him I don't particularly care what he has to say."

Lacey was thrilled with the judge's settlement proposal. "I don't mind them spending some time with their grandparents," she told me. Whitley's clients, who had left the courtroom before we did, sounded far less agreeable. Lacey and I could hear both of them yelling at him, even though they were halfway down the hall. It soon became obvious that there would be no agreement.

The hearing was continued to another day.

Gina Mandrel did her best to try to get Ronald III transported from prison to attend the rescheduled hearing, but she was unsuccessful. I was probably even more disappointed by her lack of success than she was. Ronald III's presence in the courtroom would only have aided my case. Lacey told me that Ronald and his father looked very much alike, so the optical effect alone would have been a nice touch. And watching him be subjected to my cross-examination might well have been the highlight of the event. The fact that Ms. Mandrel thought it was a good idea to have her client attend the hearing told me that she wasn't a very good lawyer. I realized I didn't have to worry about the ratio of lawyers being two against one.

When the rescheduled hearing date arrived, we had to persevere without the prisoner. The Berringtons, as the plaintiffs, got to put on their side of the case first. Mrs. Berrington took the stand, devoting most of her testimony to maligning Lacey—for the dank smell in her home, for the holes in the walls, for her "unwillingness" to get broken appliances fixed, and for her inability to protect her children from harm.

My goals for the cross-examination of Mrs. Berrington were three-fold: to put on stark display her total refusal to acknowledge her son's culpability; to give her the opportunity to reiterate her complaints about the condition of Lacey's home (because I had a CYS worker waiting to contradict her); and to showcase her haughty air of privilege and superiority. It didn't require much skill on my part to achieve all three goals.

Mr. Berrington didn't testify, but one of the parties' acquaintances did. The woman attested to how admirably the Berringtons took care of their grandchildren. She summed up her testimony by saying, "They're fabulous parents!"

When it was my turn to cross-examine their witness, I simply asked: "Are Loretta and Ronald J. Berrington Jr., these friends of yours who possess the sterling parenting skills you just told us about, the same people whose parenting skills helped make their *son* the man he is today?"

The witness appeared panic-stricken when this question was posed to her, looking desperately to the Berringtons' lawyer for guidance he was not permitted to give, before finally blurting out, "I don't know what you want me to say."

"I'm satisfied with that answer," I said. "No further questions."

She was the Berringtons' final witness. From my point of view, the plaintiff's side of the case had ended on a perfect note.

My first witness was Lacey. She testified to the physical, verbal, and emotional abuse that Ronald had subjected her to during their marriage, how his repeated threats to kill her and the children if she ever tried to leave him had made her too fearful to attempt to escape, and of the many times that his parents had seen the bruises on her face and neck and arms and legs without evincing the slightest interest. She told of the horrifying moment when she learned, from the guidance counselor at Mary's elementary school, that her husband had been sexually abusing her young daughter, silencing the child with threats to kill her and her mother and brothers if she ever told anyone. She described how difficult it had been, in the midst of trauma, to convince her employer to allow her to work more hours at her low-paying job, and how desperately she had struggled financially until a co-worker became a renter, augmenting the family's income and saving them from homelessness. Through it all, Lacey testified, Loretta and Ronald Berrington Jr. never offered a word of encouragement or a penny's worth of assistance. Lacey also talked about her three children—two sons and a daughter—and about how close the siblings were to her and to each other. Officially, Mary was the boys' half-sibling, a fact that Ronald and his parents frequently made a special point of noting as a way of relegating Mary to a lesser status. But it was a fact that had no meaning to Lacey's young sons, who adored their big sister.

At the time of the hearing, there was a long-standing presumption in custody law that it was best not to separate siblings, half-siblings or step-siblings that had been growing up together in the same household. It was a *rebuttable* presumption, meaning that it was assumed to be true unless sufficient evidence could be produced to contradict it. While on the stand, Loretta Berrington had tried to contradict the presumption by claiming that Mary was a disturbed and unruly child, whom her half-brothers feared. Although Mary would have had reason to be disturbed and unruly, it was a fabricated claim that did not survive Lacey's loving description of her daughter. It was further demolished by my introduction, one by one, of piles of photographs Lacey had taken, showing her three children lovingly interacting with each other over the years.

I had John Mason testify, too. I wanted the judge to see what a fine person he was, and to give him public credit for the many steps he had taken to undo the damage done by Ronald Berrington III. Besides explaining the multiple repairs he had made to the house, he was able to tell us what a good mother Lacey was to all her children, and about how charming her children were. He said he felt honored to be a part of their lives and to be in a position to contribute to their happiness.

John Mason had been worried about testifying, afraid he'd be too nervous to talk when he got on the stand, but he turned out to be a model witness. Loretta Berrington had spoken demeaningly of him, characterizing him as an "unskilled laborer" that Lacey had "picked up at work" and thrust upon her children. But in the end, I think, it was John Mason who got to deliver the final blow to that insidious myth that wealth and worth are intrinsically connected.

My last witness was social worker Jerry, who carried with him the supreme authority of the Bucks County Children & Youth Social Services Agency. It's always best to end on a strong note, and Jerry did not disappoint. By the time the hearing was finally held, Jerry had bonded with Lacey and John and the children, and also with me. He had become more than our witness. He was our friend.

I felt confident, even before Jerry testified, that Loretta and Ronald Berrington Jr. would not be getting primary custody of Lacey's sons, that they would not be raising another generation of Berrington boys. On that main issue, I knew we had already won the case. Lacey was not opposed to the Berringtons having periods of partial custody of the boys, and I expected that the periods granted to them by Judge Palmer would not be excessive. But I did have one strong remaining concern. In my opinion, it was imperative that Ronald III be prohibited from having any contact whatsoever with the children, and I was worried that Judge Palmer did not share that opinion.

Through his attorney, I learned that Ronald was still denying any wrongdoing on his part. According to him, Mary had lied about the sexual molestation and Lacey had lied about having been physically abused. It was them and not him who belonged behind bars. That was Ronald's official story, and I thought he would try to convince the boys of its veracity any chance he got. Not only that, I was concerned that Mary's recovery from trauma could be jeopardized by the knowledge that her rapist had access to exert influence over her little brothers. That was why at least half of my closing argument was an urgent plea to Judge Palmer to include a provision in his order that not only forbade the Berringtons from discussing their son or bad-mouthing Lacey or Mary in the presence or hearing of their grandchildren should they be granted any visitation, but also banned Ronald Berrington III from having any form of contact with the children, either directly or indirectly through third parties.

Judge Palmer entered his order from the bench as soon as closing arguments were completed, granting primary physical custody and sole legal custody of the children to Lacey. He gave the Berringtons partial custody of the children for two non-consecutive weeks in the summer, starting the following year, and one Saturday-to-Sunday visit every non-summer month.

As we sat at the defense table together, Lacey leaned in and squeezed my hand in a silent gesture of exultation and relief. But I was apprehensive, waiting for what might come next. And then it came: Judge Palmer granted Ronald the right to have supervised contact with the children during his parents' custodial periods.

Ronald J. Berrington III had repeatedly raped his children's sister and beaten their mother, but the fact that he was their biological father was enough for Judge Palmer to conclude that the children's best interests would be served by having contact with him. The only protective feature in the order was the "no bad-mouthing" provision I had requested, which Judge Palmer also applied to Ronald.

I was bitterly disappointed, but not surprised.

Unlike me, Lacey wasn't upset about the judge's decision to allow Ronald to have contact with the children when they were with his parents. She was certain the Berringtons were far too self-involved to ever go to the trouble of traveling hundreds of miles to visit their son in jail, where he would be residing for at least the next five years, and she had ascertained that Ronald's access to a telephone, and the length of time he could speak on one, was severely limited. She was also certain that the children would tell her if Ronald or his parents said anything bad about her or Mary, which would be a violation of Judge Palmer's order.

Because Lacey was happy with the order, I accepted it. But I didn't like it. It was one of the cases that led me to join the legislative committee of the Pennsylvania Coalition Against Domestic Violence (then headed by famed attorney Barbara Hart). I was able to help draft the wording of crucial proposed changes to the Child Custody Statute and the Protection from Abuse Act. Aided by PCADV's talented lobbyist, the required majority of Pennsylvania's senators and representatives who make the laws of our commonwealth have seen the wisdom of adopting all or significant parts of many of the amendments that PCADV has proposed or supported over the years. Now, a judge in Pennsylvania is not permitted to issue an order granting any kind of custodial rights to a convicted rapist, unless the judge has considered the criminal conduct involved and has specifically determined, on the record, that contact with that parent does not pose any threat of harm to the children.

While amendments to child custody statutes over the years have usually improved those laws, child custody statutes are still a virtual minefield when it comes to truly protecting the best interests of children. A Pennsylvania judge with the mindset of Judge Palmer, for example, could still issue the same order today that Judge Palmer issued back then, the only difference being that now he would need to defend his decision on the record, and an attorney would potentially have stronger grounds for an appeal to the Superior Court. Needless to say, the relative strength of an appeal is a purely academic issue when the client is happy with the outcome of the hearing. Sadly, it is also a purely academic issue for the many low-income people who don't have access to free representation or the means to hire an attorney to file such an appeal.

Lacey *was* happy with the outcome of the hearing—extremely happy—and her happiness finally made me less upset. As one would expect, the Berringtons were extremely unhappy with the outcome. It was obvious they were furious that Lacey, who couldn't afford an attorney (and therefore, they believed, did not *deserve* an attorney), had gotten one anyway; that their high-paid New Jersey attorney had been unable to keep the case in New Jersey; and that their two high-paid Pennsylvania attorneys had been unable to win the case. The Berringtons had expected to be taking Lacey's sons away from her when the day was done, and instead all they could do was storm angrily from the courtroom.

Their great wealth had failed them, exposing their impoverished souls.

19. Fetal Alcohol Syndrome

Rosemarie knocked on the door to my office. "A woman just walked in without an appointment, begging to talk to our family law attorney. She's too upset to tell me what it's about. Can you see her?"

I was engrossed in preparations for a major hearing in two days. A stack of work to do on other active cases was piled on the side of my desk, urgently awaiting my attention. I had to think about it for a second. Then I said "Sure," because this sounded like it was an emergency. Emergencies always had to be handled.

I hurried to the waiting room, where a young woman was anxiously pacing with two little boys who seemed to be attached to her, each holding onto one of her hands and pressing his small body against her legs. All three of them looked shell-shocked.

"I need to get custody of my children," the young woman blurted out when she saw me. "I need to get custody right away!"

I guided them into my office and pointed to a large basket in one corner of my room, filled with an assortment of toys, books, dolls, and crayons. "Would your children like to play with some toys while we talk?"

"That would be nice," she said, letting go of their hands, but the children instantly wrapped their arms around her legs and clung more tightly.

"Would you like to play with some toys?" I asked them directly, softly and without approaching. They buried their faces in their mother's skirt.

I went to the basket and pulled out two handfuls of miniature toy trucks and spread them on the floor near the children. "Come play with these trucks," I urged. "You can each pick one to take home with you when your mommy and I are done talking."

The children did not move. They looked too afraid to let go of their mother.

I have always done my best to shield children from the conversations I have with adults during legal consultations. When people called Legal Aid to schedule an appointment, they would be asked to please try not to bring children. I felt it was important to exclude children from these meetings for a number of reasons: to allow me and the client to take as much time as we needed, without distraction or interruption; to preserve the client's confidentiality; to ensure an environment safe enough for clients to provide uncensored information about the issues that brought them to see me; and to protect the children from hearing that uncensored information. Unfortunately, poor people can rarely afford to hire a babysitter, so if no friend or family member is available to help, they usually had to bring their children with them. When that happened, as it frequently did, there was a secretary who was willing to play with them in her room, armed with supplies from my basket. But that wasn't going to be doable on this occasion. These children were clearly too traumatized to be separated from their mother, who appeared to be just as traumatized as they were.

"Will you help me?" she pleaded. "Will you help me get custody of my children?"

It is not my practice to commit to representation before I have obtained and assessed the facts of a case. But I did so in this case. I had seen enough to know for a certainty that these children belonged with their mother. So I answered without hesitation. "I'll do everything I can to help you get custody of your children."

My new client began to cry. "Thank God! Thank God! Thank God! Thank God!" she kept repeating.

"Well, you're *welcome*," I interrupted finally, hoping to make her smile. She laughed instead, and at the sight and sound of it, the smile I had been aiming for grew shyly on the faces of both of her children. The heavy weight of anxiety that had filled the room began to lift.

Not long after that, tentatively at first, the children began playing gently together. They carefully maneuvered their toy trucks around one another in peaceful concentration, avoiding the loud crashes that most little children seemed to savor. While they played, I gathered the information I needed from my new client. The story she told was hard to hear.

Jami Steele was only twenty-three years old, but she was so tiny and slim she barely looked like a teenager. Her children were Henry, who was four and a half, and Paul, who was three. She was not married to their father, Hank Roeger (the only good thing about the situation; at least she wouldn't need a divorce). From the behavior that Jami described, it was evident that Hank was a sadist, as viciously abusive as any abuser I had previously dealt with. In the five years they had been together, Jami told me, he had beaten her at least a hundred times, once so badly that she had almost died. He had brutally raped and sodomized her, cut her with a razor, and crushed out cigarettes on her body. He had threatened, countless times, to kill her if she ever tried to leave him, and to bury her body where only rats and worms would ever find it.

Finally one day Jami managed to escape with the children, preferring death to life with Hank. She hid from him, but he tracked her down, slashed the tires on her car, and broke into the home where she was staying, snatching the sleeping children from their beds. Awakened by their screams as he ran carrying them out the door, she had tried in vain to catch up to him. She had been left to watch helplessly as he threw them into his truck, threatening that he would kill them if they didn't shut up. She could hear them screaming for her as he drove away.

It was Lily, all over again.

Her call to the police had elicited the response that by then I had heard from the police so many times: "Fathers have as much right to their children as mothers do." The atrocious circumstances surrounding the exercise of that "right" were rarely of any interest to the police. Unless a court order is being violated, there is no such thing as a "parental kidnapping."

When Jami realized that the police would do nothing to help her, she rushed to the courthouse to file for custody. She couldn't afford an attorney and did not yet know about Legal Aid. Three months later, when the custody hearing was finally held before the Honorable Michael J.

Kane, Jami was alone and too frightened to speak out, while Hank Roeger had a lawyer—a cagey, nasty lawyer, who, it seemed to me, specialized in representing sociopaths in family law cases. The lawyer obtained a letter from a local doctor which stated that Henry, who had minor facial abnormalities, had been born with fetal alcohol syndrome. Hank testified that Jami was an extreme alcoholic who had refused to reduce her consumption of liquor during the pregnancy, leaving little Henry to endure a lifetime of deformity.

Understandably, given the information presented, Judge Kane granted legal and physical custody of the children to their father. Jami was permitted to have contact with them only under Hank Roeger's supervision.

Later that same day, Hank had called Jami and asked, mockingly, "When are you coming to visit my children?"

Jami knew how unsafe she would be "under Hank Roeger's supervision" so she told him: "Never." It was the smartest thing she could have said, because Hank Roeger didn't want the children. He wanted Jami.

Two weeks after the hearing, Hank drove to the front of Jami's residence, flung the children out of his truck, and sped away. Jami wasn't home, so the children huddled together on a step until a neighbor, who had witnessed the event, took them into her apartment. It was the middle of January, and the children were dressed only in T-shirts and ill-fitting pants. Paul had no shoes. When Jami returned home three hours later, she was overjoyed to see them.

Paul, shoeless, was the lucky one. Henry's feet had been crammed into a pair of shoes that Jami had left behind when she fled because Henry had outgrown them. The shoes were so tight he could barely walk in them, and he cried out in pain as she removed them. All of Henry's toes and the back of both heels had bleeding gashes. Two of his toes showed signs of infection from the untreated wounds. The children were so caked in dirt that Jami was sure Hank had never bathed them. They smelled of grime and alcohol. They clung to her and kept crying: "Don't let Daddy come back!"

I had long before perfected the ability to never show fear in a client's presence, but I have been far less successful at suppressing feelings of anguish. Jami's account was so devastating that I wanted to weep, and I couldn't block the tears that pooled in my eyes. I was feeling more than anguish. I was feeling rage.

As horrendous as it was, there was a serious problem with the case. If we went to court, I might succeed in getting the children removed from the custody of Hank Roeger, but they might be placed in foster care, not with Jami, because of Jami's alcoholism. Litigation is rarely devoid of risk, but in this case it was fraught with danger. As it was, without taking any legal action, the children were now in Jami's physical custody. But Hank had a court order, so he could come and take the children any time he wanted. Unlike Jami, he could readily obtain the assistance of the police.

"Do you have any reason to believe that Hank will simply leave the children with you from now on?" I asked.

"No," she said. "I know he doesn't want them, but he'll take them again to hurt me."

I suspected that Hank would take the children again not only to hurt her, and not only to flaunt the power that the court order had given him, but also because he would calculate that being with her children again, however briefly, would break Jami's brave resolve to never see them again if it had to be under his supervision.

If Henry and Paul needed to be either in the custody of Hank Roeger or in foster care, there was no question that the choice had to be the latter. But my job was to fight for them to be in the custody of their mother, where they belonged. So we needed to deal immediately with Jami's alcoholism.

"We have to talk about your alcohol addiction," I told her. "Tell me what steps you have taken to overcome it."

"I don't have an alcohol addiction," she said.

I spoke sternly. "You won't be able to get custody if you deny you're an alcoholic."

"But I'm *not* an alcoholic," Jami insisted. "I never drink alcohol. I'm not allowed to. I have epilepsy."

I was stunned. "How long have you had epilepsy?"

"I've had it ever since I can remember," she said, "and I've never in my whole life taken one sip of alcohol."

It took a few minutes for me to process what she was telling me and to-decide that she was telling the truth. My apprehension about the case was swept away in a sudden surge of excitement. Fetal alcohol syndrome is caused by exposure to alcohol during pregnancy. That fact is indisputable. If I was right to believe that Jami did not drink alcohol during her pregnancy, then another fact was equally indisputable: Henry did not have fetal alcohol syndrome.

"When was Henry first diagnosed with fetal alcohol syndrome?" I asked.

"It was right before the custody hearing, when Hank took him to see that doctor, and that's when Hank started telling everyone that I'm an alcoholic."

Because I believed Jami, I was convinced the doctor was wrong. I just had to find a way to prove it.

I made arrangements for Jami and her children to stay at A Woman's Place's, the Bucks County shelter. They had to be kept safe until I gathered the ammunition I needed to win this custody case. The children left my office with all the tiny toy trucks, tucked in a bag, because I decided they needed more than one each. As a thank you, Henry shyly gave me a little hug before he and Paul reclaimed their spots by their mother's side. And I made a silent vow that anyone who tried to rip these sweet, wounded children from their mother's side would have a battle on their hands. As I so often found myself thinking, in this work: *over my dead body.*

Having learned that Jami was on a lifetime regimen of anti-epileptic medications, a hunch began forming in my mind. Like a diabetic on insulin, the drugs weren't something she could just stop taking, so she had taken them throughout her pregnancies. Could *those* drugs have caused Henry's birth defects?

I called a friend who worked at a drugstore. She talked to the pharmacist, who confirmed the accuracy of my guess. Exposure to anti-epileptic medication during pregnancy can, indeed, cause a child to be born with facial abnormalities. In fact, facial abnormalities were not the only possible birth defects associated with what's called fetal hydantoin syndrome.

So I was right! Now all I needed was a doctor to verify the new diagnosis. But not just any doctor was needed; it had to be one whose opinion would hold more weight than that of the general practitioner who wrote that letter. I needed a specialist.

The problem with finding a specialist to examine Henry and to render an expert medical opinion about his condition was that Jami was indigent and had no health insurance. She had been eligible for medical assistance for herself and the children when she had physical custody of them originally, but now that Hank had a court order giving custody to him, Jami was no longer eligible. Hank had the medical coverage now, even though he didn't really have the children, and Jami had no access to the children's current medical cards.

I thought about the doctor I would pick if money were no object (because money *was* no object, since we didn't have any). And the answer was obvious: I would pick a top specialist from a nationally renowned institution. As luck would have it, we happened to have one of those institutions in our vicinity. The prestigious Hospital of the University of Pennsylvania (HUP) was located an hour or so away, in Philadelphia, the City of Brotherly Love.

After ascertaining that I needed a neurologist with a subspecialty in epilepsy, I called HUP and asked the receptionist for the names of Penn doctors that fit that description. She gave me three names. I then inquired if they all had the same position in the department, and was informed that one of them held the highest ranking. "Put me through to him, please," I said.

Dr. Daniel Feldman's assistant answered the phone. I introduced myself as an attorney and told her I needed to speak to the doctor. I knew that doctors would always take a call from another doctor, but I was banking on the possibility that the title of "attorney" would suffice. "He's seeing patients until four p.m.," his assistant told me. "Can you call back then?"

When I called again at 4:15, Dr. Feldman came to the phone. I laid out the story as quickly as I could and literally pleaded with him to agree to examine Henry for free. The children's lives were at stake, I told him. It was then I learned that I had picked the right doctor. Dr. Daniel Feldman was not only a brilliant and highly credentialed neurologist, acclaimed for his expertise in the study and treatment of epilepsy, he was also a good person. Without a moment's hesitation, he agreed to my request. Because of the pressing nature of the case, he evaluated little Henry Steele just three days later, early in the morning before his normal hospital hours, and called me after the evaluation was completed.

"In my opinion," Dr. Feldman said, "Henry does not have fetal hydantoin syndrome."

I was shocked. And I was devastated. I had been so positive about my deductive diagnosis. I had been so sure that Jami was telling the truth.

"So Henry really *does* have fetal alcohol syndrome?" I asked, wanting desperately not to believe it.

"That's not what I'm saying," Dr. Feldman responded. "I'm quite certain that Henry *doesn't* have fetal alcohol syndrome. In my opinion, his facial abnormalities are birth defects that are totally unrelated to either syndrome. I'll mail my report to you today, with these findings."

Overjoyed, I shouted: "Bless you, Dr. Feldman!"

"Bless you, too, Attorney Groff," he responded with a laugh. "Let me know if there's anything else I can do to help Henry."

Nothing more was necessary. I hung up the phone and began drafting an emergency petition. I knew it would contain all the evidence needed to modify the custody order. When it was finished, I consumed a very large chocolate bar in celebration of the day's spectacular events.

I am aware that it is more traditional, at times of celebration, to consume a glass of champagne. But I too, like Jami, have never in my whole life taken one sip of alcohol.

20. The Burdens of Teresa

I knew that Teresa Ruiz was in Legal Aid's crowded waiting room because I could hear her booming voice above the steady din, demanding to see me. She didn't have an appointment, of course. Teresa never showed up for an actual appointment. I didn't know if her refusal to keep appointments was a form of rebellion against other people's schedules, or if she just preferred to materialize when no one was expecting her. But one thing was certain: a new bad thing had happened, or she wouldn't have come.

A lot of bad things happened to Teresa, some of which were not her fault. Depending on how you looked at it, maybe none of it was her fault.

Teresa was in her early thirties. I could tell she had been attractive once, before the harsh realities of her life had intervened. There were traces still. Her lovely blue-gray eyes were framed with long, dark lashes, and her wavy ebony hair was lush. But the strains of poverty were deeply engraved on her pinched face.

Teresa was one of the poorest people I encountered in my years at Legal Aid. She and her two young children subsisted on an insufficient allotment of food stamps and a monthly welfare grant of less than three hundred dollars. For a rental fee of two hundred dollars a month, her parents allowed her and the children to live in a small, dilapidated trailer on a minuscule patch of arid land they owned, without which she would have been homeless. Any apartment in Bucks County, no matter how small or rundown, would have cost many times more than the paltry sum she received from welfare.

Teresa loved her children, a little boy and girl who were exceptionally beautiful and were just two and three years old when I first met her. Whenever I saw her with them, I was struck by how patient and tender she was with them. Patience and tenderness were not traits that Teresa tended to exhibit towards anyone else. Besides looking beautiful, her children always looked happy. Yet I knew Teresa struggled, largely unsuccessfully, to give them the physical comforts that can help children thrive.

Besides her oppressive poverty, Teresa was burdened with a mental illness—borderline personality disorder—and an abusive boyfriend. Carlos Rodriquez was not just her boyfriend. He was also the father of her children, but she and Carlos had never revealed that fact to anyone except me. If the authorities had known the identity of the children's father, they would have forced Teresa to sue him for child support as a precondition for receiving any welfare benefits. And if Teresa had sued Carlos for child support, he would have disappeared from her life, which she was not prepared to have him do.

Carlos caused crushing problems for Teresa, in more ways than just their need to hide his paternity. He was physically abusive to her, ate the food she bought for herself and the children, and lived with her in the trailer despite her parents' unbendable edict that he was never to set one foot on their property. Teresa's parents warned her that they would evict her and the children if she ever dared to disobey that prohibition, and from what I could gather they were not the forgiving types. Not only that, but Teresa's meager welfare funds would also have been cut off if it ever became known that Carlos was living with her. Welfare grants did not go to intact families, no matter how impoverished they were—a public policy that effectively mandates that poor children grow up in broken homes.

So Teresa's life was a toxic blend of dangerous secrets, devastating poverty, and domestic violence, topped off with a mental illness. The mixture did not leave her with many resources to mother her children, but still she tried. She loved them. Unfortunately, she also loved Carlos.

Actually, Teresa loved and hated Carlos with equal passion, wildly and erratically, their interactions intensely dramatic yet strangely superficial. They were a terrible pair, constantly on the brink of breakup but impossible to separate.

Teresa was a deeply injured person, clinging by her fingertips to a world she could not afford, pummeled by forces she could not control. I did everything I could to help her, always knowing that in the end it would not be enough. She needed more than my empathy and legal skills. She needed therapy. She needed medication. She needed friends. Most of all, she needed money. I bought a lottery ticket every week, with her name at the top of the list of people with whom I would share my winnings, but odds being what they are, I never held out much hope that luck would save the day.

I felt great compassion for Teresa, but I cannot truthfully say that I was ever happy to see her. I didn't want to admit it, but the fact that she broke every scheduled appointment sometimes brought with it a small sense of relief.

I could only sigh when I heard her loud voice rising above all others in the waiting room, demanding to see me immediately, brushing aside the receptionist's question, "Do you have an appointment?" That was an irrelevant question for Teresa, and one that she might very well consider rude. I rushed to the waiting room to escort her to my office before a scene erupted.

No news was good news with Teresa, so of course the news was bad. Her children were in foster care. Teresa fluctuated between being irate and being contrite as she told me the twisted tale of how her children had been taken away by CYS.

It had happened three weeks before, on a Friday night. Carlos had told her he planned to spend the evening at a local bar, and they argued about it. He began punching her, because physical violence was his surefire way of winning every argument, and Teresa ran from the trailer and hid in the bushes of a neighbor's yard. She waited for what seemed like a very long time for Carlos to leave for the bar so she could return to the trailer, but Carlos didn't leave. Finally, she crept through the darkness to ask the storekeeper at the corner store to let her use his phone to call her cousin. Teresa's cousin was her one and only "support system." She was going to ask him to come to her aid so she could safely re-enter her trailer, but her cousin wasn't home.

When she returned to the trailer, Carlos was gone. So were the children, who had been sleeping in their shared twin bed when she left the trailer. She thought Carlos had taken them to upset her. They would be at his mother's house. That was the only place he would take them. It was late, and she was tired, so she locked the door and went to bed, proud of herself for not letting it upset her.

It wasn't until the next day that Teresa discovered what had really happened. When she did not return quickly to the trailer, Carlos concluded that she had gone to the corner store to call the police to report his abuse. That's when he got the clever idea to call the police before she did, to tell them that he had come by for a visit and had found the trailer door unlocked, with the children asleep inside, alone, and with Teresa nowhere in sight. It was a believable story, since Carlos allegedly did not live at the trailer. And when the police arrived in response to his call, they found the scene exactly as he had described it: the children were asleep, ostensibly alone, and Teresa was nowhere in sight. The children, deemed neglected, were roused from bed and placed in foster care.

The next day, CYS instructed Teresa to come by herself to their offices, where no one was willing to listen to her story. Instead, she was presented with a so-called family service plan to sign. It was routine practice for CYS caseworkers to tell frightened parents that they had to come alone, without an attorney. This ensured that their family service plans would get signed without a critical assessment. The title of this document, which implied that services were going to be provided to the family by CYS, was a cruel and cynical misnomer. Once signed, it had the weight of a contract, its conditions ironclad. Frequently the conditions dictated in the family service plan were impossible for the impoverished parent who signed them to fulfill, such as "obtain a two-bedroom apartment" and/or "obtain a road-worthy automobile."

Not all, but a large number of the caseworkers at CYS were young, White, recent college graduates from middle- or upper-class families, sorority girls who led privileged lives. They were, in fact, too privileged to know what privilege is. Now they were suddenly granted enormous power over parents who were almost always poor and with whom they shared no common bonds. They were often inclined to wield that power without compassion or contemplation.

The CYS cases I handled at Legal Aid were limited to those involving accusations of neglect, as opposed to abuse, unless the abuse accusation was clearly bogus, because I could not in good conscience represent anyone who had intentionally abused his or her children. But, it bears repeating, when CYS caseworkers accused a parent of neglect, what they almost always meant was that the parent was poor. For CYS, poverty and neglect were virtually synonymous concepts. And when it came to poverty, few people could outdo Teresa Ruiz.

"I wish you had contacted me sooner," I told Teresa. "You've already waived your right to a hearing challenging the foster care placement. Now we have to deal with the family service plan."

Teresa had not brought her copy of the plan with her, and she had no idea what she had agreed to accomplish before she could get her children back. I asked her if she could return home to get it so I could make a copy. Even as I asked this, I knew it wouldn't happen. Whatever kept Teresa from keeping appointments would prevent her from returning to Legal Aid at my request.

After Teresa left, I tried to get through to someone at CYS about her case. I wanted to advocate on her behalf, and I wanted a copy of the family service plan, but no one would talk to me. So I decided to emulate Teresa's no-appointment approach. The next day, after court, I drove uninvited to the Agency's offices, where I was able to bully a secretary into giving me a copy of Teresa's family service plan.

It was every bit as outlandish as I had feared. Teresa had agreed to get that two-bedroom apartment that CYS loved to demand, and to secure a full-time job, despite having only an eighth-grade education and a debilitating mental illness, not to mention that the cost of all-day child care for her two young children would, by itself, far exceed what that imaginary job could possibly pay her.

A few provisions in the family service plan were conceivably attainable. The most significant was Teresa's agreement to get drug-tested every two weeks, a procedure whose cost would be covered—because ordered by CYS—by the medical insurance Teresa had from welfare. I was actually pleased about this requirement, if only Teresa could follow it, because I knew that Teresa was not a drug user.

It was too late to get a hearing to challenge the initial foster care placement. We would have to wait three months for a status review hearing, at which time Teresa's "progress" at satisfying the terms of her family service plan would be on trial. I tried to disrupt the process by filing for a hearing to challenge the family service plan, but my petition was denied as "untimely" by the court. Having already been signed, the family service plan was now sacrosanct.

Despite the rigid procedural roadblocks we faced, I hoped to convince the court that Teresa had not really left her children unattended and that therefore CYS hadn't had an initial legal basis for putting the children in foster care. It was the truth, and Carlos wasn't smart enough to lie in detail. I hoped this argument could overcome, or at least offset, Teresa's subsequent failure to fulfill the terms of the family service plan.

But there was another roadblock. Teresa refused to allow me to tell anyone what really happened. She feared that too many of the secrets she felt compelled to keep would be revealed. I beseeched her to change her mind. Unless her parents attended the hearing (which they would never have bothered to do), how would they find out that Carlos had been staying at their trailer? No one from welfare would know about the hearing. And what would it matter if Carlos disappeared to escape paying child support? He paid nothing anyway, and his presence in her life was only causing her grief. But Teresa was too afraid, too much was at stake. The whole story could not be told.

There was nothing I could do to help her except advise her to make attempts to address the attainable provisions in the family service plan, especially the drug testing, in preparation for the review hearing.

Teresa made no discernible attempts to address any of the provisions of the family service plan, nor did she answer any of my phone calls. But one day, when she was in the neighborhood, she stopped by Legal Aid to tell the receptionist to inform me that she had waived the review hearing. She didn't say why.

Months later, Teresa returned to Legal Aid, unannounced, demanding to see me. I was in court in Doylestown, so I missed her visit. I telephoned her the next day, and the day after that, leaving messages asking her to call me back, but she didn't call.

Another month passed before Teresa showed up again. This time she brought "some papers" with her, which turned out to be the petition that CYS had filed to terminate her parental rights to her children. Attached to their petition was an order that set a hearing date. I could tell from the date on the envelope that she'd had notice of the hearing for weeks.

The hearing was set to occur in seven days.

I was surprised the agency had moved so fast. Termination of parental rights was supposed to be a last step, taken after every reasonable effort to reunite the family had failed. I doubted that any efforts with that goal in mind, reasonable or not, had been taken by CYS. They were relying on using Teresa's failure to achieve the goals they had made for her in the family service plan, which she had supposedly agreed to achieve.

And I was now required to prepare a defense in the week remaining before the hearing. My calendar was already completely booked for most of those days. But I couldn't ask for a continuance without divulging to the court, and to CYS, that my client had not informed me of the hearing before today, a fact that CYS would surely use against her, as evidence that she did not care. It might have seemed like it, but it was actually *not* evidence that Teresa did not care. It was evidence of her need to live in denial, because her profound sense of powerlessness left her no other place to live.

I spent the next few hours trying to get a full picture from Teresa of the events that had elapsed in the months since her children had been taken from her. How many times had she interacted with CYS caseworkers? What had they said and done? What had *she* said and done? What was Carlos saying and doing? Besides CYS and Carlos, did she know of any other people who might come to court to testify negatively about her or her parenting skills?

According to Teresa, Carlos was sorry. He might be willing to admit that he had lied to the police, although neither he nor she were willing to tell the truth about why he was at Teresa's trailer that night.

Knowing that Carlos and Teresa could not go more than a few days without a skirmish, I thought it best to get to him while he was feeling some remorse. Teresa reported that Carlos was at home, waiting for her to return, so I commandeered my secretary and a tape recorder and drove to Teresa's trailer. Teresa got to the dirt driveway moments before we arrived, and the three of us entered the tiny dwelling together.

Carlos, shirtless, was sprawled out on a thread-bare loveseat, watching television. He looked up at us with mild interest. I tried to act nonchalant, as if it were an everyday event for me to show up suddenly, secretary in tow

There was no emotion in Carlos's voice when he asked, "Is this about the hearing?"

"Yes, actually, it is," I said, as casually as I could manage. "I talked to Teresa about it, but I have a few questions to ask you."

My secretary and I took a seat at the small round table in the area designated as the kitchen (although the interior of the trailer had no walls), and I motioned for Carlos to join us. There were only three chairs, so Teresa remained standing, hovering near us nervously.

"Amanda and José were put in foster care because of the story you told the police," I told Carlos. "They'll be taken away forever unless the judge hears what really happened. Do you understand that?"

It took him a while to respond, but finally he said, "I'll tell the judge that I didn't tell the truth. But no one can know that I live here."

He was at the trailer that evening, whether he lived there or not, so I was willing to accept the restriction. The essential truth about the incident did not require a full confession concerning Carlos's residency status.

I told Carlos I was going to tape our conversation so I wouldn't have to take notes. My secretary turned on the tape recorder, and I treated the meeting like a formal deposition. In reality, I taped our conversation because I needed to have Carlos clearly on record admitting that he had given false information to the police. The rules of evidence would not allow me to introduce the tape in court if he didn't show up to testify, but Carlos didn't know that. I figured his awareness that the recording existed would be enough to prevent him from changing his story on the day of the hearing, and if it didn't, I could use his own recorded prior testimony to impeach him on the stand.

The taping went well. Carlos was surprisingly forthcoming, admitting that Teresa had fled from the trailer because he was assaulting her, and that he had lied to the police about the children being left alone to keep himself from getting into trouble. It wasn't like Carlos to accept blame for anything, but maybe, in his own way, he loved the children, too.

When the hearing date arrived, I felt hopeful. A miscarriage of justice had occurred; Carlos was to blame; and Carlos was willing to acknowledge his fault. There was no reason for Teresa's parental rights to be terminated, and there was no reason for the children to remain in foster care.

The courthouse was about a fifty-minute drive from Teresa's trailer, which was a problem. Teresa had a car, but it was older than she was, uninsured, had a taped-on sheet of cardboard in place of the driver's side window, and overheated if driven for more than twenty minutes, requiring at least five minutes to cool off. Teresa used it to go places locally, if it would start and if she had any money for gas. All in all, I think it is more accurate to say that Teresa did *not* have a car. Carlos's mode of transportation was an ancient bicycle. And the only public transportation from their location to the courthouse was a train which, while within walking distance, Teresa and Carlos could not afford to ride.

This problem was not uncommon. The majority of my Legal Aid clients lived in lower Bucks County, and getting to mid-county for legal proceedings was a serious challenge for many of them. It goes without saying that this was not a problem our legal system deemed worthy of the slightest consideration. Having no viable means of transportation is just one more in the long catalog of challenges that poor people must face on their own.

As a family law attorney for Legal Aid, I needed to be more than just an attorney if I was to have any chance to win my cases. I needed to be a therapist, too, and a social worker, private investigator, and occasional chauffeur. This hearing was one of those occasions. If I wanted Teresa and Carlos to come to court, I was going to have to drive them there.

Teresa and I lived on opposite ends of the county; from my house to Teresa's trailer and then to the courthouse involved more than a two-hour drive. Extra time had to be added to get them both hustled into my car, and then there was the additional time it would take to hike the long uphill block with them from the parking lot to the main courthouse. To be safe, I needed to add another forty minutes to accommodate the vagaries of traffic on such a long trip and to hopefully give my client and my witness (and me) a little time to acclimate to the courthouse environment before we had to enter the courtroom. I was up the night before until two a.m., putting the final touches on my prepared questions, reviewing all the relevant documents, and committing the outline of my closing argument to memory. So I was already tired when I left my home in darkness at 6:15 a.m.

It was a relief to find Teresa and Carlos both at the trailer, looking relatively composed and actually ready to go when I arrived. I did not realize, until I saw them, how concerned I had been about the state I would find them in—if I found them at all. During the lengthy ride to the courthouse, I went over the direct examination questions I intended to ask them and gave them advice about the cross-examination questions they might face. I welcomed the long trip as my only chance to prepare them for the hearing.

We got to the courthouse with time to spare, and I was feeling almost relaxed sitting with Teresa and Carlos in the waiting area near the courtroom, engaging in some decompressing small talk, when Charlotte Simpson, the new solicitor for CYS, walked by, accompanied by five well-dressed, professional-looking people and a police officer. The sight of this unexpected crowd was alarming. I could feel my face flush as my blood pressure rose. I thought CYS would have two witnesses: one of their caseworkers, and the policeman who came to the trailer. Who were all these other people? Before I had a chance to ask Teresa if she knew any of them, she shouted out indignantly, "Why is Dr. Dunlap here? Who told Mrs. Reese about this hearing? Hey! There's the guy from the therapist's office!"

"Who is Dr. Dunlap? Who is Mrs. Reese? *What* therapist's office?" I asked in a panic.

Teresa was highly agitated and in no mood to answer my questions. I was agitated, too. Teresa had assured me she could think of no one that could possibly testify against her at the hearing besides the police officer and the CYS worker assigned to her case. I tried again to question Teresa about who the people were, but she was engrossed in her growing indignation and could not be distracted from angrily yelling out their names. The sense of calm that I always strive to achieve for myself and my clients before the start of a hearing had been blown away as if by a cyclone. I had prepared so diligently for this hearing yet now felt wholly unprepared.

Aside from the horde of unknown witnesses, I was well acquainted with the cast of characters for this hearing. The judge was the Honorable Harriet M. Mims, the first woman to ascend to the bench in Bucks County. She was tall, with a regal bearing and hair the stunning color of newly fallen snow. I was very fond of Judge Mims, who showed kindness and respect to all who entered her courtroom. She was unfailingly considerate to every lawyer and litigant, which I especially appreciated as a Legal Aid lawyer. A number of the other judges had difficulty hiding their disapproval of poor people, and there were a couple who made no effort whatsoever to mask it.

Two lawyers besides me were involved in the case, both supremely skilled attorneys. Charlotte Simpson, the new solicitor for CYS, was a veteran trial attorney who epitomized the expression "smart as a whip." The other attorney, Curt Van Sciver, had been appointed by the court to represent the Ruiz children. Van Sciver was a long-time member of Legal Aid's board of directors, so I knew him rather well. He had the gentlemanly manner of an old-timey lawyer, which he used to remarkable effect, especially during his legendary cross-examinations. Carefully, methodically, always the courteous gentleman, he had an amazing ability to extract the truth from witnesses who did not want to tell it. Once, after having answered a series of seemingly unassuming questions put to her on cross-examination by Van Sciver, a CYS caseworker suddenly realized she had been astutely led to a spot she could not wiggle out of. "You've backed me into a corner!" she protested, to which Van Sciver very politely responded: "That was my *effort*, Ma'am."

I felt fortunate to have the chance to share a courtroom with this judge and these lawyers. All three of them were brilliant, and there is much to be learned from brilliant people. Beyond that, all of them were ethical and fair-minded. And I felt sure that Van Sciver would end up on my client's side. He was a tender-hearted person. He didn't serve on Legal Aid's board of directors to add another notch to his résumé. He did it because he cared about poor people and their access to quality legal services.

But my confidence had been severely shaken by the slew of mystery witnesses who'd come to testify against my client. And no trace of Teresa's original composure remained as we entered Judge Mims' courtroom. The witnesses were sequestered, so we had to leave Carlos in the waiting room. I ordered him to stay put, and not to talk to anyone.

It was CYS's petition, so they went first, which was fortunate because Teresa had begun hyperventilating. I gave her a pen and a pad of paper so she could communicate with me without speaking, and kept quietly reminding her that she needed to stay silent and calm.

The hearing began with the testimony of the officer on the scene the night the children were taken into foster care. He acknowledged, on my cross-examination, that he did not know why Ms. Ruiz had not been present when he arrived, and that he had simply accepted Carlos Rodriquez's account. He acknowledged that Mr. Rodriquez had a criminal history of assault and disorderly conduct.

Next on the stand was the CYS caseworker assigned to the case, a classic example of the type. Young and blond, with a self-important manner, she was pleased to report that Teresa had not achieved any of the goals in the family service plan. I was able to repeatedly make the point that the family service plan was rife with "goals" that required more money to achieve than Ms. Ruiz was capable of earning. While the CYS worker never conceded the point (and seemed in fact not to grasp its significance), I could tell the issue was not lost on Judge Mims.

Next up was Dr. Dunlap, who turned out to be Teresa's family doctor. CYS had gotten Teresa to sign a release that allowed her physicians to provide them with information about her, although I am sure she'd had no idea what she was signing. Dr. Dunlap was there to testify that he had referred Teresa more than once to a psychiatrist for treatment of her borderline personality disorder. He acknowledged, on cross-examination, that he did not have the training to diagnosis alleged mental illnesses, and further that many individuals who were accurately diagnosed with borderline personality disorder were nevertheless able to successfully parent their children.

There were a lot of other people in the waiting room who had arrived with Simpson, but she did not call any of them as witnesses in her case in chief. I did not know if they were being saved as rebuttal witnesses, or if they were just there to throw me off stride. But at one p.m., CYS's solicitor finished putting on their case, and Judge Mims adjourned court until 2:15 p.m.

Carlos was waiting where we had left him. I'd been a little worried about his staying power, but my concern was mostly alleviated by the comforting knowledge that he had no financial means to actually go anywhere. Sitting there for hours had left him bored and annoyed, and upon seeing us he immediately declared that he was starving. Certainly they both needed to eat lunch, and just as certainly they both had no funds. We took the elevator down to the cafeteria area in the basement of the main courthouse, where there were vending machines with an assortment of food and drinks, and I gave each of them five dollars. I knew better than to give one of them all the money; that could only lead to strife. I also told them that after court was over I would give them money for train fare. I felt too tired to drive back and forth across the county twice that day.

Leaving Teresa and Carlos in the courthouse cafeteria, with instructions that I would return to retrieve them at two p.m., I took the elevator up to the lawyer's lounge on the fourth floor. I wanted a quiet spot to reflect on the testimony that had occurred and to review my case. I thought the day was going well, and that Carlos's surprise testimony might bring a decisive defeat to CYS's effort to terminate Teresa's parental rights.

Returning to the basement at two p.m., I immediately heard shouting as the elevator door opened. I recognized the voices. Teresa's voice was naturally loud, but when she was agitated her voice could be deafening. Carlos was holding his own, shouting profanities above her shouting. When I got to the cafeteria, I was shouting, too. "What's happening?" I demanded. But it was obvious what was happening. Carlos and Teresa had been in the same small space for too long. Whatever their argument was about, which I never really got to know, it was inevitable. What had I been thinking when I left them alone together? Teresa was screaming at Carlos to "Get out!" and he was yelling back at her, "I'm outta here!" Their faces were contorted in anger.

We had fifteen minutes before court was to resume.

Somehow I managed to physically separate them. I may have become more crazed than they were, because when I started shouting, they stopped. "We're going back to the courtroom now," I yelled, "and you, Carlos, are going to be telling the truth about what happened—just like you did when I tape-recorded you. Otherwise, neither of you will ever see your children again."

I took Carlos by the arm and ordered Teresa to follow us as I moved quickly to the elevator. They remained perfectly silent in the elevator, but as we approached the benches outside the courtroom, Teresa began hyperventilating again. She had become convinced that Carlos would incriminate her in some way, and she was desperate to keep him from testifying. He assured me that he would tell the truth, and I believed him. Besides, as long as he testified, the tape-recording could refute any lies. But his testimony was crucial to the case. He had to testify. "Please trust me," I pleaded to Teresa. She relented at that moment, but her trust was reed-thin. She was shaking and unsteady on her feet as we made our way to our seats at the defense table, with everyone watching.

I called Carlos Rodriquez to the witness stand.

As Carlos reached the stand, Teresa suddenly abandoned all pretense of sanity. She leaped up, shrieking wildly, and ran from the room. A courthouse guard, who had been stationed in the courtroom, ran after her. We could hear them wrangling outside the door. More guards arrived. Teresa was screaming, "No! No! Get away from me, you pigs!" A guard's voice could be heard yelling, "Take it easy! Take it easy!"

My case crashing around me, I asked for a continuance. Simpson objected. "If we stop these proceedings because Ms. Ruiz is behaving in accordance with her borderline personality, when will we ever be able to finish?"

I objected to the characterization, and argued that my client was simply overwrought from a long day facing the loss of her children. Judge Mims took a middle road. "Let's hear what Mr. Rodriquez has to say. I won't require Ms. Ruiz's presence in the courtroom. After he testifies, we will reschedule."

It was hard to hear Carlos above the ongoing pandemonium outside the courtroom door, and Judge Mims had to repeatedly ask him to speak

up. But he told the truth, as he had promised he would, and it had a powerful effect. It was painfully clear that the entire initial rationale for taking the children into foster care had been based on a lie. If Teresa had
not been screaming uncontrollably outside the courtroom, I was certain
that Carlos' testimony would have clinched the case.

But Teresa *was* screaming uncontrollably outside the courtroom.

When Carlos was finished being questioned and cross-examined,
Judge Mims asked him, kindly, "Would you prefer to leave through the
back door, so you don't have to pass by Ms. Ruiz at this time?" He answered yes with visible relief. But as the tipstaff began to escort him out
the door normally reserved for the judge and her staff, Carlos realized
that if he left that way he would not pass by me, either. "Wait!" he cried
out. "I need the money Meg said she'd give me."

Everyone in the courtroom froze, including me.

Van Sciver came first to my rescue: "We all know Ms. Groff's dedication to the law," he said. "I'm sure there's an explanation."

Simpson quickly concurred: "Yes. There must be an explanation."

"Yes, certainly," said Judge Mims, turning her face to smile at me
benignly before looking again at Carlos. "But tell us please, Mr. Rodriquez, what *is* the explanation?"

Carlos piped up before I could unfreeze. "Meg said she'd give me
money for a train ticket. I don't have any way to get home."

There was a palpable release of tension in the room. I thought I
could hear everyone exhaling.

"May *I* cover that cost, this time?" the gallant Van Sciver asked Carlos, rushing towards him with wallet in hand.

"Thanks," Carlos said, as he took the money and was ushered swiftly
out the back door.

Teresa's day in court would be rescheduled for a later date. For now,
the exit plan worked. Carlos was able to escape unnoticed from the courthouse, successfully avoiding a confrontation with my client, whose
screams outside the courtroom continued undiminished until I drove her
home.

21. The Rights of a Rapist

The so-called Fathers' Rights Movement was already in full swing when I arrived at the Bucks County Legal Aid Society in 1984, and a number of Bucks County's judges supported its cause. The county's premier father's rights group was named F.A.C.E., originally an acronym for Fathers and Children for Equality. I liked to say a more suitable moniker was Fascist Abusers Complaining about Everything.

As far as I could tell, the Bucks County branch of F.A.C.E. was mostly made up of men who despised the mothers of their children, were embittered about having to pay child support, and were incensed at the "man-haters" who ventured to suggest that their lack of parenting skills should have an impact on the terms of their custody orders. I know it wasn't a prerequisite, but almost every F.A.C.E. member I crossed paths with at that time had a current or past protection from abuse order entered against him. It was the opinion of these fellows, it seemed to me, that no behavior a man chose to display, no matter how reprehensible, should ever interfere with his God-given ownership rights to his children. Unfortunately, some of our judges seemed to share this point of view. Custody decisions were often based more on solicitude for fathers' rights than on the best interests of children.

After historically having few or no rights under the law, there had been a brief period of time in Pennsylvania when, in certain circumstances, mothers were favored over fathers in custody cases. For a number of years before 1976, when our state passed the Equal Rights Amendment, which was supposed to ban unequal treatment based on gender, mothers were presumed to be the better caretakers of very young children. This legal presumption was known as the tender-years doctrine. Like other presumptions in the law, the tender-years doctrine could be rebutted by sufficient contradictory evidence, but the burden to do so was on the father. The doctrine perfectly reflected the culture of the times, when women were expected to be in the home taking care of children while men were out in the world doing more important things. Fathers who actually played a nurturing role in the lives of their children had every right to protest against this presumption, and had I been a lawyer before 1976, I would have supported them.

But by the early 1980s, the tender-years doctrine was dead and gone, and so too was that brief period of time when fathers, as a class, were treated less favorably in custody cases. In fact, the opposite soon began taking hold again. A number of academic studies conducted across the United States have found that men win a sizable percentage of contested custody cases, despite rarely having been the children's primary caretaker previously. The most obvious reason for this is the fact that women remain less likely than men to be financially able to hire an attorney (or a capable one) to represent them. But another obvious reason is our culture's unconscious bias: it is much harder to be deemed a good mother than to be deemed a good father. Often all a father needs to do to earn the enduring admiration of the court is to once have been seen changing a baby's diaper.

Mothers would never receive kudos for such a feat. Quite the opposite: often all a mother needs to do to earn the court's enduring contempt is to have once been seen *not* changing a baby's diaper . . . *in a timely fashion*. Mothers are *supposed* to change diapers, and to bathe and clothe and feed their children, and to get up at night when their children wake crying. Mothers are supposed to be the ones who make and keep the doctors' and dentists' appointments, attend the parent-teacher conferences, and make sure the children do their homework. And when children get sick, it is their mothers who are supposed to watch over them and nurse them back to health.

People do not get a lot of credit for doing what is expected of them.

Fathers' rights became so powerful after the demise of the tender-years doctrine that the request for representation I received from Lloyd Jefferson—the murderer of Annette—was not completely far-fetched. There was more than one higher court case where the father had murdered the mother and had then successfully sued for visitation with his now motherless children; where the mother's family members, who had become the children's caretakers, were ordered to transport the children long distances back and forth from a prison so that the man who murdered their loved one could exercise his custodial rights.

Thankfully, Pennsylvania's custody statute has changed over the ensuing years in ways that have sometimes helped to impede—and, at least in *some* cases, to prevent—such outrageous outcomes. But the original Custody and Grandparents Visitation Act was still the law of the state when I participated in a certain contested custody hearing before Judge Link, my least favorite judicial member of the Bucks County Court of Common Pleas at that time.

I have an exceptionally vivid memory of this particular custody hearing, partly because, before it was over, I nearly got thrown in jail.

It all began when our receptionist, Rosemarie, rang through to me from her desk to ask if I could possibly squeeze in another client consultation that day. She knew the answer would be yes, because there was no fixed time for my workday to end. So an initial consultation with Vanessa Roberts was scheduled for eight that evening.

Vanessa arrived more than an hour early for her appointment. I was alone in the office, meeting with another client, and the entrance to Legal Aid was locked, so Vanessa had to ring the front doorbell, and I had to leave my inner office to open the door for her. Embarrassed, she explained that she hadn't been familiar with Legal Aid's location and wanted to make sure she wouldn't be late. Being a compulsively early (and always lost) person all my life, I assured her I completely understood and very much appreciated her effort to ensure that no one was left waiting but her.

When my client meeting ended, I was able to turn my attention to Vanessa Roberts. She was a young Black woman, plainly dressed and wearing no makeup, with a wholesome beauty that needed no adornment. As we walked together down the hall to my office, I noticed how she held her arms tightly across her chest, each hand gripping the opposite elbow as if armoring herself. I could tell she felt intimidated by her surroundings, even though Legal Aid's Bristol office was as far from fancy as any law office imaginably could be, and I was clad, as usual, in blue jeans. Vanessa Roberts was too apprehensive to be comforted by such inconsequential details.

After we were both seated in my office, I tried to relieve her anxiety. I asked her to call me Meg and told her how glad I was that she had chosen to come to Legal Aid. Then I very gently asked her to explain the reason for her visit.

"I need a lawyer . . . but I don't have enough money to pay for one," Vanessa said, almost in a whisper. Her voice quivered, and her head was bent down as if in penance.

It is common for poor people to believe that their poverty makes them undeserving. This is understandable, because so many people who aren't poor keep imposing that belief upon them. It is a belief shared by many of our judges and prosecutors—an insidious, intrinsic bias, conscious and unconscious, that devalues the lives of the poor and corrupts our legal system. It is a bias those of us who advocate for the indigent must constantly confront and overcome as we battle for the rights of our clients. Sadly, our clients are often the first people who need to be convinced of the simple truth that they are as deserving as anyone else.

It was distressing to see how ashamed Vanessa was about not having enough money to pay for a lawyer. My first impulse was to reach over and give her a comforting hug, but I was afraid that would be intrusive. So I said playfully: "It sounds like you need a lawyer who *can't be bought.* So you've come to the right place. . . . I'm your *man!*"

Vanessa Roberts raised her head just enough to look at me directly for the first time. She had an astonished expression on her face.

I laughed. "Actually, I'm not really 'your man' . . . but I *am* your *lawyer!*"

When I finally saw her smile, I decided it might be okay to ask if I could give her a little hug. We hugged, and she told me her heartbreaking story.

When Vanessa was thirteen years old, a chaste and innocent child from a very religious family, she was raped. She was grabbed off the

street on her way home from Bible study by a man from the neighborhood she knew only by sight, and half carried, half dragged into a trash-
littered lot behind a shuttered row of houses. The man, whose name she
later learned was Aaron Johnson, easily weighed twice her ninety-eight
pounds. He had a shimmering knife that he held to her throat. After rap-
ing her, he left her there, in that dirty lot, to gather her torn clothes and
cover herself as best she could as she stumbled home.

She told me her parents were terrified of the retaliation the family
might face if the crime was reported. They were poor, and the man was
not. They had migrated only three years earlier from Alabama, where the
authorities didn't much care what happened to Black folks. Her mother's
sister had been raped there by the chief of police after going to report a
burglary. The family had good reason to believe there was danger in taking action when you have no power. So they did nothing. They told no
one, not even their pastor.

After a few months had gone by, it became apparent that Vanessa
was pregnant. Her parents had to explain what was happening to her,
because the only thing Vanessa had ever been told about "where babies
come from" was that angels delivered them from God.

The rapist's baby was not wanted, but the family never considered
an abortion. Instead, Vanessa was sent to stay with her grandparents in
a small town in Alabama for the remainder of her pregnancy. The plan
was to place the infant for adoption there. But after Vanessa gave birth
to a beautiful baby girl, her grandparents decided to keep the child and
raise her as their own. Two days after the delivery, Vanessa returned
home. She went back to school, repeating seventh grade. No one spoke
of it again.

Twelve years passed. Then the grandmother was stricken with a
cancer that the family did not have the means to try to fight. The grandfather had grown too old and frail to take care of both his ailing wife and
his great-grandchild. So it was agreed that the child, named "Faith" by
her great-grandparents, would be sent to Pennsylvania, to live with her
grandparents and a mother she had never met. Which is why, six months
before our meeting, Vanessa's parents had travelled to Alabama to bring
Faith home.

Faith's sudden separation from her great-grandparents and her long trip north with virtual strangers must have been incredibly difficult for her. And now, Faith had to adjust to a whole new world. I could see, from Vanessa's description of the events, that she understood how traumatizing all of this felt to a shy and sheltered twelve-year-old child. Tragically, in some ways it was as traumatic for Vanessa as it was for Faith. To Vanessa, Faith was the child of rape, a living memory of the awful crime that had been committed against her. A crime she and her parents had desperately tried to forget.

As I reflected on this terrible situation, I noticed that Vanessa had fallen silent. A long minute passed before she spoke again. "Can I tell you something?" she asked hesitantly.

"I'm your lawyer," I assured her. "You can tell me *anything*."

Vanessa leaned towards me and whispered, "I had questioned God. All those years, I had questioned Him."

I wanted to cry. I reached across my desk to put my hands on hers. "That's completely understandable, Vanessa. *Everyone* would feel that way."

"Do you think He forgives me?" she asked.

"Yes," I said. "I'm sure of it."

Some clients believe that lawyers know everything. I usually try to disabuse them of that misconception. But I welcomed it that day, seeing the relief on Vanessa's face. She trusted her lawyer.

She told me then that over the past six months she had succeeded in overcoming her initial feelings about Faith's arrival. She knew Faith was blameless—an innocent child who needed a mother who loved her; needed one even more than children always do, because for so long she had been denied one. Vanessa had met privately with her pastor, seeking his guidance, and he had said many helpful things. What had helped her the most, she told me—what she remembered and recited to me by heart—were the words of Martin Luther King Jr. that Pastor William had quoted: "Darkness cannot drive out darkness; only light can do that. Hate cannot drive out hate; only love can do that."

Vanessa's recitation of those words touched me so profoundly I could no longer suppress my tears. I did not even attempt to wipe them away. I was so thankful for what seemed to be a happy ending. Everything was going to be all right.

But then I glanced at the label affixed to the cover of Vanessa's file, which Rosemarie had prepared for me earlier and left on my desk. The label said: "CUSTODY." I was confused.

"It sounds like things are going well. Why do you think you need a lawyer?"

"He filed for custody," Vanessa said.

"*Who* filed for custody?" I asked, puzzled.

"Aaron Johnson."

I was flabbergasted. "Are you *sure*?"

Vanessa reached into her pocketbook, pulled out the custody petition, and handed it to me. It was unbelievable, but it was true. Aaron Johnson was seeking partial custody of Faith. A custody hearing was scheduled in three weeks' time.

"How did he *know*?" I asked.

"One day, when Faith and I were coming home from the grocery store, I saw him standing across the street from our house, staring at us. It scared me, the way he looked at us. He must have heard talk in the neighborhood. I know there was gossip. A few weeks after that, someone handed this petition to my dad outside of church."

"But what proof does Aaron Johnson have that Faith is even *your* daughter?"

Vanessa explained that her parents had originally intended to introduce Faith to their neighbors and fellow parishioners as their niece, but Vanessa had objected. She thought a lie like that would be another kind of cancer. She told her parents: "Faith doesn't need an aunt and uncle. She needs a mother."

So everyone knew Faith was Vanessa's daughter. Aaron Johnson, the rapist, had simply done the math to figure out who the father was. Now he was demanding his "father's rights."

Vanessa had already attended the custody conference. Her father had gone with her to the conference, but not being an attorney, he hadn't been permitted to attend. So Vanessa was unaccompanied as she sat in one of those little windowless rooms, at a small table across from her rapist, with the conference officer at the head of the table asking the same tedious, mundane questions that conference officers always asked of each party in custody cases: age, employment, income, type of housing, other members of the household, child custody arrangement requested. The conference officer was thoroughly uninterested in the history of this child's conception. "He *is* the father, isn't he?" was all he had to say on the topic. No agreement having been reached at the conference, a hearing was scheduled—by chance, on Faith's thirteenth birthday. The case was assigned to Judge Link.

I wouldn't have chosen Judge Link to be the presiding judge in this case. In truth, I wouldn't have chosen Judge Link to be the presiding judge in *any* case. We disliked each other intensely. On my part, it was because he was a hateful, narcissistic, misogynistic racist. (This is only a partial list of my reasons.) On his part, it was because I was a Legal Aid lawyer. Judge Link made it clear to me and others on a number of occasions that he didn't think poor people deserved to get free lawyers. According to him, poverty was people's own fault, and they shouldn't be "rewarded" for it.

For Judge Link, the color of people's skin defined them, hierarchically, with White people innately superior to all others. Once, during a conference in his chambers with two White lawyers, he took the opportunity to comment on the campaign of a young Black man who was running for a local school board seat, asserting, "Colored people don't have the brains to be on school boards." He was speaking, as always, with the supreme confidence of a man incapable of questioning his ignorant prejudices.

In one sense, it could have been argued that Judge Link might be a good judge to handle this particular matter, because he liked to tout the importance of "family values" and decry the depravity of modern-day mores. Sex outside of marriage, for example, was a crime in his book. If he'd had the authority to do so, I am sure he would have banned it nationwide. Certainly a person holding such beliefs would be horrified by the circumstances of this case. Except that, for Judge Link, family values were inherently unattainable for some categories of people, and therefore inapplicable.

Judge Link didn't have a lot of opportunities to act on his racial animus because Bucks County is largely a Caucasian enclave. But we have a fair share of poor people, and Judge Link never felt the need to hide his disdain for my clients. Vanessa, poor *and* "colored," had two strikes against her.

If I had attended the custody conference, I could have kept the case from being assigned to Judge Link's courtroom. Due to my friendship with certain staff at the prothonotary, I possessed a powerful secret weapon: a copy of the court schedule. This was an internal document published every few months that mapped out the daily calendar of every judge. Only a handful of need-to-know court workers were allowed access to it, and lawyers did not fit that description. Armed with my illicit copy of that priceless document, I could look at any day of the month and see exactly which judge was sitting that day in family court.

When a custody case didn't get resolved at the custody conference, making a hearing necessary, the conference officer would give the attorneys three or four possible hearing dates to choose from. I would surreptitiously check not only my work schedule but also the court schedule and would declare myself available only on the days when a judge I preferred was sitting—which was certainly never Judge Link.

Unfortunately, Bucks County's population kept growing over the years, causing more judges to be added to the Court of Common Pleas. When two or three judges were sitting on any given day instead of one, I could no longer use the court schedule to hand-pick my judge. But until then, my secret copy of that document granted me a long and rewarding run.

The court schedule couldn't have helped me pick a judge in the matter of *Johnson vs. Roberts*, however, because I hadn't attended the conference. Once the date for a custody hearing was set and the judge assigned, that was the judge you were stuck with.

I'm ashamed to admit it, but in preparing for the hearing I was heartened by the fact that my client wasn't the only "colored" person in the case. Aaron Johnson was also Black, although he wasn't poor like Vanessa. But he was a *rapist*, and Vanessa was not. That had to count for something. Actually, that had to count for everything. It didn't matter what the law said or didn't say or who the judge was. What mattered was this: I was determined that Aaron Johnson would never get his filthy hands on my client's child.

Vanessa and her father met me at the courthouse early on the morning of the hearing. We were sitting together in the large waiting room down the hall from the courtrooms when Aaron Johnson came swaggering in. He was heading in the direction of Vanessa until he realized I wasn't just a random person who happened to be sitting next to her. I could see from the surprised look on his face that he hadn't expected her to have an attorney. He hadn't bothered to retain one, which didn't surprise me. It wasn't uncommon for abusers to feel so much power and control over their victims that they felt no need to further buttress their advantages.

When court began at ten a.m., there were only two cases still scheduled on Judge Link's list. Since the plaintiff in the other case had been unable to serve papers on the defendant, she and her attorney were in court only to request a continuance to a later date. So by 10:15 a.m., our case was called.

I immediately asked Judge Link if I could give an opening statement.

The purpose of an opening statement, delivered before testimony begins, is to provide the judge (or jury) with a summary of your case, signaling how the facts and evidence you intend to produce will validate the verdict you are seeking. It's a chance to pre-tell the story from your client's perspective, a head start in the process of convincing the judge (or jury) to see things your way. Essentially, I approach every hearing like a play being performed in a courtroom instead of a theater. Opening statements set the stage. Yet while they are an expected and integral practice in criminal cases, opening statements are the exception in family court in Bucks County, where judges tend to start all hearings with the simple command, "Call your first witness."

This practice of skipping opening statements in family court is, in my view, one of the many clear indications that family law cases are held in low esteem. Thus, it is *my* practice to request permission to give an opening statement at the start of every custody hearing. And I've found that when such permission is specifically requested, it is always granted. But when I asked Judge Link if I could give an opening statement, he did not hesitate before responding with a thunderous "No!" As swiftly as that, the opening salvo I had so painstakingly drafted was officially quashed.

Judge Link turned his attention to Aaron Johnson, saying brusquely, "You're the *plaintiff* in this case. If you intend to testify, come to the stand." His tone was predictably condescending. But I noticed that Aaron Johnson was much lighter skinned than Vanessa. I wondered and worried whether that would matter.

Aaron Johnson's testimony was as follows: He'd had sexual relations with Vanessa Roberts. She'd left town without telling him she was pregnant. He didn't know he had a daughter until she showed up in town. Since he was the child's father, he intended to exercise his parental rights. He thought every other weekend would be fair.

It was time for me to cross-examine.

"Do you know how old Ms. Roberts was when you raped her?"

Before he had a chance to respond, Judge Link bellowed at me: "Has he been *convicted* of rape?"

I answered, firmly, that my client was only thirteen years old when Aaron Johnson raped her, which would have been statutory rape regardless, but she had not reported the rape to the authorities.

Judge Link bellowed at me again, even louder this time: "Your question will be *stricken from the record!* You will not utter that word ever again in my courtroom! The plaintiff was not *convicted* of rape—and it wouldn't be relevant if he *had* been."

Judge Link was livid. But not quite as livid as I was.

"The plaintiff is a *rapist*. He raped and impregnated a *child*, and now he wants partial custody of the child born as a *result* of that rape. How can that not be *relevant*?"

Judge Link rose from the bench. The color of his face had changed from its customary blotchy white to a crimson red. He was screaming. *"I'm warning you!* If you say that word one more time, I will hold you in *contempt!"*

I had never been held in contempt. I had never seen anyone else be held in contempt. But maybe this was the right time to have the experience. I knew it involved jail and possibly a fine I couldn't afford, but it would be a small price to pay in exchange for the reward of such a newsworthy story. Front page in our local paper, I thought, if I handled it correctly. Plus the hearing would have to be postponed, and possibly Judge Link could end up feeling forced to recuse himself. Being held in contempt was starting to sound like a good idea.

"Your Honor, with all due respect," I began. (Isn't that what we always say, when no respect is due?) I then proceeded to argue that the plaintiff was a clear and present danger to the child in this case—a young girl, like his original victim. I argued that muzzling me would hinder my ability to effectively cross-examine him about the vileness of his past acts and the chilling audacity of his current efforts to get access to the child. And muzzling my client would keep her from being able to testify truthfully about what the plaintiff had done to her. I told him I was obligated, as an ethical attorney *and a human being*, to make a strong and accurate record of the menace this man posed. Because then, when the entire transcript of these proceedings was sent to the Superior Court, the record would clearly show that granting Mr. Johnson any contact with this young girl would be an extreme judicial error.

Even though I had somehow managed to get through this argument without actually saying the word "rape" again, I fully expected to be held in contempt then and there. Because I had just told Judge Link, in so many words, that I intended to continue making it clear that Aaron Johnson was a rapist, and that, if he tried to give a child rapist partial custody of a child, I was going to file an appeal to the Superior Court—where his disgraceful order would (I hoped) be overturned.

We both knew my allusion to an appeal was an outright threat.

Judge Link liked to strike fear in the lawyers and litigants who landed in his courtroom, glorying in the command he had over people's lives. I had observed many times the perverse pleasure it gave him. A tiny, almost imperceptible smirk would flicker across his face when the terror he struck became palpable, causing the upper left side of his puffy mouth to curve upward ever so slightly. It would all pass in a flash, but I always caught it. And for me that tiny smirk was a manifest sign of how small and ugly and pitiful he was, which is why his tactics of intimidation never worked on me.

On the surface, Judge Link held all the power in any battle in family court. But when he couldn't strike fear, I sensed it made him fearful. And the threat that a decision of his would be overturned by a *superior* court, whose opinions were published for the entire legal community to see, was an unambiguous declaration of my fearless resolve. If he planned to punish me for contempt, I wanted my contempt to be blinding.

I am sure Judge Link had initially been more than ready to order me hauled out of his courtroom in handcuffs. But now he glowered at me instead, and said, "You can *describe* the act but not name it."

I accepted his compromise.

It would be nice to believe that my arguments about the obligations of an ethical lawyer were what convinced Judge Link to stop trying to erase any hint of rape from the record in our case. But we both knew better.

I was mostly successful at avoiding the offending word throughout the remainder of the proceedings (I committed only one slip-up—inadvertent or otherwise). In answer to a cross-examination question posed to her by Aaron Johnson, Vanessa also said "rape" one time. Judge Link glared at me on each occasion, but he let it go.

When the hearing ended, Judge Link issued his order. He granted Aaron Johnson one hour of visitation with Faith every week, supervised by Vanessa's pastor, at a time, day, and location to be chosen by the pastor. It was Johnson's responsibility to contact the pastor to initiate the supervised visits.

I have no doubt Judge Link had initially intended to grant that rapist liberal partial custody of Faith. Given the judge we had and the state of the law at the time, this extraordinarily restrictive order was undoubtedly the best we could have gotten. Still, I was devastated. I felt I had failed to fully protect my client's child. As we left the courtroom together, Vanessa put her hand in mine and said quietly: "Don't worry. Faith will be safe with Pastor William."

I asked her to call me every week to let me know how each visitation went. Although I was certain the custodial rights given to Johnson were far too limited to successfully appeal, I planned to file a petition to modify the order if the visitations went badly.

Week after week, Vanessa called to tell me, "He hasn't called Pastor William yet."

After a few months passed in this fashion, we came to a wonderful realization: Aaron Johnson would never have a moment's visitation with Faith. He had no interest that survived supervision.

So it all turned out well in the end. The custody order, although unpardonable, proved sufficient for our needs. I managed to escape imprisonment. And every year thereafter while I was at Legal Aid, on the anniversary of our hearing date, I got a cherished letter from Vanessa Roberts and her daughter, blessing me and bringing me joyful news about their lives.

22. "We're Done Now"

A wealthy attorney who was a long-time member of our board of directors decided to donate an office in Doylestown to Legal Aid. I can't say for sure, but I think he did it because he felt sorry for me. He had recently dropped by the tiny room that another nonprofit agency let Legal Aid borrow on Wednesdays to meet with family law clients from upper and middle Bucks County. When he arrived that day, I was sitting on one of the two chairs in the room (there was no desk), trying to steady a legal pad balanced on my lap, writing a petition during a brief lull between client appointments. The attorney had come to hand me a packet of documents that he wanted delivered to David Tilove when I returned to Bristol the next day. He was taken aback by the diminutive dimensions of the space.

"Aren't you feeling claustrophobic?" he asked, sounding genuinely surprised that I was not attempting to jump out the window.

Being a rational person, I was certainly aware that, objectively, the room was exceptionally small. But it was actually close to the size that my beloved office in Lewistown had been, so—as anyone familiar with the theory of relativity would understand—I experienced it as quite roomy enough for my needs.

"It would be nice to have more space, but beggars can't be choosers," I said cheerfully.

Shortly after our brief encounter, the board member announced his decision to lend Legal Aid a free office in Doylestown.

Our new office was on the second floor of a two-story building on Main Street, directly across the street from the back entrance to the main courthouse. It had three small individual rooms and a private bathroom. It was about five times the size of the cubby-hole where I'd been camping out on Wednesdays, although still rather small. Theoretically, though, two other people could have been there (snugly) with me, if Legal Aid had had two other people to spare.

All of a sudden, there was no reason for me to commute to the Bristol office four days a week. We now had an office at the county seat, halfway between the upper end of the county and our main office at the lower end of the county. For poor people and victims of abuse living in upper and middle Bucks County, Legal Aid was now easily accessible. So after we got this office, I went to Bristol only once or twice a week.

When I first came to Bucks County, a number of the judges who heard family law cases had courtrooms in the main courthouse. But now all the family law matters took place in a separate family court building. Unlike the large and architecturally impressive courthouse, family court was housed in a narrow, nondescript building, identified only by an inconspicuous sign, located directly across the street from the front entrance to the main courthouse. To get to family court, I simply had to cross Main Street, walk through the courthouse plaza, and then cross Court Street. It took about three minutes. It seemed unbelievable, but I was now closer to the courthouse in Doylestown than I had been to the courthouse in Lewistown. As often as I was in court, it made my life much easier.

Viola Jaffe, an elderly woman who lived near Doylestown, had been volunteering at A Woman's Place for a number of years. After sitting in on many of my meetings with shelter residents, she had learned everything there was to know about the Protection from Abuse Act. When she heard I was yearning for a coworker at Legal Aid's new Doylestown office, she offered to split her volunteering time between the two agencies. I had observed Viola's quick intelligence and the great rapport she had with victims of domestic violence, so I was delighted.

Viola became my paralegal for two or three days a week, interviewing abuse victims and drafting their PFA petitions. She was very good at her job. She would call me into her room when a tricky legal question or tactical issue needed to be assessed, or when she wanted me to talk to the client before going forward. Sometimes a warning letter to the abuser might be a better step to take in a particular case, or there might be a question as to whether the abusive behavior the client described met the definition of abuse under the act. Occasionally, a client might distrust Viola's knowledge of the law because she wasn't a lawyer. But often an entire day would go by without Viola needing any advice or assistance from me.

One morning, Viola called out to me while she was on the phone with a client. The client had come to the office the day before, and her PFA petition against her husband had already been filed. "I'm going to have the lawyer talk to you about this, okay?" Viola was saying. She held up a piece of paper for me to look at. On it she had written: "She wants to withdraw her petition. The abuse was VERY BAD."

Clients often decided to withdraw their petitions for protection, but I had a knack for convincing them not to. When a client's decision to withdraw was made at the direction of her abuser—a voice she was used to obeying—frequently all that was needed to restore her initial conviction was for her to have a different strong voice to listen to. When the client's decision stemmed from her own second thoughts about severing the relationship because she still loved the abuser or was financially dependent on him, I would explain that the PFA order did not necessarily have to *evict* the abuser, or deny him all *contact* with her. If she wished, she could withdraw her request for those provisions. The abuser could simply be ordered not to abuse, threaten, stalk, or harass her. They could continue to live together or spend time together, but without violence. It was not an optimal arrangement, but it was an option that kept many clients from totally withdrawing their petitions for protection.

Some clients would respond that they had no choice but to withdraw their petition, because their abuser refused to continue living with them if they didn't.

"If he refuses to agree that he won't *abuse y*ou, how can you possibly live with him safely?" I would ask. The undeniable truth contained in that question helped many victims choose not to return to their abusers, or at least not to do so without obtaining a modicum of protection.

Still, it's important to respect a client's independent appraisal of her readiness to proceed in any fashion. No one should ever be pressured into getting a protection order against her own judgment. These orders have saved countless lives, and I wholeheartedly endorse them, but it is also true that for the kind of abuser who is deranged and desperate enough, who thinks that "if I can't have her, no one else will," a PFA order can potentially be like a red cape waved before a raging bull.

As soon as I got on the phone with Viola's client and heard the sheer terror in her voice, I knew the type of withdrawal request this was.

"You have to withdraw my petition right now!" the client screamed. She was screaming and sobbing at the same time.

I had never before heard anyone sound that terrified. I knew instantly that her husband was there, in the room with her, and that she believed her life was in danger.

"Is your husband there with you?" I whispered into the phone.

"No! No! Just withdraw my petition!" she shouted.

Now I knew that her husband could hear me.

"Okay, there's no problem at all," I said, mimicking nonchalance. "I'll go over to the courthouse right now to withdraw your petition."

"Do it now!"

"I'm going there right now to withdraw your petition. Please stay on the line with Viola while I'm gone, so I'll be able to let you know as soon as I get back."

There was a brief delay when all I could hear was the muffled sound of sobbing. It was the time it took, I knew, for her to see her husband shake his head no.

"I can't stay on the line," she shouted. "Just go do it now!"

"Of course. I'll call you as soon as I get back from the courthouse," I said.

The call disconnected.

I called the police. I told the officer that our client had filed a protection from abuse petition against a very violent abuser and that he was forcing her to beg us to withdraw it.

"He's holding her against her will—right now! You have to go check on her *immediately*. Her life is in danger!"

"We'll send some guys out right away," he said.

Thankfully, the police station was just a few blocks from the client's home.

"Please *hurry*," I said, "and please call me back to let me know if she's safe."

I ran to family court to withdraw the petition and rushed back to the office. I was gone less than twenty minutes. The police were already on the phone with Viola when I got back. All color was gone from her face.

"The lawyer is here now," Viola told the officer, handing me the phone.

"What's happening?" I asked. "Is my client okay?"

The policeman's reply was matter-of-fact: "Your client killed herself."

"What? Oh my God, her husband killed her!"

The officer corrected me. "Her husband didn't kill her. She killed *herself*."

"She didn't kill herself!" I yelled at him. "I *told* you she was in danger! I *told* you her husband was holding her against her will!"

The officer remained blasé. "Sorry, but no one else is here. Your client committed suicide. She shot herself in the mouth. The gun is in her hand."

"Women don't shoot themselves in the mouth!" I yelled.

"Well, *she* did," said the officer, annoyed at my insistence.

"If she was planning to kill herself in a minute, why would she call Legal Aid, scared to death, begging us to withdraw the PFA petition she had filed against her husband?"

"How am I supposed to know why your client acted the way she did?" the officer replied. "I'm not a mind reader."

I wanted to scream and curse at him. I wanted to call him a fucking idiot. But I was still trying to change his mind.

"I called you because I could tell she was petrified that her husband would kill her. And now she's dead! Her husband was there when I was talking to her. You have to arrest him!"

"Lady, her husband had nothing to do with this."

"How can you know that?" I demanded.

"Because he just happened to walk by here a minute ago, with a friend, and I talked to him. He's been with his friend all morning. He told us his wife's been threatening to kill herself for a long time. He said she's crazy."

I lost all control at that point and began yelling hysterically. "Are you kidding me? You're taking the word of her husband, who just happened to be strolling by when you were finding his wife's body? You're at a crime scene! You need to get your detectives out there!"

"I gave you the courtesy call you asked for, lady," the officer said. "We're done now."

I had dealt with enough police officers in domestic violence cases to know the way they routinely demeaned and dismissed victims, but this was a new level of indifference. This was beyond my comprehension. I had wasted precious time talking to him, because there was nothing I could have said that would have changed his mind.

I called the district attorney's office. The receptionist wouldn't put me through to the D.A., only to the assistant D.A. on call. I told him everything that had just happened. I said I wanted to come to the courthouse to give my statement. I said the crime scene needed to be preserved.

The assistant D.A. on call thanked me for my phone call. "We'll get back to you if we need to," he said.

Apparently they didn't need to, because although I left three follow-up messages, no one from their office ever got back to me.

I saw the client's obituary in the local paper a few days later. It said she had "died suddenly at home," the code phrase for death due to suicide or drug overdose. I immediately called the newspaper, asking to talk to a reporter. None were available. I left an urgent, detailed message about the murder, and asked to meet with someone about the case as soon as possible. I left two more urgent messages the following day, and two more after that.

No one ever called me back.

23. Failing to Not Be Poor

Everyone was afraid of the Honorable Isaac S. Garb, who, despite his small stature—he was approximately five feet four—was a towering figure at the Bucks County Court of Common Pleas. He had been elected president of the judges shortly after I moved back to Bucks County, and he remained the head judge for many years thereafter, using his position to brandish an outsized influence over every facet of the court system. He managed to maintain his reign long past the term restrictions for that position, the rumor being that none of the other judges were willing to challenge him for the post.

Judge Garb famously had no patience for fools, and he was thought to be so smart that everyone else was a fool by comparison. Some judges act kindly towards newly-minted lawyers, recognizing that the practice of law can be difficult and take time to master. Judge Garb was not one of those judges. His impatience with new lawyers was legendary.

I was still very much a new lawyer when I joined the staff of the Bucks County Legal Aid Society, but luckily Judge Garb spent most of his time either sitting in criminal court or presiding over the child dependency cases that CYS filed. Those cases were on Legal Aid's priority list, and Rita Andover handled them, while I handled all of Legal Aid's custody and domestic violence cases. Only an occasional CYS case would go to me, when Rita was unavailable. This made my interactions with Judge Garb infrequent. But not quite infrequent enough, because I happened to be given a couple of those occasional CYS cases shortly after I arrived.

No one had warned me about Judge Garb beforehand, but it wouldn't have mattered. A decade and a half older than the average law school graduate, I was a new lawyer who didn't *look* like a new lawyer, which was the worst kind of lawyer to be in his courtroom. Nonetheless, our first hearing together seemed to be going smoothly until I objected to a cross-examination question my client was asked by CYS's solicitor. I didn't like the question and I thought the judge might not like my client's answer, so I interrupted with a loud: "Objection!"

Judge Garb turned to me, obviously annoyed. "What in the world is the *basis* for your objection?" he asked sharply.

The list of proper legal objections is reasonably long, each one distinctly defined. It seemed to me that there *should* have been an acceptable basis for objecting to that question (besides the fact that I didn't like the question), but nothing came to mind. Trying to visualize the applicable chapter in the textbook from my rules of evidence class, I began to mentally scroll through the official objections as quickly as possible. But not quickly enough for Judge Garb.

"Do you need more time, counselor, to *make one up*?" he asked, to the great amusement of everyone in the courtroom. Sarcasm was Judge Garb's forte.

I laughed too, because his quip was admittedly funny and, really, there wasn't much else I could do. "It just felt objectionable to me, Your Honor," I said finally.

"Interesting," said Judge Garb, instilling the word with so much derision that for a moment I was sure he said "idiocy." He sighed audibly, as if to ask, "How much incompetence must one person endure?" Then he rose from the bench and loudly announced, "We'll take a recess."

When he returned after a fifteen-minute break, I girded myself for what he would say or do to me next. But he seemed willing to let bygones be bygones. He began by asking my client a question of his own, which was in no way related to the solicitor's previous question, then turned to the solicitor and said, "Do you have any further questions of this witness?" His tone made it clear that he did not want there to be any further questions, and the solicitor responded, "No further questions."

I could hardly believe my good fortune. I had miraculously averted a significant reprimand from on high, a potentially damaging answer to the solicitor's question had somehow been avoided, and, best of all, at the end of the hearing my client was completely released from CYS's supervision. My client was thrilled, and so was I.

I managed to learn something important from that incident about the value of finding a way to interrupt the flow when it's not flowing in your direction. Still, I never again objected to a question in court without being ready to recite its legal basis.

I had survived my first dose of demoralization at the hands of the Honorable Isaac Garb. My undying distaste for dressing like a lawyer would deliver me straight to the next one.

It was my settled practice to wear a suit only on days when I was scheduled to be in court. I'd found that new clients responded to this policy in one of two ways. Many were noticeably relieved when they were ushered into my office for an initial consultation and saw me in an old pair of jeans. They were intimidated by people like lawyers, who they thought were too different from them to understand or care about the problems they faced—but here was a lawyer who looked like them. I perfectly understood how they felt about people like lawyers because I had felt the same way before becoming one. It made me feel good to see their nervousness dissolving at the mere sight of me.

However, some Legal Aid clients were convinced that free lawyers weren't "real" lawyers. They were resigned to the fact that, because they were poor, they would never be able to afford a real lawyer and would have to settle for someone like me. With these clients, my apparel underscored the point.

With both sorts of clients, I would begin the consultation by pointing to my law school diploma, which was hanging on the wall in the beautiful frame that Jim had made for it, and also to the impressive-looking document from the Supreme Court of Pennsylvania that hung beside it, which admitted me as an attorney in good standing to the Pennsylvania Bar. And then I promised them that I'd fight for them until my dying breath. Regardless of which camp clients started out in, they quickly ended up knowing they *had* gotten a real lawyer, no matter what clothes she chose to wear.

While my out-of-court wardrobe was not a lingering issue for my clients, it led to my second run-in with Judge Garb.

It happened one day when a badly beaten woman walked into Legal Aid in desperate need of immediate protection. I dashed off an emergency petition, removed the bright blue bandana holding my long hair in place, hurriedly stuffed that hair into a makeshift bun, and reached into my closet to grab my standby courtroom outfit. I had to take my new client to a judge's chambers to seek a temporary protection order. That's when I remembered I had taken my suit home the day before it get it dry-cleaned—and had forgotten to bring a replacement.

Nothing could be done about my attire. The client needed immediate protection, so I would just have to explain my situation to the judge. When we got to the courthouse, I went straight to the prothonotary to find out who was available to hold an in-chambers ex parte hearing. As fate would have it, the available judge was Isaac Garb.

Judge Garb's secretary ushered me and my client into his inner sanctum. I immediately blurted out, "Please pardon my garb."

There was a moment of shocked silence as we both stood there motionless, me and Judge Garb, assimilating what I had just said. I was sure he was trying to decide if I'd chosen my words purposely, as some strange sort of taunt. The terrible interval finally passed. He took the petition from my hands, read it, questioned my client briefly, and signed the temporary order. "Thank you *so much*," I said, trying my best to look the picture of penitence as I backed hastily out of his chambers with my client in tow. As I reflected on the fiasco later, it struck me that I was probably saved from retribution for one simple reason: Judge Garb was now positive that I was an idiot.

Soon he and I would be meeting a lot, because Rita Andover left for greener pastures about a year and a half after I arrived, causing all of Legal Aid's child dependency cases to go directly to me. At first, I was relieved when a CYS hearing was scheduled before a different judge. But that changed the day Judge Garb expressed outrage that CYS had deemed the temporary homelessness of my client, a young woman fleeing from an abusive partner, reason enough to immediately put her son in foster care.

"That's the first 'service' you thought to provide?" he yelled at the CYS worker. My attitude towards him swiftly shifted and my spirits soared. I had never heard any of the other two judge question the merits of CYS's interventions. So despite his irascibility, I was now glad whenever Judge Garb was on the bench.

All the CYS dependency hearings were held on Tuesdays and Thursdays. Certain CYS caseworkers frequently pressured indigent parents to forgo obtaining legal representation at those hearings, hoping to ensure that the agency's decisions would go unchallenged in court. Parents were told they didn't need to talk to a lawyer, or that it looked bad to the judge if they got a lawyer, or even that they weren't *allowed* to have a lawyer. As a result, less than half of the income-eligible parents in these cases contacted Legal Aid.

The caseworkers who did this always denied it, and we could do nothing to stop them except making empty threats to sue (which Legal Aid's funding guidelines would not permit us to do). So there were many Tuesdays and Thursdays when hearings were held without a lawyer from Legal Aid being present for indigent parents.

After I inherited this additional caseload, I suggested to David Tilove that I just show up outside Juvenile Court every Tuesday and Thursday morning, whether or not I had a client scheduled for a hearing there, in order to meet with unrepresented parents in neglect cases before they entered the courtroom alone, and offer to be their free lawyer. I could come with Legal Aid intake files and fill them out on the spot, instantly making these parents my clients. David was opposed to the idea. He thought we shouldn't be "soliciting" clients. He also thought we didn't need the extra business. I had already been working more than sixty hours a week before Rita's departure, and CYS cases were extraordinarily labor-intensive. Clients typically needed assistance that went far beyond mere legal advice and representation, including continually intercepting and protecting them from CYS's actions.

So I often spent Tuesdays and Thursdays in my Doylestown office rather than in court—contentedly clothed in a comfortable pair of jeans.

The other judges presiding over dependency cases at that time weren't bothered by the absence of a lawyer on the parents' side, but Judge Garb always asked unrepresented indigent litigants if they wanted an attorney. It was lot easier for judges to rule by rote in favor of CYS when the only lawyer in court was CYS's solicitor, but Judge Garb never ruled by rote. So I would periodically get a telephone call from him at the

Doylestown office, demanding that I come to his courtroom immediately. I'd schedule client appointments very early in the morning and after hours on the Tuesdays and Thursdays when Judge Garb was presiding, so I could be available if he called. When he did, I'd tell him, "It will just take me a few minutes to put on a suit," in response to which he would yell impatiently, "I don't have a few minutes! Just get over here *right now*!"

Which is why I would often come running into Judge Garb's courtroom, out of breath and dressed like a hippie. He would glance at me up and down, looking aggravated, but he never said a word about what I was wearing. I couldn't really be blamed for following his orders and coming "as is."

Usually, I would try to get these newly assigned hearings continued to a later date. I needed time to meet individually with my clients, to get to know them, and to understand what was happening from their perspective. I needed time to meet with any potential witnesses. And I needed time to meticulously review CYS's records, to evaluate the actions taken (or not taken) by the agency and the attitudes shown by the caseworkers involved.

Whenever I asked Judge Garb for a continuance so I could properly prepare, he would approve my request. We both knew it was an issue of due process. But for understandable reasons, many clients in dependency cases didn't want me to ask to have their hearings postponed. Either their children were already in foster care, making them unwilling to delay trying to get them out, or, due to the nature of the charges against them, their children would be taken into foster care until the rescheduled hearing could be held. Due to such heart-rending considerations, a majority of these hearings ended up happening on the day I came running into court.

Now I must pause to explain the nature of the cases I had to deal with on these Tuesdays and Thursdays. It's a slightly complex story that reflects some of the strange distortions of reality prevalent in both the American system of justice and the broader society.

Almost all Tuesdays and Thursdays cases involved CYS's endeavors to take, or keep, custody of the children of impoverished parents who were charged with child abuse based on neglect. On the rare occasions when a case landing in Judge Garb's courtroom involved a charge of physical abuse, I'd tell him I had a conflict that made me unable to provide representation, compelling him to snare a lawyer from the public defender's office to replace me. Appropriately, I was never asked the nature of my conflict, but it can be stated here: I believe, unequivocally, that the legal system must judge everyone innocent until proven guilty, and that everyone has an absolute right to a competent attorney and a fair hearing. But not everyone has an absolute right to be represented by me. When it comes down to the word of an injured child versus the word of a parent, I know whose side I belong on.

I also refused to represent a parent charged with *sexual* abuse of a child, but the situation almost never arose because child dependency cases based on parental sexual abuse are so rare. Unless accompanied by unequivocal physical injuries or the testimony of an eyewitness, there is little chance in such cases that a child will be believed and that charges will be filed. The simple reason for this is that most judges (and custody evaluators) do not *want* to believe that a parent would sexually abuse his own child. The idea is too uncomfortable for them to contemplate, so they refuse to do so. They prefer to stick with the widespread misconception that only a pedophile would sexually abuse a child, when in reality the sexual abuse of a child by a parent usually has nothing to do with pedophilia. It is, instead, a tactic of domestic abusers, designed to cause crippling emotional injury to the child and the protective parent without leaving visible bruises.

The accusation that an abusive parent has sexually abused his child instantly places the protective parent in extreme jeopardy. Such allegations are almost invariably viewed across America as unforgivable lies by the adult accuser, contrived to alienate the child's "natural affection" for the alleged perpetrator. Judges, then and now, routinely order protective parents not to say anything to the child that might lead the child to think that such depraved accusations would ever be believed, and to reprimand the child if the allegations are repeated. If the protective parent disobeys such an order—if she, or the child, dares to persist in accusing the other parent of sexual abuse—such behavior is often considered sufficient reason, in family court, to grant full custody of the child to the molester.

It also wasn't happenstance that there were so few child abuse cases based on actual physical abuse and so many cases based on neglect. Then and now, for an act of physical violence against a child to be considered abuse under the law in many states, including Pennsylvania, the child must sustain a bodily injury that either causes him to suffer substantial pain or actually impairs his physical condition. According to Pennsylvania case law, a broken arm (for example) doesn't necessarily cause enough pain or impairment to meet this standard.

Thus, it was largely acceptable for children to be victims of domestic violence. And just in case the original statute didn't make this sufficiently clear, Pennsylvania's current statute specifically states that none of its provisions should be construed to restrict the "rights" of parents to use "reasonable force" against their children for purposes of *discipline, supervision, order*, or *control*.

Pennsylvania's Child Protective Services Law is not an outlier. Some states are a little better, some even worse. In New York today, for example, acts of physical violence against a child are not considered abuse unless they place the child at "substantial risk of death." Consequently, according to a comprehensive 2019 study by Human Rights Watch and the American Civil Liberties Union, only about 13 percent of child removals in the United States occur due to physical abuse. In our society, parents everywhere are still free to beat their children under the guise of discipline as long as the beatings do not cause permanent injury or death.

In stark contrast to the multiple protections against being charged with child abuse due to physical abuse, it remains incredibly easy to charge an impoverished parent with child abuse due to neglect. The concept of "neglect" has always been both broadly and vaguely defined. There are certainly true examples of dangerously neglectful parenting, but in the vast majority of cases, the accusation of neglect generally amounts to "failing to not be poor." This is an ugly truth.

Although statutes defining neglect vary from state to state, all include conditions that are inextricably linked to poverty, such as inadequate food, inadequate clothing, inadequate shelter, and inadequate medical care. Agencies and their caseworkers have broad discretion in determining what is inadequate. And an easy remedy to any perceived inadequacy is the removal of indigent children from their parents, usually to be placed in foster care. Sometimes, this leads to the termination of their parents' parental rights, legally turning children into orphans.

Child abuse charges based on neglect are not *supposed* to be due to environmental factors that are beyond a parent's control. Like many states, Pennsylvania's law includes a statement to this effect. But this disclaimer does not really protect parents living in poverty from being accused of child abuse based on neglect, because child protection agencies (and, by and large, our courts) do not think poverty is *ever* truly beyond a parent's control.

Too many in control at child protection agencies believe in the myth that people in need are not only perfectly capable of "pulling themselves up by their own bootstraps" but also morally obligated to do so. The physical impossibility of this feat does not disturb true believers. Faith in this doctrine is integral to policies for dealing with poor families. It explains why family service plans don't offer impoverished parents the types of services and resources that might help their children thrive. Instead, the plans typically itemize all the things poor people need to do for themselves if they want to keep their children. The plans also set tight deadlines for parents to accomplish these self-bootstrap-pulling-up directives, so their failures can be timed and documented for use as evidence against them in court.

Over the years, I've met many CYS caseworkers in Pennsylvania and elsewhere, and even at least one solicitor, who were kind and caring and did their best to buck a system they were forced to work within. But the system itself has stayed solidly in place, still often driven by the holier-than-thou, delusional belief that poverty is a personal choice and that the people who choose it deserve the brutal consequences. Many of these unworthy people, my clients, are victims of domestic violence: poor, single mothers, whose efforts to flee from their abusers render them unstable (and therefore neglectful) in CYS's eyes. And many of these unworthy people, my clients, are victims of racism or other monumental instruments of discrimination that repeatedly rob them of the right to equal treatment and opportunity. Always, they are victims of a system that seems designed and structured to keep poor people poor.

Like most child protection agencies in counties throughout our nation, then and now, the Bucks County Children & Youth Social Services Agency behaved like an arm of government and wielded enormous power. It was accustomed to being on the receiving end of deference from judges and lawyers alike. Its interpretations of the law were almost invariably assumed to be correct, and its decisions to remove poor children from their families elicited little second-guessing.

As a result, many attorneys routinely opted to negotiate with CYS's solicitors, always from a position of weakness, rather than face the agency in the courtroom. I understood why they made that choice. I never forgot how intimidated I felt the first time I stood up against CYS to fight for the O'Neil family, for little Josie. But I also never forgot the outcome of that fight, and that memory carried me willingly into battle many times. Because court did indeed feel like a battlefield, where CYS arrived armed with all the weapons yet needed to be outgunned.

It helped me that the field was not so tilted when Judge Garb was the one presiding. It also helped when I got to wear jeans at these hearings, as the sight of me in them was noticeably unnerving to CYS's solicitors. But the odds were still stacked against poor families, no matter what I wore or which judge was presiding.

In spite of the odds, these were cases that needed to be won. And although Judge Garb never stopped being curmudgeonly, we gradually forged an unspoken truce. (A few times, I even caught him stifling a smile when I barged into his courtroom looking like a hippie.) We had something crucial in common. Judge Garb cared about equal justice under law. And so did I.

24. Back to Court with Teresa

S ydney Boisbrun was still at Legal Aid on loan from a temp agency when I dragged her to Teresa Ruiz's ramshackle trailer to help me record and lock in the testimony of Carlos Rodriquez, Teresa's abusive boyfriend. So she knew all about the eventful hearing and how it had ended abruptly before its completion.

Ten years older than me, Sydney looked ten years younger, with her cute figure, wide blue eyes and spikey, pixie-cut hairdo. For a number of reasons, David Tilove had no intention of hiring Sydney to permanently fill the secretary job she was temporarily filling. First of all, her contract with the agency didn't allow her to be permanently hired by any of the establishments to which she was sent unless the agency got paid a release fee for the privilege. Then there was the fact that Sydney's secretarial skills were not exactly top-notch. She was a slow typist, a poor speller, and had a uniquely haphazard approach to filing. But her special charm, energy, and enthusiasm made it easy to overlook such minor deficiencies. Everyone loved Sydney, including me (and, begrudgingly, David), so I repeatedly badgered him to pay the ransom and hire her.

I had only recently become an official Bucks County Legal Aid Society employee myself. During the last year of my two-year Reggie Fellowship, David promised to somehow find a way to retain me, and the voluntary departure of Rita Andover for more lucrative pursuits had freed up the necessary funds. However, my new status as a staff attorney came with a pay cut, because Legal Aid's pay scale for lawyers with two years' experience was two thousand dollars less than the yearly grand sum of seventeen thousand dollars that I had earned as a second-year Reggie. It was a small price to pay for the privilege of keeping the job I loved.

David was accustomed to being pressured by me. My coworkers had already elected me president of our union, the Bucks County Chapter of the National Legal Services Workers, District 65, United Auto Workers, causing me to routinely spend many nonworking hours haggling with management (David) over working conditions and staff benefits. I enjoyed this additional unpaid job because advocating for others is something I can never resist doing anyway, and debating with someone as smart and interesting as David was always fun.

David was a great boss and I was a great haggler, so after enough badgering from me, Sydney was hired on a permanent basis.

I was only one of the attorneys in Bristol whose secretarial work Sydney was assigned to do. So when the Doylestown office opened and I began spending the majority of my time there, I at first had to manage without secretarial assistance. But as the volume of clients coming to the new office kept expanding, the need for a secretary/receptionist became overwhelming, and David finally agreed to send Sydney to Doylestown. It was a welcome change for Sydney, who lived in Doylestown and was thereby spared a long daily commute to and from the lower end of the county. As for me, having a personal secretary for the first time in my life (along with Viola, my part-time volunteer paralegal) made the Doylestown office feel like my own private fiefdom.

Sydney had a consoling look on her face when she walked into my room one afternoon, clenching the day's pile of mail under one arm and waving a one-page document aloft.

"Sorry to be the bearer of bad news," she said, "but you got an order for a new hearing date in the Ruiz case."

I had been dreading the inevitable scheduling of that new hearing date, even as I accepted that it couldn't be avoided.

It was a little joke of mine to say that I had gravitated, instinctively and inexplicably, to the most stressful specialized corner of the law—fixating first on family law, with its fast pace, high stakes, and clients suffering from traumatic distress, and then adding poverty and violence to the mix. It was a joke that helped me deal with the stresses I had chosen.

But I'd never had a case quite as stressful—or dispiriting—as Teresa's. Because I knew I couldn't save her. Teresa needed more than I had the know-how or resources to give her, and the recognition of my inadequacies was taking its toll, chipping away at the fortitude required for the work I did.

I'd made some unproductive efforts to be of assistance to Teresa since the last hearing date. I'd left her numerous telephone messages, offering to arrange transportation for her mandated biweekly drug tests, and had sent her two letters asking her to contact me. I'd asked Rosemarie, Legal Aid's receptionist in Bristol, to call me immediately if Teresa ever stopped by unannounced (that being the only way that Teresa ever stopped by). But Teresa had disappeared into the ether.

I knew Teresa wasn't taking any of the steps she had agreed to take to try to keep her parental rights from being terminated, because she wasn't capable of taking new steps. Given her utter lack of resources, she was barely capable of surviving day to day.

I knew that CYS wouldn't help Teresa. Despite its name, in my opinion the Bucks County Children & Youth Social Services Agency rarely gave services to people. It gave *orders* to people, and expected them to serve themselves.

I also knew that Teresa's parents wouldn't help her. That Carlos wouldn't help her. And that no one could actually live on the pittance that Teresa got from the welfare department, a pittance they could snatch away at any time as punishment for breaking one of their many inhumane rules.

I was beginning to silently wrestle with a terrible, shameful question: might it be better for Amanda and José to be adopted by another family?

CYS was not averse to terminating the parental rights of parents in spite of knowing that the children had no chance of ever being adopted. It didn't seem to faze CYS when children they had legally orphaned were destined to stay in foster care until they turned eighteen, after which they would be released, summarily, to the streets. But Teresa's children were highly adoptable commodities. They were still very young and exceptionally beautiful. Maybe they would be grateful to escape from the depths of poverty they had been born into, even if it meant losing their mother.

Maybe Teresa would have a better chance of surviving her circumstances if she weren't responsible for the care of two children.

It was devastating to me to feel so defeated by a system I was dedicated to fighting—to be forced to contemplate whether, in the United States of America, some people might just be too poor to be allowed to keep their children. Yet the objective reality of the situation, as ugly as it was, was difficult to deny: Teresa needed to live in a different kind of country. One that I couldn't supply. One with a safety net strong enough to nurture and protect all of its people.

We all need to live in a country like that.

"Are you all right?" Sydney asked. I had been sitting rigidly at my desk, immobilized by dark thoughts.

"Not really." I got up and took the hearing order from Sydney's hand. The new hearing date was only three weeks away. I took a deep breath. "We have to get notice of this to Teresa."

I dialed Teresa's phone number, knowing as I did it that she never picked up. I left her a message informing her of the hearing date, telling her I needed to meet with her to prepare for the hearing, and asking her to contact me immediately. I explained that I was now based in Doylestown so she couldn't expect to see me if she just popped in at the Bristol office, but that I would still meet her in Bristol if she'd call to schedule an appointment. Then Sydney typed a letter saying the same things, which we sent both by regular and certified mail.

When I went to Bristol the following Monday, I took a long detour to Teresa's trailer. No one was there. I slid another copy of the letter under her door.

The day before the hearing, I finally stopped waiting for Teresa's call. Yet even though she hadn't contacted me, I expected her to somehow show up for the hearing. Like many clients whose experience of trials comes largely from TV, Teresa didn't understand the concept of "preparing." The lawyers on TV never needed to prepare. And I knew that Teresa would not have successfully completed or even have attempted to complete any of the actions she had unwittingly agreed to take when she'd signed CYS's family service plan.

I called David at his home at nine that night, in great need of his always sage and serene advice. I was more than a little depressed. I talked and talked, unloading all my tortured feelings about the case, finally ending with the painful admission, "I have no idea what to do. There's no way I can prevail at the hearing."

David listened patiently to my lamentations. Then he asked, "Meg, is there any lawyer you know who *could* prevail at the hearing at this point?"

It was an easy question to answer. "No," I said.

"What about in the *world*? Do you think there's any lawyer in the world who could find a way to prevail at the hearing?"

As upset as I was, I had to laugh. "Probably not."

"So we can agree that prevailing is not the issue at this point," David said. "At this point, your client just needs to feel that she did the best she could. Put her on the stand and simply ask her what she wants to say to the judge. Then don't interrupt her. Let her have her day in court."

David's advice felt like the lifting of a heavy weight off my heart. I wasn't totally powerless to help Teresa. I could help her feel that she had done the best she could.

I was at the courthouse very early the next morning. I had no notes to pore over, no witness questions to review, no client to soothe. But I stuck to my long-time practice of being the person who literally turned on the lights on the third floor of family court, where the hearing was being held. I waited for Teresa to arrive, feeling strangely calm. Feeling resigned.

The court-appointed child advocate, attorney Curt Van Sciver, arrived a little after 9:30, looking as dapper as ever. He greeted me warmly as he sat down beside me on one of the benches outside the courtroom. Charlotte Simpson, the solicitor for CYS, arrived a few minutes later with a CYS caseworker. She gave us a friendly hello before entering the courtroom. She knew that Van Sciver's natural sympathies lay on my side, but she also knew, I'm sure, that Teresa Ruiz's parental rights would be terminated before the day was over.

Normally, *both* parents' rights must be terminated before the process can be completed, but that wasn't happening in this case. I think CYS knew that Carlos Rodriguez was the children's father, but Amanda's and José's birth certificates both said "UNKNOWN" in the spot where the father's name was supposed to be listed, and CYS was perfectly willing to pretend to believe that. It spared them the trouble of holding a separate hearing to terminate Carlos's parental rights, a hearing they conceivably might have lost. Carlos could have proven his status with a paternity test, but the test cost three hundred dollars that he didn't have, and anyway Carlos didn't want to establish his paternity. He had never taken care of Amanda or José and had no desire to do so, and he had even less desire to pay child support to CYS while the children were in foster care.

By 9:50, I was starting to think that Teresa might not come after all when I saw her rushing towards me down the hall. Just then, Simpson emerged from the courtroom and told us that Judge Mims was conferencing an emergency matter in her chambers, causing our case to be declared in recess for one hour. I was grateful for this turn of events. It gave me a chance to finally talk to Teresa and gave her some time to relax, hopefully, before she had to take the stand.

But we had barely begun conversing when Teresa spotted a man exiting the courtroom adjacent to ours.

"Hey, Phil!" she yelled. The man turned to look at her.

"Teresa!" he yelled back, "What are you doing here?"

The man named Phil came sprinting over to us. He explained that he was in court to dispute a spousal support ruling and had stepped outside the courtroom to take a quick cigarette break while his lawyer and the opposing counsel were having a conference with Judge Denning.

"How do you and Teresa know each other?" I asked. I wasn't expecting the answer to matter, but you never know.

"We met at AA!" Teresa announced. Phil nodded cheerfully in agreement.

"Are you talking about *Alcoholic Anonymous*?" I asked, incredulous. Teresa had monumental problems, but as far as anyone knew, alcoholism wasn't one of them.

"Yes, ma'am!" Phil exclaimed. "We met at AA!" The "anonymous" aspect of the organization was clearly of no import to either of them.

An intriguing thought started to percolate in my mind.

"Teresa, how *long* have you been going to AA meetings?"

Teresa mulled over this query. "I think I started going after the last hearing. It's a good place to meet people."

"Nothing beats AA meetings!" Phil chimed in. "Teresa looks a hundred percent better now than when she first started coming!"

"Really? She looks a hundred percent better since coming to the meetings?"

"Absolutely! A hundred percent!"

My intriguing thought began morphing into a plan. A long-shot plan, but what other options did I have?

"Would you be willing to testify to that?" I asked.

Phil was delighted. "What a blast! I'd love to!"

When our case convened at eleven a.m., I requested a conference with the judge.

"What's this about, Meg?" Judge Mims asked. Simpson and Van Sciver were wondering also.

I proceeded to relay what I had just learned: that my client had been attending AA meetings since our last hearing date—*on her own initiative.* I pointed out that none of us had realized that Ms. Ruiz had a problem with alcohol, that CYS had wrongly accused her of using illegal drugs. Now she was going—*on her own initiative*—to AA meetings, even though it wasn't required by the family service plan. I said I would never have known about this important step my client was taking if someone from her AA meeting hadn't by chance been in the courthouse; that he told me he saw a one hundred percent improvement in Ms. Ruiz's appearance since she started attending the meetings; and that he was willing to testify about this under oath.

Then I added: "In light of this important new development, I'm requesting that this case be rescheduled to give Ms. Ruiz an appropriate period of time to advance through the twelve steps of recovery."

CYS's solicitor strenuously objected to my request, but Curt Van Sciver spoke up in support of it. Judge Mims said she needed to hear testimony from Phil before making her decision. So Phil was called out from the next courtroom to testify on Teresa's behalf. I kept it short, just having him tell the judge what he'd already told me.

Judge Mims announced that the hearing would be continued for six months.

I could hardly believe the serendipitous events that had just occurred. But as I left the courthouse, worrisome second thoughts began swirling in my brain. Did Teresa really have a heretofore unrecognized alcohol problem? Or was it one of the few problems that Teresa *didn't* have? How could Teresa possibly afford to have an alcohol problem? Had she been attending AA meetings just to make friends? (Teresa truly needed friends.) Upon reflection, I realized that Teresa had not even professed to have an alcohol problem; she had in fact just said that AA was a good place to meet people.

Had I grabbed hold of an illusion and misled the court?

But soon these bleak thoughts were replaced by the bright memory of a fable my mother once told me about a king and his court jester. According to the story, the king became angry at something the court jester said and ordered that he be executed at midnight. The court jester immediately proposed to the king, "If you let me live, in one year's time I will teach your horse to talk." Intrigued, the king agreed to the deal.

As the court jester walked freely from the castle, a friend approached him anxiously, asking, "What were you thinking? No one can teach a horse to talk!"

The court jester smiled broadly. "In one year's time, *anything* could happen," he said. "I might die of natural causes. The king himself might die. The king's feelings towards me might mellow. Or—who knows? I might teach his horse to talk."

Recalling this story, my perspective shifted. The hearing was over and, incredibly, CYS had failed to terminate Teresa's parental rights. Amanda and José still had the mother they loved. Maybe the AA meetings *were* helping Teresa, whether she had an alcohol problem or not. Maybe her new friends would have resources to provide. Maybe I had overlooked some way to get aid to her. Thanks to the continuance, I had six more months to attempt to achieve a miracle. In six months' time, *anything* could happen.

Sydney and Viola were waiting for me at the office, ready to lift my spirits. As soon as I walked in the door, they presented me with a cupcake from the local bakery, and a pretty card, inscribed by Sydney: "You Can't Win Them All—But Keep Trying!"

"If I didn't lose the case, can I still eat the cupcake?" I asked.

I called David to inform him that the hearing was over and that Teresa Ruiz's parental rights were currently still intact. David's response to this news was typically David. "So," he drawled, with the tiniest tinge of irony in his voice, "there *was* one lawyer in the world who could prevail at that hearing."

25. The Appeal

E lijah Harris was only fifty years old when he became my client, but his weathered face and stooped bearing made him look much older. He was a heavyset, dark-skinned African-American man with a bad back and a ninth-grade education, who had no problem qualifying for services under Legal Aid's poverty-level income guidelines. Yet Elijah Harris had once been famous, his exquisite baritone gracing one of the country's top R&B/soul bands. It was a band that recorded many top-ten hits, some of which sold millions of copies and reached the top of the billboard charts. The name of the band and its classic songs would be recognized instantly by music lovers, but to honor confidentiality I'll call his band The Five Tones.

By the time I met Elijah Harris, five years had elapsed since the lead singer of The Five Tones had disbanded the group, just days before Christmas, to embark on a triumphant solo career. Only one of the remaining four band members had managed to reach for stardom again. The others were left behind, unanchored and adrift.

Elijah had entered the music industry straight from the Philadelphia ghetto he grew up in. He was poor and Black, unsophisticated and undereducated, but he was endowed with a magnificent voice. His lack of business savvy had hurt him badly. Although he was an integral member of The Five Tones, his contract terms were never commensurate with the band's success. As a result, even at the zenith of his career he had not been a truly wealthy man, although it had felt like riches to him at the time. And whatever money he had earned in those glory years was long gone. Fame and The Five Tones had become a distant memory.

Now, Elijah Harris was reduced to performing on weekends at bars and rundown dance halls whenever he could get a gig, making forty or fifty dollars for each one-night stand. Sometimes he had to travel so far that the cost of gas cut deeply into his earnings.

Elijah told me that, three months earlier, his wife had taken Joey, their three-and-a-half year old son, and moved in with her parents. Since that time, she had refused to allow Elijah to have any contact with their child. When he heard that there was such a thing as a free lawyer, he came to Legal Aid hoping to find one. He wanted to see his son.

"Why isn't your wife letting you see Joey?" I asked. I needed to assess if there was anything he had done that posed a danger or was otherwise detrimental to his son or his wife.

"She says she's sick of me being a loser," he said, so softly that I had to lean towards him to hear. "She says she never would have married me if she'd known what a loser I am." He expressed no anger when he said this, just resignation. It was clear that he agreed with his wife.

Elijah had met his wife in a bar in New York where the band members had gone to unwind after performing a concert at a nearby amphitheater. Sandra had attended the concert, so she was thrilled when she and her two girlfriends were invited by The Five Tones to join them at their table. Elijah described this encounter with Sandra as a case of love at first sight. They immediately became inseparable and married six months to the day of their first meeting.

Elijah had always wanted to have children, but when Sandra confided before their marriage that a childhood condition had left her barren, he accepted it and never spoke of it again. He loved her too much.

Because the band often went on tour between local performances and recording sessions, causing Sandra to be left alone for extended periods of time, Elijah understood her desire to live close to her parents. When an apartment became available directly across the street from her parents' home in Bucks County, he had no objection to moving there to please her.

They were happy in the beginning. Sandra, who was thirteen years younger than him, was pretty and cultured and educated. He adored her and considered himself unworthy of her. For her part, Sandra always told him how proud she was to be married to a Five Tone, the one whose gorgeous baritone voice was responsible, she insisted, for all of the groups' hit songs.

When the band dissolved unexpectedly, Elijah and his wife had been devastated. But Sandra had faith in him. He still had his velvet voice, and they had money in the bank. Sandra was sure another band would soon seek him out. So when they learned a number of months later that a distant relative of Sandra's, a fourteen-year-old girl living in Tennessee, had become pregnant with a child she planned to give away, they immediately decided they wanted the baby. Elijah thought it was a precious gift from God.

Six months after that, when they were notified that the relative had gone into labor, Elijah was still unemployed. He had planned to accompany his wife on the flight to Tennessee, but recurring spasms in his back were severe enough to temporarily disable him. So Sandra made the trip to Tennessee alone. She and the young girl signed a one-page power of attorney that a local lawyer had hastily prepared, which gave Sandra the authority to leave the hospital with the baby.

Elijah and Sandra planned to officially adopt the child as soon as they could afford the legal fees, but the baby was already theirs. And they could not have been happier. Elijah's face glowed as he recounted in loving detail the first time he had laid eyes on his newborn son. They named him Joseph Azizi Harris. Sandra picked Joseph to honor her father; Elijah picked Azizi because it means "chosen one" in Swahili and because he liked the lyrical sound of it.

But the anticipated offers to join another band never materialized. The money in the bank gradually got spent. And Sandra gradually stopped being proud of her husband as it became increasingly clear to her that she was no longer married to a Five Tone. She was married instead to a man whose single skill had ceased to be marketable, an aging man with a bad back and a ninth-grade education. A loser.

It was a heartbreaking story, and it was clear to me that Elijah's heart was duly broken. So it felt good to be able to tell him that Sandra had no right to deprive him of contact with their son, and that I, his free lawyer, was going to help him get partial custody of Joey. I was positive

I would succeed in the effort, since we were in the enviable position of having both justice and the law on our side. It was going to be a slam dunk.

My new client had barely left my office before I began drafting a petition for partial custody on his behalf. Early the next morning, on my way to spend a day at the Bristol office, I stopped at family court in Doylestown to file the petition. I was determined that Elijah not wait one day longer than necessary to be reunited with little Joseph Azizi Harris, the precious gift from God.

I expected the case to get settled at the custody conference, now that Sandra knew that Elijah had a lawyer. But Sandra had no intention of sharing Joey with her failure of a husband. Her attorney, Carol McCarty, was a brand-new associate at a fancy Bucks County law firm. Despite her youth, she had already mastered the contemptuous air that attorneys from fancy firms so often adopted in the presence of lowly lawyers from Legal Aid.

Ms. McCarty had an unusual explanation for why her client was refusing to allow her husband to even see his son. "Mr. Harris doesn't have standing to sue for partial custody. He doesn't have a blood relationship to the child, and his name isn't on the power of attorney." She issued these statements haughtily, as if the entire case was beneath the dignity of her and her client.

"Standing to sue" is a legal concept that means a person who seeks to have a judge resolve a dispute needs to have a real, legally protectable interest at stake in the matter. For example, if your neighbor's landlord refuses to fix broken plumbing in his apartment, *you* do not have standing to sue your neighbor's landlord, but your neighbor does: he has a real interest at stake in having plumbing that works, and his payment of rent to the landlord makes that interest legally protectable. By contrast, a squatter in the apartment would also have a real interest at stake in having plumbing that works, but he wouldn't have standing to sue because his interest would not be legally protectable.

I considered Ms. McCarty's argument utterly ridiculous. The natural mother of the child, who had relinquished custody on the day of his birth, was a distant relative of Sandra's. Their relationship to each other was one of those third-cousins-once-removed situations that practically no one can even figure out. They had met only once in their lifetimes, when Sandra came to a hospital in Tennessee to take custody of the baby. As for the power of attorney, it was a pseudo legal document whose single purpose was to allow the removal of the baby by a third party, which had been required by the hospital solely for its own protection against liability. It had no other legal significance. For financial reasons, Elijah and Sandra had delayed initiating a formal adoption, but this fact was the same for both of them. I saw nothing of legal significance in their circumstances that would make one of Joseph Azizi Harris's parents less legitimate than the other.

I regarded Ms. McCarty's attempted justifications for her client's unjustifiable actions to be so spurious that I showed some contempt of my own. "You must be *joking*," I scoffed, stuffing as much scorn into the words as I could fit. I didn't give her legal argument a second thought.

At the time, I had been a Legal Aid attorney for four years and had never tried a case that hadn't ended in victory. Having prevailed in hundreds of cases by then, I had begun to half-believe that I could never lose. I certainly never thought I could lose Elijah Harris's case. Still, I prepared for the hearing with my usual compulsiveness and spent a great deal of time composing a passionate opening statement and closing argument. I didn't just want to win the case for Elijah. I wanted to vindicate his worth, as a good man and a good father. I felt sure I was thoroughly prepared to achieve that goal.

I hadn't given a thought to what kind of fanciful tale could be told to shore up the absurd argument Ms. McCarty had offered. But within minutes of our case being called on the day of the hearing, she was telling just such a fanciful tale. And Judge Denning had a perfectly receptive look on his face as he listened to it.

Their story was that the power of attorney was a document meant to remain in place until an unknown future date when the birth mother would deem herself ready to take the child back. The document gave only *Sandra* the right—proven by the fact that Elijah had not signed it—to temporarily take care of her relative's child for an unspecified period of time, while her relative was getting herself ready to assume the duties of motherhood. In effect, the power of attorney was part of a temporary foster care arrangement, agreed to solely between Sandra and her distant relative. It conferred no legal rights to Elijah Harris.

I was caught off guard by this trumped-up yarn, but I felt confident that Elijah's testimony and my cross-examination of Sandra would easily expose it as totally fabricated. I just needed to be able to put on my client's case. Excerpts from a transcript of the proceedings, edited and abridged, best show what happened next.

THE COURT: It is my understanding that the basis for custody in this case rests exclusively with the power of attorney.

MS. McCARTY: Yes, Your Honor, and with the agreement and consent of the natural mother for Sharon Harris to temporarily raise the child.

I was shocked. Apparently Judge Denning had already accepted Sandra's story as true, and was ready, without testimony, to rule that Elijah Harris did not have standing to sue. And if he didn't have standing to sue, there could be no hearing. My voice rose in protest.

MS. GROFF: Your Honor, we strongly contest the sudden emergence today of this alleged temporary babysitting arrangement. My client will testify that there never was such an arrangement. The power of attorney was drafted only to enable the parties to take custody of the child directly from the hospital, in accordance with the hospital's policy. The child was to be raised by them forever. His formal adoption wasn't initiated before the parties' separation for financial reasons only. Mr. Harris is here this morning seeking a court order to establish his partial custody schedule of his son. We are ready to proceed with the custody hearing.

THE COURT: Does your client advance a legal basis for any right to custody of the child?

MS. GROFF: Certainly. The fact that he has acted as the child's father since the boy's birth, exactly the way his wife has acted as the child's mother. The natural mother—a young teenage girl, a distant relative—gave the baby away to them, with no talk of reappearing. And she never did reappear. My client has always considered the child to be his son, and has always treated him as his son. His rights in this matter are identical to the rights of his wife.

THE COURT: But is there any legal basis for Mr. Harris to pursue his position? He has no blood relationship to the child. Are there any court orders, any other powers of attorney? Is there only the practice that the parties have engaged in since the birth of the child?

MS. GROFF: The practice that the parties have engaged in since the child's birth is exactly what matters. The sole purpose of the power of attorney was to allow the baby to be taken from the hospital by someone other than a natural parent.

It looked as if my argument had prevailed, because Judge Denning abruptly asked, "Are you ready to proceed?" and I quickly answered, "Yes," and called Elijah Harris to the stand.

Elijah was a good witness. It was easy to see his sincerity. He testified to how deeply he loved his wife, and how thrilled he had been when she told him there was a baby soon to be born that they could adopt. He was able to explain why he had not been able to accompany his wife to Tennessee when the child was born, and the reason they had needed the power of attorney. He got to show Judge Denning the two photographs of his son that he carried proudly in his wallet. One was taken when Joey was one day old, with the hand-written inscription from Sandra on the back: "You're a father! I love you!" The other was taken just months before Sandra left, taking their son with her. On the back of that photo, along with the date, Sandra had scrawled in crooked block letters, as if penned by a child: "TO DADDY—LOVE JOEY."

I got to ask my client: "Your wife's attorney told Judge Denning today that actually the plan was for your wife to just keep Joey in your home for an unknown period of time, until the birth mother returned someday to pick him back up. Did you ever hear that story before today?"

Elijah shook his head. "No, never. I can't believe Sandra would make up something like that."

I thought things were going well. Elijah Harris was an honest and humble man, which made his testimony about his love for his son especially touching. So I was caught by surprise, once again, when Judge Denning interrupted my next question to my client, mid-word.

THE COURT: Ms. Groff, I'm still concerned with the threshold issue. What authority do I have to enter an order for custody or partial custody of this child to your client?

MS. GROFF: Your Honor, you have complete authority to enter a custody order in this case. Mr. Harris and his wife have shared custody of this child since the child's birth. We are asking only for the entry of an order that grants primary custody to Mrs. Harris and partial custody to Mr. Harris. At the end of this proceeding today, Mrs. Harris intends to continue having custody of this child, whether or not an order is issued. But without a court order, Mr. Harris will not be able to have contact with his son.

THE COURT: I understand. And I assume that your petition was filed because as a result of the separation of Mr. and Mrs. Harris, there has been a denial of partial custody or visitation to Mr. Harris and this child. But I'm asking you to show me some legal authority by which Mr. Harris, who has no blood relationship to this child, has the right to be in court.

MS. GROFF: Mr. Harris has the right to be in court because he is the only father this child has ever known, and it is in the child's best interests that his relationship with his father be protected. This is not a unique case. There are many cases where people who have no blood relationship to children, but have been parents to them and have raised them, have been granted orders of primary or partial custody of those children. If the birth mother in this case ever really wanted to show up in Bucks County and file a petition requesting a review of the order that's been issued, she would have the right to do so. All custody orders are in effect temporary.

THE COURT: Before I can award any rights of custody to Mr. Harris, his standing to sue must be established. What legal document or citation of case law can you give me, to support your position that Mr. Harris has a legal right to any custody of this child?

I didn't have any legal document or citation of case law to give Judge Denning.

Case law is made when the losing party in a case believes that the judge made a mistake in reaching his or her decision and appeals that decision of a higher court. In Pennsylvania, such appeals are made to the Superior Court, which decides whether the lower court misinterpreted the relevant statute or in some other way failed to apply the law correctly. The Superior Court then issues a written explanation of its decision, which is called an opinion, confirming or overturning the lower court's ruling. Superior Court opinions may themselves be appealed, in certain instances, to the Supreme Court of Pennsylvania, whose opinions takes precedence over all prior court decisions. These higher court opinions are published in law books and become case law, which can then be cited by lawyers and judges to prove that a law, or a specific aspect of a law, has already been interpreted or clarified in a certain way. Although the particular facts are unique in every case, the underlying legal issues are often the same, or *arguably* the same.

Judge Denning wanted me to either produce another power of attorney or cite case law that validated my argument that the custody statute, which on its face said nothing about the particular facts in our case, gave Elijah Harris the legal right to sue for partial custody of Joey. But I hadn't bothered to search for case law to validate my argument, because I had pooh-poohed the possibility that Judge Denning would ever doubt my client's legal rights.

Standing there empty-handed, I knew that I *should* have had case law to cite to Judge Denning. Sure, I couldn't have guessed that Sandra Harris or her attorney would concoct a phony story turning the power of attorney into a temporary foster care document. But Sandra's attorney *had* informed me of her plan to argue that my client had no standing to sue for custody. Rather than search for case law involving litigants who won custody without having a blood relationship to the child, I had chosen instead to merely mock the argument.

It's hard, being a perfectionist, when one is so patently imperfect.

The realization that I had failed to properly prepare for a matter of such grave importance to my client hit me like a physical blow. I was supposed to be fighting for justice, not being the cause of an injustice. I was certain that case law existed to support Elijah Harris's right to a hearing, but I didn't have it to give. I was going to lose the case. My brain was reeling, but a single thought broke through.

MS GROFF: Your Honor, I respectfully request a brief postponement—a continuance of the hearing, to give me time to obtain the case law that you are seeking.

Judge Denning reflected for a moment on my request, and then turned to opposing counsel.

THE COURT: Ms. McCarty, do you have a position on this?

MS. McCARTY: I'm opposed to any continuance. I have researched the case law, and I found no cases where a third party was able to petition for custody under circumstances such as this, where he's not the natural father, where he's not related.

Being told that Carol McCarty had already researched the case law settled the matter for Judge Denning.

THE COURT: I assure you, Ms. Groff, I am most sympathetic to Mr. Harris's desire to have contact with the child whom he obviously dearly loves. But even assuming that he is a competent, loving, nurturing parent, I still have no basis to award any order of custody or partial custody, given the state of the record, that there is no tangential connection between Mr. Harris and the child.

MS. GROFF: I do disagree, and—

THE COURT: I understand that you disagree. But frequently counsel will disagree with the judge.

MS. GROFF: Well, I am asking only that there be a two-week continuance of this hearing, to enable me to answer your questions better to your liking, and to avoid the necessity of going through an appeal process.

Judge Denning was unmoved by my reference to an appeal. He had already been assured by opposing counsel that there was no case law to support my position, so what grounds could there be for an appeal?

THE COURT: Your request for a continuance is denied. Is there anything further you wish to present?

Judge Denning was likely expecting a resigned no, but instead I leaped at the chance to enhance the court record with an *offer of proof*. (This is a legal term not often heard in family court in Bucks County, where appeals are relatively rare.) An offer of proof, in this situation, basically means, "This is what I *would* have said or done if the judge had not insisted on stopping me." It can assist an appeals court in determining, from the record of the proceedings, whether the lower court's ruling against you was correct, because it provides a glimpse of the testimony that would have occurred, or the evidence that would have been submitted, if only the judge had not ruled otherwise. It was my last signal to Judge Denning that I intended to file an appeal: I wanted to make a record for the Superior Court.

MS. GROFF: As an offer of proof, I will tell you that I have three witnesses here today, ready to testify. I have Mr. Harris, who would have completed his testimony, explaining that the birth mother gave the child away to him and his wife on the day he was born; that there was never a question that the child—who carries their name—was always to be their son; that he loves his son very much and has never harmed him; that he is heartbroken by the loss of contact; that his son is also heartbroken; that when he goes near his son in the yard, his wife's parents grab the boy away from him and his son cries. Mr. Harris's cousin is here, to testify to my client's devotion to his son, and of the loving relationship they have. And the preacher from Mr. Harris's church came to court today, to tell you that Elijah Harris is a good father and a good man.

THE COURT: Accepting, without deciding, everything you have submitted as an offer of proof as to the case you were prepared to present today, Ms. Groff, it appears to me that I have no alternative but to deny Mr. Harris' petition for partial custody.

I detected a touch of regret in Judge Denning's voice when he issued his final decision. As he left the bench, I turned to console Elijah and to apologize to him for my failings, but Elijah spoke first. "Thank you for fighting so hard for me," he said.

It was such a kind thing for him to say at that sad moment, comforting me when I should have been comforting him.

"I'm not done fighting yet," I told him. "We're going to appeal to the Superior Court."

I had never appealed a case before and didn't actually know how to do it. So it was time for me to learn.

I was right about the case law. I can't speak to Carol McCarty's researching efforts, but I found numerous Superior Court opinions that addressed the basic issue in dispute and validated my position. While there was no reference to it in the custody statute, there was a particular phrase that appeared in each of the opinions, which described the legal relationship that my client had with Joey: *in loco parentis* status. It was a term I had not heard before. Nor, apparently, had Judge Denning.

In loco parentis is a Latin expression (the law loves Latin, no matter how long ago the language died) which literally translates to "in the place of a parent." When a biological parent has been unable or unwilling to perform the duties and responsibilities of a parent, and someone else—even someone who is not biologically related to the child—willingly steps in to perform those duties and responsibilities for a substantial period of time and without financial remuneration, that person, through his or her actions, may be deemed to have attained *in loco parentis* status. In the eyes of the law, a person who has attained *in loco parentis* status is entrusted not only with a parent's duties and responsibilities, but also with a parent's rights.

There was one potential problem with the case law that I found. In every instance where the court recognized an unrelated person's *in loco parentis* status, that person had stood in the place of a parent for an extensive period of time. There was no case where the person had not performed that role for at least five years, and usually much longer. Joey was not quite three-and-a-half years old. I would need to convince the Superior Court that, under the circumstances of this particular case, the number of years was not a relevant issue.

There was also the unusual matter of Sandra's power of attorney. The existence of that document had influenced Judge Denning's decision. To protect against it having a similar effect on the Superior Court, I would have to thoroughly disempower the power of attorney.

After researching the case law, I next needed to figure out how to correctly file an appeal. This forced me to turn to that mammoth tome, *The Commonwealth of Pennsylvania Court Rules*. I harbor highly negative feelings towards this book, a treatise that maliciously transforms English into a labyrinthine language that borders on the indecipherable. For unfathomable reasons, it was Leo Vasmanis's favorite book. It was always open on his desk in Lewistown, and more often than not when I came to the door of his office I would find Leo perusing its pages, lost in thought. When I tried to read it, I would simply be lost. Consequently, whenever I needed to understand a procedural court rule, I relied on Leo to translate it back into English for me. It was a service for which (I realized in his absence) he was never properly rewarded. But Leo was no longer in the next room. I was on my own.

Unsurprisingly, *The Commonwealth of Pennsylvania Court Rules* contained a plethora of confounding rules governing every step of the process for appealing to the Pennsylvania Superior Court. All the rules had to be strictly followed, even down to the size and type of font permitted in the legal brief to be filed. Leo-less, I spent hours reading and rereading these wretched rules and worrying about the many ways I might misconstrue or inadvertently violate one of them.

Fortunately, the crux of the appeal was not problematic. It was clearly an error of law for Judge Denning to have ruled that my client had no legal standing to sue because he was not related to the child and had no power of attorney or other authorization. Judge Denning was also wrong to have thought it mattered that Sandra Harris had a blood relationship to the child that her husband lacked. Two Superior Court opinions specifically stated that in cases of a custody dispute between two non-parents, one a relative of the child and one not, the burden of proof favored neither party over the other.

Traversing the minefield of procedural rules had felt like a punishment for my sins, but I enjoyed writing the argument part of the legal brief. It gave me a second chance to set things right.

Given the ample number of Superior Court opinions that explained the concept of *in loco parentis* status and the rights it bestowed, I had plenty from which to quote. As for the length-of-time issue, I realized I had an unassailable argument: Elijah had been standing *in loco parentis* to Joey from the first day of the boy's life. The relevant fact was not that Sandra Harris had signed a power of attorney. The relevant fact was that the birth mother had willingly given her newborn child away. She had handed him over at the hospital, whereupon Mrs. Harris had taken the infant home to her jubilant husband, who was waiting there for them, they had given the child their surname, and they had lived together from the start—as mother, father, and son.

In the final paragraph of my legal brief, I asserted that denying Elijah Harris the right to seek partial custody of the child was a manifest error of law because his *in loco parentis* status was irrefutable. Elijah Harris was the only father that Joseph Azizi Harris had ever known.

I filed my brief and crossed my fingers.

As in many states, custody cases are fast-tracked by the Pennsylvania Superior Court, so I didn't have too long to wait for the good news. The Superior Court agreed with me, overturning Judge Denning's Order and remanding the case back to his courtroom for the full custody hearing we had originally been denied.

The second hearing ended perfectly. Elijah Harris was granted liberal partial custody of Joey and was reunited with his little boy that very day.

Almost two decades later, Judge Denning and his wife attended an event for A Woman's Place at which I was receiving an award, and we found ourselves seated next to each other at the head table. As the desserts were being served, Judge Denning learned towards me and said in a whisper, "I should have given you that continuance."

26. The Ruse

Sometimes it seemed as if I lived at the courthouse. Besides all the CYS hearings, custody hearings, and custody conferences I handled, protection from abuse hearings were held two or three days a week back then and on each of those days I represented multiple plaintiffs seeking protection orders.

In about 75 percent of PFA cases, the abuser and his attorney could be convinced to agree to the entry of an order against him, thereby eliminating the need for a contested hearing. There were definite benefits to getting such an agreement. It enabled me to precisely tailor the protection order's terms and conditions to the client's particular needs and circumstances. It also spared my client the anxiety of having to testify about the abuse they had suffered. It is stressful to testify on the witness stand in any kind of case, with a court reporter documenting your every word and a judge scrutinizing everything about you. In a domestic violence case, that stress is exacerbated by a fear of speaking out in the presence of the abuser, and further magnified by the fact that women so often feel shame and humiliation about having been abused by the men they loved. (It never fails to anger me that victims are the ones suffering from shame and humiliation, when it is the abusers who should be plagued with those feelings.)

Best of all, reaching an agreement bypasses the dangers inherent in allowing a judge to decide the outcome. This was particularly true on days when the judge presiding was oblivious to the realities of domestic violence, entertaining thinking processes like, "If those things *really* happened, she would have left sooner." Or, worse, when the judge's mindset secretly coincided with the abuser's: "If those things really happened, she must have been *asking* for it."

It was harder to obtain an agreed PFA order on days when biased or clueless judges were on the bench, because experienced defense attorneys were aware of the advantages their clients had. Some lawyers for victims would urge their clients to withdraw their petitions rather than face those judges, due to how dangerous it is for a victim of domestic violence to lose a contested abuse case. Losing such a case brands the victim forever as a liar in the eyes of the court, the police, and other authorities, leaving her with no legal recourse against future abuse, which usually increases as a result. It can also cause the victim to lose primary custody of her children at a subsequent contested custody case, where her allegedly false charges will be portrayed as a malicious effort on her part to alienate the children from a loving father. If the children corroborate the abuse, the victim risks additionally being accused of having brainwashed them.

To help nullify the dangers these judges posed whenever a contested hearing was necessary, I relied on diligent preparation and a readiness to directly address and strenuously challenge the kinds of biases and misinformation that these judges harbored. I also deployed my knowledge of psychology. Early on, I had realized that the worst judges in family court felt remarkably free to show their prejudices and act like tyrants in their courtrooms, largely unconstrained by the laws they were supposed to be enforcing. Unlike in criminal court, where the filing of appeals to the Superior Court was routine and often expected, the rulings of judges in family court were almost never appealed. Most family law attorneys were afraid to "make an enemy" of a judge they had to stand before day after day, by openly questioning the judge's decisions. As a result, our uneducated and biased judges had good reason to be unconcerned about the possibility of being publicly rebuked and summarily overturned by their judicial superiors.

This is why, early on, I intentionally cultivated a reputation as someone who *would* appeal—and fully expected to *win* on appeal—if I ever lost a case in the Bucks County Court of Common Pleas. It's also why I never felt the need to advise a client to withdraw her petition in the absence of an agreement.

An appeal, or the threat of one, doesn't make an enemy of a judge. It educates them. It makes them stop and think twice before they act.

There is one downside to a PFA order entered by agreement of the parties: it is entered without a finding of fault. In other words, the defendant agrees not to commit certain acts in the future (for a specific period of time), but he makes no admission of any prior wrongdoing, and no judge has found him guilty of any past bad acts. This fact grates on me, because I believe it is important for abusers to be officially declared guilty of the crimes they've committed against the people who loved them.

Abusers do not think of themselves as criminals. In their minds, the violence they commit is not a crime. It isn't even their fault. Their wives or ex-wives, girlfriends or ex-girlfriends, are always looking at other men, or late getting dinner served, or talking back, or otherwise "pushing their buttons," and as a result they deserve what they get.

Abusers are not alone in this way of thinking. In the minds of many, domestic violence is differentiated from "criminal" violence. That's why, when victims are stalked, assaulted, or even murdered, they are typically described as having been involved in a "domestic dispute." How many times have you seen the newspaper headline or heard the newscaster using that trivializing, euphemistic phrase? *Woman Hospitalized after Domestic Dispute. Man Shoots Wife during Domestic Dispute. Domestic Dispute Leads to Stabbing Death.*

Imagine a robber holding a gun to a bank clerk's head and ordering her to open the vault. Imagine him shooting her when she hesitates for a second or refuses to comply. Now picture the headline in the morning paper. Is there any chance it will say *Clerk Shot in Banking Dispute?*

When bank robbers are apprehended, we expect them to go to jail. Jail is the right place for abusers to go, too.

This is not to suggest that I approve of the mass incarceration that our criminal justice system so tragically preserves by targeting minorities for arrests, coercing the poor into unfair plea deals, imposing harsh sentences for minor infractions and non-violent crimes, criminalizing drug addiction and mental illness, compelling pretrial detention and money bail, and investing far more in prisons than in the kinds of human services that could help keep most people out of them. Millions of our citizens have been unjustly incarcerated.

But robbing another person of her autonomy, through violence, fear, and intimidation, is not a minor infraction. And for the average abuser, a little time in jail does wonders. It causes him to actually experience a negative consequence for his actions. Even more important, it tells him, likely for the first time, that society thinks his behavior is criminal. The views of the community are central to everyone's self-image. If he does not want to be looked upon as a criminal in the eyes of society, he needs to stop abusing his partner.

Lou Greco was one of those abusers. He looked like a nice guy, and everyone thought he was a nice guy. No one imagined he was a narcissistic control freak who threatened, bullied, and stalked his wife. But that's exactly who he really was. And he felt justified in everything he did. One of those things he did, repeatedly, was violate his estranged wife Muriel's PFA order.

Pennsylvania's Protection from Abuse Act offers a number of punishments for abusers who violate orders, including the possibility of being sent to prison for up to six months—a length of punishment that is almost *never* imposed. But Muriel didn't want Lou to go to jail. She had her reasons, lots of them. She still loved him; she feared he would lose his job or that he would retaliate or never forgive her; she didn't think a wife should ever be responsible for sending a husband to jail.

Each time Lou Greco violated Muriel's PFA order, we would go back to court, and an agreement would be reached to extend the order for another year (or as long as the statutory limit for orders was when his latest violation occurred). This ritual didn't bother Lou. Muriel's PFA order had no real impact on his life, so why would he care if it got extended?

In cases where an original PFA order has been willfully violated, I have always considered it inappropriate to merely agree to extend the order, so I urged Muriel against taking that approach every time. I wanted Lou Greco to be found guilty and sent to jail, even if it were only for a brief period of time. But those things had no chance of happening without a contested hearing, to which Muriel was opposed. It didn't matter how many times I told her that she would not be the one sending her husband to jail; by his contemptuous actions, he would be sending *himself* to jail. But since Lou knew that Muriel would protect him from those penalties, the end result, I kept telling her, was that Lou was being protected and she was not.

And so Lou continued to stalk Muriel, intimidate her, threaten her, and commit acts of vandalism against her property. He had not hit her yet, but during the most recent incident he had grabbed her arm violently, leaving a bruise. The use of physical violence had never been Lou's predominant method for enforcing his iron control over Muriel. He had actually used it sparingly, as a last resort, if disobeyed, relying more on bullying, emotional degradation, financial deprivation, isolation, and the setting of hundreds of restrictive rules she was required to follow. He was a master of the art of coercive control. Through it, the *threat* of violence had kept Muriel in a constant state of fear.

The seventh time I represented Muriel—the first time to obtain the original PFA order, the rest for contempt proceedings when Lou violated the order—I got to the courthouse with Muriel to see Lou conversing with a young attorney I did not recognize. For some reason, Lou hired a different attorney for every court proceeding. The lawyer told me he worked for a firm I'll call Kendel & Donmoyer, a ubiquitous legal franchise that seemed to have a storefront office on every other street corner. It was a good place for a new lawyer to get some experience.

"It's a shame you missed the previous five contempt hearings," I said to the young lawyer, whose name was Tyler. "You'd have a better idea of the kind of guy your client is."

"I think I can tell that just from reading your current petition," he said.

This unexpected response caused me to assess him more closely. He looked almost young enough to be a child of mine, his face friendly, unlined, and unguarded. He didn't have the arrogance that so many experienced criminal defense attorneys in private practice took pride in exuding. On the contrary, I could sense the discomfort he felt with the role he was required to play. He had not yet learned how to detach himself from his moral compass, a skill that lawyers too often learn to value. For his sake, I hoped that he would ward off such an education and would grow up instead to have a career like mine, rewarded with the honor of seeing justice done. In the profession of law, mine can be an aberrant path, but I had a feeling this young man had the capacity to choose it. This time, I thought, Lou Greco had picked the wrong attorney.

An idea began forming in my mind, fine-tuning itself into a plan. To have a chance to enact it, I would need a reason to request a conference with the Honorable Ward F. Clark, Sr., who was presiding over abuse court that week.

Judge Clark was near the end of his tenure when I arrived at Legal Aid, but during the few years that we shared time in family court he emerged as one of the judges I liked. He had some understanding of the dynamics of domestic violence, which few judges did, and he was bright, tough, and cared about people. But what I loved about Judge Clark was his mischievous sense of humor. Many amusing stories circulated around the courthouse about his escapades, and if my plan worked I thought it might add another one to his collection.

I wanted to prepare young Tyler enough to keep him from feeling blindsided. So I took him aside and told him that I genuinely feared for my client's safety; that his client's escalating lawlessness and anger against her could easily lead to tragedy for both of them; and that, in my opinion, nothing would stop him except a belief that any further violation would send him straight to jail.

"I'll gladly inform him that any further violation *will* send him straight to jail," Tyler said.

I told him I appreciated the offer, but it wouldn't help. Lou Greco was well aware of the control he still held over his wife. He knew she'd never seek a hearing.

Tyler was sympathetic. "It's a shame you can't convince her to have one."

"Maybe this problem can actually be solved with just a conference," I responded. "Let me talk to my client a little more."

I didn't know if I could persuade Muriel to let me try to carry out my plan, but I was optimistic. If it didn't work, I told her, nothing would change. If it did work, the fabulous change would not be "her fault." She was resistant at first, but as I continued to lay out my plan, she grew more and more receptive. Finally she said, "Go ahead and try it!"

So I informed Tyler that one small provision needed to be added to the parties' usual agreement to extend the PFA order. At *my* insistence, I stressed, his client had to agree to pay for his wife to receive ongoing, weekly therapy sessions with a counselor from A Woman's Place. If he didn't agree, we would need to have a conference with the judge to resolve the issue before we could enter into another agreed order.

Tyler gave me a knowing look. "I guess now we'll be needing that conference you said might solve the problem of Mr. Greco's recidivism, because you know he won't agree to that provision."

Of course I knew. If his wife got counseling, it might change her, and he liked having her exactly the way she was. He wouldn't want her talking, for even a minute, to one of those no-doubt radical feminists from A Woman's Place. I was equally certain that the Protection from Abuse Act did not envision a provision of this kind, and that no judge on our bench would order such an open-ended financial obligation as a punishment for contempt.

But none of that was really of any consequence to my client, because I also happened to know that victims of domestic violence were never charged a fee for therapy sessions with counselors from A Woman's Place. What I really wanted was a plausible excuse to compel a conference with Judge Clark—just Tyler and me, without our clients.

I smiled at Tyler. "Maybe your client will surprise us and agree to start paying."

Lou Greco did not surprise us.

When our conference began, I immediately told Judge Clark I was willing to withdraw any counseling request, thereby settling that issue, but that there was a more pressing problem that needed his guidance. I then asked opposing counsel if he would agree that it was in *everyone's* best interests for this defendant to stop violating PFA orders. When Tyler quickly agreed, as expected, I said to Judge Clark, "As you can see from the court's file, Your Honor, this is Mr. Greco's *sixth* contempt of a PFA order. I believe there's a simple warning you could give him that would put an end to these violations once and for all."

Judge Clark was interested. "What do you have in mind?"

I waited a few seconds, for effect.

"When we stand before you with our clients, putting the agreement to extend Ms. Greco's order on the record, you could interrupt us. You could say you refuse to allow another order to be entered that does not include a term of imprisonment for the defendant. I would quickly interject that my client does not want her husband to be sent to jail, but you could say you don't *care* what Ms. Greco wants, because you cannot allow court orders to be violated with impunity. My colleague here would no doubt beg you to show mercy, this one time, eliciting Mr. Greco's promise never to disobey another order. Then you could give him one last chance, warning him that he will spend six months in jail if he ever again violates another protection from abuse order."

"Is that all you're looking for to solve this problem?" Judge Clark asked.

"Yes, Your Honor," I said. "I don't think anything more is needed." Whereupon Judge Clark announced, with a gratifying degree of enthusiasm, "Consider it done!"

As we exited his chambers he called after us merrily: "Don't forget your lines!"

Returning to the courtroom, I glanced over at my fellow lawyer as he huddled with his client. I watched as a smug expression came over Lou Greco's face, so I knew he was being told that the order would have no provision about paying for his wife's counseling. It was not the first time I had observed that smug expression on this defendant's face, but I had reason to believe it would be the last.

When our case was called, we all performed admirably, but Judge Clark emerged as the star of the show. He interrupted our recitation of the agreement with a bellicose roar that startled the entire courtroom.

"This agreement is a travesty!" he bellowed. Glaring at the defendant and pointing a finger at his face (a face now devoid of any remnant of smugness), Judge Ward snarled, "You're going to jail, Mr. Greco, where you belong!"

Lou Greco's knees buckled and he started to fall. Tyler barely managed to catch him before he hit the ground. The shock of his response threw off my timing, but eventually I chimed in with my part, followed by the impassioned pleas of the associate from Kendel & Donmoyer. Prodded to speak, Lou wailed fervent apologies for all the wrongs he had committed and begged the judge for leniency. He was still being propped upright by his lawyer when Judge Clark finally told him, "Don't ever ask for forgiveness again! If you violate the extended protection from abuse order I am about to enter, nothing anyone can say or do will keep you from spending six months in jail!"

As I watched Lou Greco leave the courtroom, half-carried in the arms of his promising young attorney, I knew with an absolute certainty that he would never, at any location, abuse, threaten, stalk, or harass my client again.

27. Supervised Visitation

T he first time I saw Maria Price, she had a black eye, a cut lip, and a large, burgundy-colored bruise on her jaw. Her lip was swollen on the side of the cut, making her face look lopsided when she talked. She and her three children had just arrived at the shelter at A Woman's Place after her husband had beaten her for the third time that week. She told me that the severity of the beatings had mounted with each attack.

Edward Price did not get arrested, and no criminal charges were filed against him, even though the local police department was the first place Maria had gone the morning after the last attack, when she had finally been able to escape from her husband.

"How can we tell what *really* happened?" the police officer had said to her when she finished describing the events to him. "You could have been drunk and fallen on your face. If your husband was really hitting you, you should have called us while it was happening. Now it's just your word against his."

I wasn't surprised to hear this. I'd heard the same thing, in various versions, hundreds of times (and would continue to hear it, decade after decade). When it comes to domestic violence, the police are always ready to find alternative explanations for the origin of any injuries they can't pretend not to see. I called the police department the next day, in an effort to convince the chief to arrest Edward Price, but the effort proved futile. The chief agreed with his officer.

"It's just her word against his."

The canard that nothing can be done because it's a he said/she said dispute has always been law enforcement's go-to justification for not enforcing the law. It's their way of conveying that domestic violence allegations are either fabricated, exaggerated, or simply not worthy of further inquiry.

"So if she told you that he's planning to bomb this police station, and he said he isn't, would you decide that, since it's he said/she said, we should all just leave it at that?" I asked the chief.

I always asked this question in these circumstances, but I never received a thoughtful answer. Still, I asked it. I hoped it might eventually sink in.

The original officer had at least given Maria a brochure from A Woman's Place, which had the phone number for their emergency hotline. She called the number from the police station, and within an hour she and her three frightened children were shelter residents.

I arrived at the shelter that evening on my way home from work. When I introduced myself, Maria began to cry. The response from the police that morning had made her think the law was on her husband's side. She thought no one would be willing or able to help her. But then the wonderful women at AWP had given her and her children what they so urgently needed at that moment: people who understood, a safe place to stay, a private bedroom, plenty of food to eat, toys and toiletries, and, most important, a budding belief that the future could be better than the past. And now a lawyer had come to see her, free of charge. I held her as she cried.

We spent three hours together as I gathered a history of her life, explained the provisions of the Protection from Abuse Act, and got all the details she could remember about each of the many times her husband had physically abused her or the children, or had threatened to do so. I learned that Edward had been physically abusing Maria for eight years, starting with her first pregnancy. (Pregnancy is a classic time, in domestic violence cases, for physical abuse to begin.)

He had also abused the children. Maria told me she had to be careful not to be noticeably affectionate with them when Edward was present, because it enraged him. "Stop fawning over the fucking children!" he would shout. He constantly complained about the time she spent caring for them, and his resentment was often directed as much towards the children as towards her. He would look for reasons to punish them, the most common being making unrealistic demands and hitting them when his demands were not met.

I arranged to call Maria early the next morning to read her the petition I was going to draft when I got home, and to coordinate our meeting at the courthouse to file the petition and seek a temporary protection order. I wanted to get her husband evicted from their apartment as quickly as possible. As nice as the shelter is, it is a shelter. Maria and her children deserved to be back home.

The next morning, the children's counselor played with Maria's children while she drove to the courthouse to meet me. Judge Denning was the on-call judge. As Maria and I entered his chambers, I saw him wince instinctively at the sight of Maria's battered face. He signed the temporary protection order before he finished reading the many incidents I had described in her petition. The order evicted Edward Price from the marital residence and prohibited him from abusing, threatening, stalking, or having any contact with Maria or the children. It would remain in place until the final hearing, which was scheduled for the following week.

The process continued, swiftly and successfully. Later that same afternoon, deputies from the sheriff's office went to the parties' apartment, served Edward with a copy of the temporary order, and evicted him from the premises. Retrieving Edward's keys to the apartment, the deputies escorted him to his car and informed him that he'd be arrested if he tried to come back. The next morning, Maria and the children returned home.

At the hearing one week later, I got to meet Edward. As was often the case with abusers, especially when they showed up for court, he didn't *look* dangerous. He was only about five foot eight and a little pudgy, well-groomed, well-dressed, and seemingly well-mannered. He looked like an average sort of guy. But Maria's facial injuries were still visible. I'm sure that played a strong role in Edward's decision to agree to the entry of a final protection from abuse order against him.

Among other provisions, the final order granted Maria sole custody of the children, but when she and I left court that day, we didn't know how long the custody provision would last. In reality, the term "final," as applied to Pennsylvania's final protection from abuse orders, is a misnomer. While the lifespans of these orders are relatively short—currently never more than three years—their custody provisions are potentially far shorter because they are subject to total modification in family court. At any time, either party can file a complaint in custody, asking to have the issue of custody decided anew at a custody hearing. Although judges were (and still are) extraordinarily resistant to granting custody of children to only one parent, no matter how toxic the other parent might be, sole custody will sometimes be granted in abuse court because the provision is viewed as an interim measure. However, if neither party ever files a complaint in custody, the custody provisions in a final PFA order will remain in place for the order's duration.

Victims of domestic violence are the only crime victims who, if they have children, are routinely required by a court order to continue to interact with their assailants, and risk losing custody of their children if they ever disobey that mandate. Thanks to judges and custody laws that habitually minimize or deny the real dangers that victims and their children face, many victims are forced to spend years of their lives dealing weekly or even daily with their abusers, and are constantly being judged by how cooperative their communication is.

We fully expected Edward to file for his custodial rights after the PFA hearing, and I was prepared to fight ferociously for a custody order that gave him only visitation supervised through an accredited supervision program. Bucks County did not have such a program, but the neighboring counties of Montgomery and Philadelphia each did, and Bucks County residents were permitted to utilize their services.

It is extremely difficult to convince a judge in family court to limit a father to supervised visitation. And trying to get a judge to understand that supervision cannot be performed safely by a family member (or worse yet, by the abuser's new girlfriend) almost always requires a herculean battle. It was a battle I was ready to wage. Maria had told me she couldn't trust her in-laws to do the supervision.

"They're as afraid of Edward as I am," she said. "They would *never* try to tell him what he can or can't do."

In the end, however, no custody battle was necessary. To our great relief, Edward Price did not file for custody.

At the time of our first meeting, Maria had been less than a year away from completing the courses she needed to fulfill her dream of becoming an elementary school teacher. If she had stayed with her husband, I have no doubt she would never have graduated, given the extent to which he was determined to sabotage her efforts. He couldn't risk having his wife become financially independent, or be in a position to forge real relationships with people outside of his control. One of his many acts of sabotage was to destroy Maria's costly college textbooks, which he did several times.

"Edward liked to hold my books inches from my face," Maria told me, "and tear out their pages one by one."

His favorite maneuver was to beat Maria badly on the night or morning before an important exam was scheduled, leaving her either in too much pain to take the test or too embarrassed by her appearance to show up at school.

Edward had been relentless in his efforts to keep his wife from graduating college, but in the end he was unsuccessful. Maria left him, excelled in her classes, and earned her college degree.

I really liked Maria. She had a quirky sense of humor, which made her fun to be around, and we ended up spending a number of Saturday afternoons together, sitting and chatting while her children played. I also really liked Maria's children. The boys—Teddy, age five, and Seth, age four—looked almost like twins because Seth was tall for his age and both boys had dimpled cheeks, big brown eyes, freckled faces, and mops of curly brown hair.

Their personalities, however, were very different. Teddy was shy but inquisitive. He wondered about everything.

"What do you have in *those*?" he asked, in his soft voice, the first minute he was in my office, pointing to the row of four-drawer file cabinets lining the wall behind my desk. My answer immediately elicited more questions. "Where did you *get* them? . . . Why do you need so *many*?"

When he learned that I was a lawyer, Teddy needed to know what exactly a lawyer was. And then, "How did you learn how to be a lawyer?" "Can *I* be one when I grow up?"

Seth, in contrast, was sassy and rambunctious, always skirting trouble by the narrowest of margins. He wasn't the sort to ask what was inside a file cabinet. He would just open each drawer and peek inside for himself.

Sally, the oldest at age seven, was a mini-Maria in looks and mannerisms, and a second mother to her little brothers. She was a sweetheart, so grown-up and thoughtful for her age. Like her little brothers, her eyes were big and brown, but like her mother she had dark hair, straight and shiny, and skin the color of honey. I loved watching how caring she was with her brothers. I thought it a lovely trait for such a young child to possess, to be so kind to her siblings.

One day I told her, "You're *such* a good kid!"

"It's good to be good," she said, earnestly.

I almost laughed, but I didn't dare diminish the gravity of her statement. Because it *is* good to be good. And Sally was a serious and responsible child, facing life bravely.

As the months passed after Maria received her final protection order, our contacts gradually became less frequent. We were both far too busy. She came over for dinner once with the children, and we met for a quick coffee a few times (Diet Coke for me, really; I don't like coffee). She invited me to her college graduation, and called me excitedly with the news when she got hired to teach third grade. But after she moved to Philadelphia, to be near the school where she was teaching, we lost touch. We were living more than an hour away from each other.

Maria's new job provided her with a salary that made her ineligible for Legal Aid's services. By then, it didn't seem to matter. The only family law issue remaining for Maria was divorce, and she intended to wait a while longer before taking that step. It is dangerous to live with an abuser, but the period of time around the act of leaving him—when his anger and feelings of abandonment are at a peak—can be even more dangerous. One protective measure, after leaving, is for the victim to lie low as much as possible until emotions start to defuse and the abuser begins to adjust to the fact that the relationship is over. So in many cases (not all) it is better for victims to delay a bit before initiating the final severing that divorce signifies, to allow for that recovery time to pass. Maria and

I agreed that, in her case, this wasn't the best time for her to file for divorce.

Because I had lost touch with Maria, I didn't know that, two years later, Edward had decided to file a complaint for custody. Nor did I know that the attorney Maria hired did not share my belief that Edward's contact with the children needed to be supervised by a qualified agency. Edward's attorney, as one might expect, didn't think Edward's contact with the children needed to be supervised at all. I didn't find out about any of this until after everything was over. It wasn't until then that I learned an agreement had been reached for Edward to have partial custody supervised by his parents.

On the day of one of the scheduled visits, Sally and Seth both had bad colds, so Teddy was the only child who attended. Edward's parents were supposed to physically supervise the visit at all times, but they didn't. On this occasion, Edward insisted that he and Teddy were going to the park by themselves.

That was where they were, in the neighborhood park, when Edward pulled out a gun and shot Teddy in the back of the head. Then he shot himself.

Maybe he considered it some kind of victory over Maria—that he had the power to take the life of a child she loved so dearly. That he still had the power to rip her world apart.

David Tilove called to tell me. He'd seen a story about it in the *Philadelphia Inquirer*. "Wasn't that mother a client yours?" he asked.

That's how I found out that Teddy was dead. It felt as if I'd been stabbed in the heart.

Teddy was dead, and I had done nothing to save him.

Friends and colleagues argued that there really wasn't anything I could have done, that Maria's income was over Legal Aid's guidelines, that she wasn't even a Bucks County resident. They said I couldn't have represented her without breaking all the rules. I appreciated their attempts to ease my guilt, but it was futile. We all knew that rules would not have stopped me if I hadn't lost touch.

I was a Legal Aid attorney. I was accustomed to having clients in danger, with no one but me to help them. I felt compelled to disobey rules

when they conflicted with morality. Like the Pennsylvania Rules of Professional Conduct, which forbade lawyers from giving anything of value
to their clients. That rule was not written with Legal Aid clients in mind.
If its authors' clients were as destitute as mine, they'd have done exactly
what I did. They'd have given them everything of value they possibly
could.

Many times I had no choice but to be a scofflaw, because who could
have qualms about breaking rules when lives were at stake? And I would
have done anything to protect Maria and her children. Except that I
hadn't. All I had done was lose touch.

For a long time after Teddy was murdered, I tried desperately to
never lose touch with any of my clients. But given the numbers, it was a
feat I failed to achieve. I also tried not to care so deeply about my clients,
to keep their deaths from feeling like my own. That, too, was a feat I failed
to achieve.

28. One Small Thing

"**G**et out of your house!"

I was emphatic. She had to get out of there immediately.

It began with Emily Maxwell's call to Legal Aid early one Saturday evening. If I hadn't been working at the office all that day, trying to get ahead of my ever-burgeoning caseload, no one would have been there to answer the phone. Her plea for assistance would merely have been a message on the answering machine, retrieved on Monday morning.

Emily was anxious to talk to a lawyer. She was only twenty-one years old, and Joe, her boyfriend of less than a year, was becoming increasingly controlling and abusive. He had just stormed out of her house after another argument over an imaginary affair he was convinced she was having. He had hit her for the first time, and she had told him it was over. "Don't come back," she had said when he yelled that he was leaving. But he had been very angry when he stormed out of her house, kicking the front door open in a fit of rage as he left and breaking the latch. She was afraid of what he might do next.

On weekends, victims of domestic violence in Pennsylvania can request an emergency protection order from their local district judge. However, the orders that district judges have the authority to enter remain in effect only through the weekend, expiring on Monday. To keep the protection in place, victims then need to request a temporary protection order on Monday from a judge of the County's Court of Common Pleas, which, if granted, will remain in effect until the final hearing date.

Emily clearly needed a protection from abuse order. I explained the law to her and discussed the protective provisions that an order might provide. I told her I would draft a petition and file it with the court on Monday morning, but first she needed to go to her local district judge to request an emergency order.

"The district judge is Joe's uncle," she said.

That was very bad news.

"Do they have a close relationship?"

"Very close. He's Joe's godfather."

Few things are more endangering to a victim of domestic violence than having the abuser be notified of an unsuccessful effort to get a protection order against him. I wasn't going to gamble with Emily's safety by putting it in the hands of Joe's uncle and godfather. We would have to wait until Monday morning, when I could file the petition directly with the county court.

We spoke on the phone for more than two hours as I got to know Emily Maxwell and gathered the information I needed to draft a strong petition on her behalf. She had been living on her own since she was nineteen, when her mother and grandmother had died together in a car accident. Emily had inherited her grandmother's mortgage-free home and a modest trust fund, which was enabling her to attend college full-time. She was in her junior year at the local community college, with realistic dreams of becoming a social worker. She had a good relationship with her father, who lived nearby. She was an intelligent, amiable, level-headed young person, with everything going for her except for Joe.

Joe was Emily's first real boyfriend. In the beginning, she had thought he was a great guy. Good-looking and romantic, he brought her flowers and chocolates for every occasion. His doting attentions, so typical of abusers during the courtship phase, had made her feel loved. But gradually Joe began wanting Emily to be with him all the time, becoming bitterly jealous of anyone who might take her away from him, even for a day, an hour, or a minute. He sulked when she spoke to her father on the phone and treated her friends so rudely that they stopped spending time with her when he was there. He threw a tantrum whenever she suggested she might want to visit her father by herself or, inconceivably, have a girls' night out.

Joe lived with his mother when he didn't live with Emily and had a job at the neighborhood McDonald's, but he didn't like the job and he didn't like his mother. It upset Joe that Emily was going to college, and he did his best to disrupt it. He didn't trust the kind of people he thought she would meet there. He demeaned her for thinking that college was important and constantly pressured her to skip classes so they could spend more time together. He said people with college degrees think they're better than other people, and began accusing Emily of looking down on him. Recently, he had grown convinced that she was having an affair, either with a fellow student or with one of her professors. To ward off arguments, Emily avoided talking to him about her classes and was cautious never to allude to any interaction she might have had with a male teacher or student, but Joe came to view her self-censorship as acts of concealment, deviously designed to keep him in the dark. He was convinced her college courses were serving as a cover for her affair. As time went by, nothing Emily could do or say could dissuade Joe from believing that she was sleeping with at least one other man.

The more I learned about Joe, the more uneasy I became. Abusers generally have low self-esteem, often deeply concealed, which makes for a hidden feeling of desperation, but Joe's desperation was sitting on the surface. It was apparent that he was depressed, angry, and seething with resentments. And the person he now resented most was undoubtedly Emily Maxwell, the college girl who didn't love him enough, who was sleeping around and thought she was better than him. His efforts to completely control her had failed, as all such impossible efforts are destined to do.

The physical abuse was not severe, mostly involving Joe grabbing Emily hard enough to hurt her but not leave a bruise, or pushing her with enough force to sometimes cause her to fall. He had only hit her once, that day, and she described it as "not too painful." That blow was an elevation in the level of his violence. If nothing was done about it, I had no doubt that the level would continue to rise. But it was his threats that troubled me more than anything else. He had uttered the one classic threat that always worried me the most: "If I can't have you, no one else will!"

For many victims of domestic violence, *"If I can't have you, no one else will!"* are the last words they will ever hear.

"Does Joe own a gun?" I asked.

"Yes," she answered.

I didn't need to know anything else. I told her to get out of her house.

"I *can't* leave," Emily responded.

"Why not? This is just temporary."

"I can't leave because Joe broke the latch on the front door when he kicked it," Emily explained. "Now the door won't stay closed. The inside chain lock is the only thing holding it in place. If I leave, the front door will be half open. Anyone could break in and steal my stuff."

"Is there someone you know who can come over to fix it?"

"My best friend said her boyfriend could fix it, but not until Monday night," Emily said. "I'll be okay until then. I'll keep the chain on the door."

"You can't stay in that house," I said firmly. "A little chain won't keep Joe out if he comes back and kicks the door in."

Emily kept insisting she couldn't leave her house with the door ajar. "Listen to me, Emily," I said sternly. "Your stuff can be replaced, but you can't be. Take some things that are valuable with you, if you can, but you must get out of your house immediately."

She started to argue once again about the broken door latch, but I interrupted. I was yelling at her now. "Emily! Listen to me! Get out of your house *immediately!*"

"Okay," she said finally. "If you feel that strongly about it, I'll leave."

I stopped yelling. "I do feel that strongly about it."

"I could stay with my dad. He wants me to stay with him," Emily said. I asked her for her father's address and telephone number, telling her I would call after I finished writing her PFA petition so I could read it to her for her verification. "I'll try to get it done sooner, but it will probably take me until tomorrow," I said. "We can talk more then, about how the whole process works."

I stayed on the phone while she gathered the things she was taking with her.

"I'm going now," she told me.

"Thank you, Emily," I said, feeling a tremendous sense of relief.

It took me almost until midnight to finish drafting the petition. I'm a two-finger typist, which slows the final production of typed documents. It wasn't until Sunday morning that I got to call Emily back.

When she picked up the phone, I asked: "Are you ready to listen to your petition?"

"I won't need it now," she said quietly.

I was taken aback. It wasn't the first time that a victim's change of mind had caught me by surprise, but I really hadn't expected it of Emily. She and Joe had not been a couple very long; they weren't married; she was not financially dependent on him; there were no children involved; and his behavior towards her was becoming ever more menacing. She had seemed very sure the day before that she wanted nothing more to do with him. So I girded myself for a long conversation, because I was determined to try to change her mind back.

I began launching into a gentle lecture about the dynamics of domestic violence when Emily interrupted me, saying quietly, "Joe killed himself last night."

It took a few seconds to process what she had said, and then that same sense of relief flooded over me. My fear had been that Joe might commit homicide, not suicide. Suicide is frequently a final gesture, but only after the murder has been successfully carried out.

"How do you *know* he killed himself?" I asked.

The police had informed her. At about nine the night before, less than an hour after Emily had left her house, a neighbor called 911 to report the sound of a gun firing. The police found Joe's body in Emily's bedroom. He had shot himself in the mouth.

"Thank God you weren't there!" I said.

"That's what the police said, too, when they located me. They told my dad that they'd searched the house for my body. They said I was lucky to be alive."

We were both silent for a minute or two as the narrowness of her escape sunk in.

"I only left my house as a favor, because of how much it meant to you," Emily said, breaking the silence. "I really didn't think I was in danger. But you were doing so much for me, I just wanted to do one small thing for you."

At times of great emotion, words often fail me. "That's the best thing that anyone has ever done for me," was all I could manage to say.

29. Counsel to Hitler's Wife

E sther Blum, a full-figured, middle-aged woman with bleached blond hair streaked with emerald green highlights, arrived at my office with an unusual legal problem. Judge Kane had scrawled "DE-NIED" in black marker across the most recent custody contempt petition she had filed. Judge Kane had deprived Esther of the right to have a hearing or even a custody conference on the issues addressed in her petition.

I had never seen anything like this before.

Judges can certainly deny petitions that do not allege a legitimate cause of action under the law—for example, if someone filed for divorce against a person to whom they were not married. But there was nothing improper about Esther's custody contempt petition, which had been filed against the father of her child for allegedly violating one of the provisions of Judge Kane's custody order. I was baffled.

"Do you have any idea why this happened?" I asked Esther.

"I know exactly why it happened. It happened because Judge Kane hates me," she replied.

I shook my head no. "If a judge doesn't like you, it's certainly a good reason to avoid pursuing litigation in his courtroom if at all possible, but a judge can't just refuse to hear your case without some reason."

"I'm telling you, Judge Kane won't hear the case because he hates me. He hates Larry, too, by the way." (Larry was Esther's ex-husband, the one that was violating the custody order.)

I asked how many times she and Larry had had custody hearings with Judge Kane presiding. Esther counted on her fingers. "About seven times so far."

Seven was definitely a large number.

From a series of further questions I learned that those seven hearings had occurred over just three years. The reason there had been so many hearings was that Larry kept filing (without success) seeking to modify the custody schedule, and Esther kept filing (without success) seeking to have Larry punished for violating provisions of the order. The last hearing had been held three months earlier, as a result of Larry's seventh petition to modify the order and Esther's seventh petition for contempt. Esther's eighth petition was the one now lying forlornly on my desk, DENIED.

"What happened at the last hearing?" I asked. "What did Judge Kane say or do?"

"He didn't modify the order, and he didn't hold Larry in contempt. He told us we should go to a therapist and follow the therapist's recommendations. I think he was being sarcastic."

"Did Judge Kane make it part of your custody order that you and Larry go to a therapist and follow the therapist's recommendations?"

"No. He just said we should do it."

"*Did* the two of you go to a therapist?"

"No. Larry would never go anywhere with me if he could help it."

It was obvious that Judge Kane was fed up with these parties. But if Larry was doing the things that Esther told me he was doing, he was blatantly violating the custody order and should have been sanctioned for his contemptuous behavior, which no therapist had the authority to do. The only person who could sanction Larry Blum for violating this court order was the Honorable Michael J. Kane.

Esther had never had a lawyer before. Everything she filed had been filed *pro se*. She'd had no one to advise her on courtroom etiquette, and her manner was somewhat brusque. Maybe her petition just needed to be better drafted; maybe her demeanor in court just needed a bit of tailoring.

"You're the third attorney I've met with since this happened," Esther informed me. "The other two said they couldn't do anything for me, that they didn't want to make Judge Kane mad."

Their stance was not surprising. Judge Kane was an extremely formidable individual, notorious for storming out of hearings when someone or something piqued his ire. And despite their tough-guy personas, many lawyers are remarkably obsequious in their dealings with judges.-When dealing with judges like Judge Kane, they can become downright spineless.

My attitude is different. I look at judges simply as people whom the populace has elected to a particular position for the important purpose of meting out justice. Judges have great power, to be sure, but that is all the more reason to stand up to them. "Speak truth to power" is more than a catchy slogan. It's a moral imperative borne by each of us.

So I wasn't afraid of Judge Kane. In fact, as I've said, Judge Kane was secretly my favorite judge. I was attracted to how smart and perceptive he was. Manipulative abusers and their truth-spinning attorneys could never con him. I appreciated how diligently he prepared for every hearing, reading the entire court file for every case and recalling each critical detail. I admired the vastness of his knowledge of the law. And I valued the respect he seemed to show for the fact that righteous causes made me fearless.

Judge Kane wasn't the only judge on our bench who responded positively to my strong advocacy on behalf of important issues and deserving clients. In a conference in her chambers before the start of a contested hearing, Judge Cecilia D. Smith once asked me what result I would agree on to settle the case. I told her I would settle for nothing less than justice. She responded, half-mockingly, "Oh, Meg! Didn't they teach you in law school that there's no such thing as justice?"

"They tried to teach me that, but I refused to learn it," I responded.

A shocked look spread across the opposing counsel's face at what he clearly viewed as my impertinence. After a long pause, Judge Smith quietly said, "I knew that about you."

The matter was settled that day without the need for a contested hearing—and justice was done.

I thought I knew how to handle the puzzling situation Esther Blum faced. I agreed to file another petition on her behalf, this time a *motion for reconsideration.* Whether or not the Blums might benefit from a therapy session (if Larry Blum would ever agree to participate), both parties were legally entitled to a hearing before a judge.

A motion for reconsideration must be based on a strong legal argument that the judge's prior decision was in error, and it must be filed within thirty days of the issuance of the order in question. If the request is granted, a reconsideration hearing is held, at which time oral arguments are made by each side of the case as to whether or not the judge's original order should be vacated. If the party who filed the motion prevails, the order will become null and void, and a new hearing on the original petition will be scheduled.

Judge Kane granted my request for a reconsideration hearing. I served the motion and order for hearing directly on Larry because he, too, had been unrepresented by counsel at all the previous hearings. Seeing that his ex-wife had hired an attorney, Larry hired one too—a fast-talking shyster from Philadelphia who I'd never met before, and who seemed to run his law firm like a fast-food business. The answer he filed to my motion was a generic form document that he obviously used interchangeably for all occasions. It didn't address the issue I raised about my client's right to due process under the law. Instead, it simply stated that the judge's decision was right. I had to wonder how much he'd charged his client for that worthless printout, which he had loftily titled, "Respondent's Answer to Petitioner's Motion for Reconsideration."

Five cases were scheduled to be heard in Judge Kane's courtroom on the day of our reconsideration hearing, and ours was at the bottom of the list. But Judge Kane announced that ours would be the first case he was taking.

"I'll conference the Blum matter in my chambers," he announced.

Oral arguments are performed in open court, not privately in the judge's chambers. Conferences with the judge on the day of a hearing usually serve the purpose of narrowing the contested issues in a case or seeing if the matter can more easily be resolved in a less formal setting. In our case, there was only one issue (the right to have a hearing), and the only way for the matter to be resolved was for Judge Kane to agree that he needed to hold that hearing. Given the situation, I didn't know

why Judge Kane was choosing instead to hold an off-the-record conference, but I feared it wasn't a good sign.

We were hardly seated when Judge Kane turned to me and said,
"You're new to this case, Meg. You don't know how insufferable these
people are."

Without question, Esther had sized up the matter correctly. Judge
Kane definitely did not like her or Larry.

Judge Kane proceeded to explain that he firmly believed there was
no order he could enter that would make the slightest difference to either
of these parties. He could see that Mr. Blum was purposely violating his
order by bringing the son home late from every visit, but he didn't think
those violations were really hurting anybody. As far as he was concerned,
Mr. Blum was passive-aggressive, Ms. Blum was inflexible, and the parties richly deserved each other.

"I'm sick and tired of Mr. Blum trying to modify the order and Ms.
Blum trying to put him on a timer. They need to find another solution to
their ongoing civil war besides coming to my courtroom every few
months so they can call each other names in a public forum."

I was glad we were all sitting down in the judge's chambers. If Attorney Shyster and I had instead been in the courtroom, standing in front
of its elevated bench, I was fairly sure that this would be the moment that
Judge Kane would have risen summarily from his seat and exited, stage
left, in a huff. But although talking about the Blums obviously aggravated
him, he didn't have the option of storming out of his chambers and leaving us to lounge there in his absence.

Clearly this was not the perfect time to press my point, but it was
the only time I had, so I had no option.

"I understand what you're saying," I began, "but Mr. Blum—who by
the way refuses to go to counseling—now knows he can violate the custody order in any way he wants and get away with it. Banning the parties
from court gives him a virtual license to do far more than be continually
late returning the child. It tells Mr. Blum that the rule of law no longer
applies to him. Today, at least, he needs a stern warning from you about
the dangers of willfully violating your order. You can certainly lecture my
client about the need to be more flexible, and I will talk to her about that

also. But, really, you can't flatly deprive the parties of their legal rights to due process under law."

Until that point, Attorney Shyster had not said a word. When I finished speaking, Judge Kane turned to look at him and ask, "Do you have any argument to present?"

"I'm with you, Judge," Mr. Shyster said. "Esther Blum shouldn't be allowed to step foot in this courthouse ever again."

Now it was my turn to be aggravated.

"Ms. Blum no doubt has her faults, as do we all, but the real issue here is that Mr. Blum continues to flaunt his contempt for court orders. And, despite her 'inflexibility,' my client is willing to try to resolve their differences with a therapist, which Mr. Blum refuses to do. So, Judge, if your suggestion that the parties go to a therapist was not given facetiously, it is again Larry Blum who is behaving badly, not Esther."

"Do you think your client is blameless, Meg?" Judge Kane asked.

"No, I don't. But it's a false equivalency to suggest that she's as much to blame as her ex-husband is."

Judge Kane made a "harrumphing" sound as he stood up from behind his desk. "Let's go back to the courtroom," he said. "I'll give both of these people those lectures you asked for, Meg, but I'm telling you here and now, I don't want to ever see either of them again."

It wasn't a win, but it was the best I was going to get. Judge Kane obviously knew I was right, legally, but he wasn't happy about it and he wasn't prepared to completely yield his ground. As the three of us walked out of his chambers together, Judge Kane grumbled aloud about how unlikable the parties were.

"My client is actually a very decent person," I said, in Esther's defense.

Judge Kane rolled his eyes. "If you were representing Eva Braun, you'd be telling us how sweet she is."

We were at the back entrance to Judge Kane's courtroom when he shot off that remark, leaving me no time to respond. He took his seat on the bench, ordered the Blums to approach, and delivered my requested forceful warning to Larry and an equally forceful lecture to Esther. Nothing was said about banning them from court, nor did he tell them to go to a therapist.

Esther was pleased with the result, hopeful that Larry would be careful thereafter not to violate their custody order. I thought the lecture might have upset her, but she accepted it gracefully. "I guess I *have* been a little inflexible," she admitted.

It would have been a relatively happy ending, were it not for Judge Kane's snide remark about Eva Braun, the loyal mistress whom Adolf Hitler married the day before he died.

It has always been very important to me that no one ever think I am the kind of lawyer who would represent anyone as long as they paid me, or spin the truth to make a bad act look good. I attribute the success I've had to the fact that everyone knows the exact opposite about me: that I would never argue in favor of anything I didn't believe in. So I couldn't let Judge Kane's remark go unanswered.

Back at my office, I immediately drafted a terse letter to the Honorable Michael J. Kane.

Dear Judge Kane:

Please know that I would only represent Eva Braun if she were suing Hitler for divorce.

Sincerely,
Meg Groff, Attorney at Law

I rushed over to the courthouse to hand-deliver the letter to Marge, the judge's secretary. Marge and I were buddies. "What's this?" she asked.

"Probably the kiss of death," I answered.

Later that day, my secretary buzzed my phone extension, announcing: "Judge Kane is calling. I'm connecting him now."

I can always feel when my blood pressure rises suddenly. This was one of those times. Judges rarely call an attorney directly.

"Good afternoon, Judge," I said warily,

"I read your letter twenty minutes ago," Judge Kane said. "I would have called you sooner but I was laughing too hard to speak. All I really have to say is *touché!*"

I cannot tell you how good that was to hear.

Many years later, on his last day at the courthouse before retiring, Judge Kane told me he still had that letter about Eva Braun. He had kept it in a drawer of his desk, he said, and every time he saw it, it made him laugh.

30. Candlelight Vigil

O ctober is Domestic Violence Prevention Month. Every year, on an early evening in October, A Woman's Place held a candlelight vigil in Doylestown, starting at the plaza across from the courthouse. Hundreds of people would attend.

As darkness fell, people would be directed to gather in a wide circle around an area at the center of the plaza, where a podium with a microphone was placed, lit by a single spotlight. The first person to go to the podium would be either a representative from the governor's office or a local member of Congress, who would issue a proclamation concerning domestic violence prevention. One of the county commissioners would speak next, to express the county's appreciation for the work of AWP.

After those formalities were over, the keynote speaker—usually a recognized authority on domestic violence—would deliver a short speech. But the truly inspirational speakers came next. They were the survivors of domestic violence in the crowd who would be invited to come forward to tell their stories. Typically three or four women would respond, coming to the podium one by one, sometimes tentatively, sometimes resolutely, to speak extemporaneously about the abuse they had suffered and about the life-saving, life-affirming help they had received from A Woman's Place. Their stories would bring many listeners to tears, including me.

After the last person spoke, everyone would be given a lit candle, and the crowd would leave the plaza, two by two, to walk silently through the center of Doylestown, shimmering candles held aloft, in tribute to the many domestic violence victims who had not survived. The long line of people, illuminated by candlelight, walking slowly and solemnly down the streets surrounding the courthouse, was always a stunning sight.

I attended AWP's candlelight vigil every year. On many of those occasions, I was the keynote speaker; other years, I assisted at the event by manning a literature table before the speeches began and helping to distribute candles.

One year, our friend Gilbert Winner (he of the promised time-stretcher machine) asked if he could go with me. He had never been to the event before. It felt impolite for me to be occupied with other matters when bringing a first-time guest, so I didn't offer to participate that year in any way. For the first time ever, I would be just one of the crowd.

I didn't see Dick Kohler amidst the throng at the plaza that night, but I heard him. His voice was distinctive—abrasive and seemingly always very angry. The keynote speaker had just reached the podium when Dick Kohler's voice suddenly boomed out:

"Man-hater!"

The speaker stopped momentarily, scanning the crowd. We all did. But the crowd was enveloped in darkness, obscuring the source of the angry voice. She resumed her speech, but she didn't get far before Dick Kohler shouted out again, louder this time:

"Home-wrecker!"

I recognized Dick Kohler's voice because I had recently represented Marianne Kohler, his abused wife, helping her get the PFA order that evicted him from the marital residence and forbade him from having any contact with her. I had been stuck listening to that angry voice both inside and outside of the courtroom.

Marianne had filed for protection many times before coming to Legal Aid. Regrettably, her prior lawyer had never bothered to seek an immediate temporary PFA order for her, and during the week-long delay before each of the scheduled hearings, she had lost her courage and withdrawn her petitions. Her husband had grown comfortable with this repeated outcome. So he was infuriated when a temporary PFA order kicked him out of "his house" only one day after he had punched Mari-

anne in the stomach for the hundredth time. He was even more infuriated when she didn't then withdraw the petition I had drafted for her.
Her final PFA order extended her husband's total expulsion for the full
eighteen months the law then allowed, during which time Marianne di-
vorced him.

Dick Kohler blamed me. And although I didn't deserve all the credit,
I was happy to claim it. But now he was venting his outrage at AWP's
candlelight vigil, a reverent and celebratory affair that had never before
been disrupted. The keynote speaker was trying to soldier on when she
was interrupted by another shout from Kohler:

"Meg Groff destroyed my marriage!"

"Damn it," I thought.

I had heard that accusation from abusers before, but it felt surreal
to hear my name yelled out like that here, at the AWP candlelight vigil.

Two courthouse guards stationed in the plaza managed to spot
Kohler when he stepped into the lighted area as if advancing to the podium. They rushed over to him, each grabbing one arm, and got him to
go with them to the platform where the politicians had been seated before the ceremonies began. It was located directly across from the podium, and it was elevated but dimly lit, making it difficult for the crowd
to get a clear view of the man who had been yelling. The two courthouse
guards were doing their best to restrain him, but I doubted they would
prevail if he chose to fight—he was six foot three, with the physique of a
bodybuilder. That probably explained why they made no effort to remove
him physically from the plaza. They obviously had not come prepared to
handle a situation like this. None of us had.

The keynote speaker began speaking again. But almost immediately, Kohler resumed shouting, sounding even louder and angrier:

"Meg Groff is a man-hater!"

"Meg Groff is a home-wrecker!"

"Meg Groff must be stopped!"

The keynote speaker abruptly ended her speech and hurried from
the podium. In the faint light, I could see the guards trying to talk to
Kohler. But they couldn't keep him quiet.

He seemed to settle on "Meg Groff must be stopped!" screaming it
louder and louder, four or five more times in quick succession.

He was starting to sound like a rage-filled broken record.

I had forgotten about Gilbert until he put a hand on my shoulder and whispered to me, "You've got to get out of here! We need to leave *now!*"

We were at the point in the proceedings when victims of abuse in the audience would normally have been invited to come to the podium to tell their stories of survival. But the podium stood empty.

"Meg, we need to get out of here!" Gilbert repeated, grasping my arm and starting to pull.

Gilbert was mistaken. I knew what I needed to do. For Marianne Kohler. For Lily. For Teddy and Annette, and Maria and Jami and Lacey. For the hundreds of domestic violence victims I'd had the privilege to represent, and for the many hundreds of thousands more in need of defending.

Maneuvering past the people standing in front of me, I walked quickly to the podium, leaned into the microphone, and declared, "I'm Meg Groff."

A huge cheer went up from the crowd. It felt like getting a standing ovation (except that, of course, everyone had already been standing).

"I wasn't planning to speak here tonight," I said, "but I need to say something. Tonight we've all gotten a little glimpse of what life is like for victims of domestic violence. Imagine having to *live* with that man"—I pointed to Kohler's shadowy figure. "Imagine being his target and being *alone*, with no guards to protect you. This is why all of us *must* do our part to help victims of domestic violence!"

There was another roar of applause. I was feeling rather triumphant as I walked back to where Gilbert was waiting. One look at Gilbert's face was enough to inform me that he did not share my sense of satisfaction. All he said was: "I would really like to go home now." Gilbert was my guest and he had come in my car, so we made our way out of the plaza together.

"Stay on my left side," Gilbert told me. "I'm left-handed. If I need to punch him, I don't want you getting in the way."

When we were safely seated in my car, seat belts fastened, Gilbert turned to me and said, wryly, "Thanks for the adventure, Meg, but I think I'll skip it next time."

I learned, shortly afterwards, that Gilbert wouldn't be the only one not attending another candlelight vigil. The disturbance Dick Kohler had caused made AWP decide that the event could no longer be held safely. Their commemoration of Domestic Violence Month would be reduced to a modest affair, held at a small indoor venue and attended by only a select group of people. Never again would throngs of people from our community be invited to gather in the center square to herald their solidarity with victims of domestic violence. Never again would we all march together through the nighttime streets of Doylestown, candles lit and spirits ablaze, inspired and united by the significance of this cause.

I was strongly opposed to the evisceration of this signature event, but there wasn't anything I could do about it. Beth and Amy, my fellow grassroots advocates, were no longer at AWP, having both moved on over the years to posts at other advocacy organizations, so our *Little Women* alliance was gone. The folks who replaced Beth and Amy were wonderful people, and I remained grateful and devoted to AWP, but the abandonment of our traditional candlelight vigil was difficult for me to accept.

I understood the rationale for this decision. Kohler had introduced the threat of violence. But I thought a better way to deal with the potential for future problems would have been to request increased security at the site. In my opinion, Kohler's actions had provided indelible proof that events like the Candlelight Vigil *needed* to be held.

Admittedly, I might have had a skewed perspective. My job as a Legal Aid lawyer came with two distinct realities. The first was that my clients were *always* in danger—from the rage of abusers, the harshness of poverty, and, often, the inequities of the legal system. The second was that, sometimes, I was in danger, too. When your task is representing victims of domestic violence, the word "violence" is right there in the job description. Eventually, it loses the power to intimidate.

Dick Kohler's angry outbursts did put an end to the candlelight vigils. But I was comforted by the fact that he never got what he really wanted. Because his wife was free. And Meg Groff would not be stopped.

Epilogue

I t was my intention to work at the Bucks County Legal Aid Society forever. When asked, I often declared that if they ever wanted to get rid of me, they'd have to carry me out. But after David Tilove left to become the executive director of a larger Legal Aid in another county, and the new E.D. in Bucks County tried to limit my advocacy on domestic violence issues, I decided it was time for me to leave. I had been at Legal Aid for twelve years.

When Judge Susan Devlin Scott heard I had decided to open my own law office, she called me into her chambers and asked me if I was insane. She knew I had little money for such a venture, because I had worked for years for Legal Aid and was not independently wealthy. She told me that when she'd opened her law office, years before becoming a judge, she and her law partner had waited *five months* before receiving their first call from a prospective client. Fortunately, both of them were married to men who had high-paying jobs, but it had still been difficult to keep their office open all that time. By contrast, my husband was the ranger for a Girl Scout camp (or, as Jim liked to call himself, the janitor-in-the-woods). It wasn't a high-paying job.

"Don't do it, Meg!" Judge Scott said.

Her warning was sobering. But I had to leave Legal Aid, because I couldn't let anyone muzzle my advocacy for justice for victims of domestic violence. And I didn't want to work for anyone else. So on September

1, 1996, I opened my office on Main Street in Doylestown. To do it, I completely emptied my meager bank account (and even my piggy bank) and crossed my fingers.

Hearing about my plans, Judy Griffith, a volunteer paralegal from A Woman's Place, offered to be my free secretary for a year. I thought that was too steep a price for her to pay, so we wrangled it up to minimum wage. We were both excited about this new venture. But after paying the first month's rent and security deposit on the space I rented, and spending hours and hours moving in, I discovered it was too late for my firm's phone number to be listed in that year's telephone book. I would have to wait until late January for the book's 1997 edition to be published and distributed. (There was no such thing as Google back then. The only way to find a phone number was to look for it in the phone book.)

When I got this news, Judge Scott's warning flashed in my mind like a neon sign. Was I insane to have tried to open my own law office?

Later that first day, a technician came to install my office phones. Judy and I watched as he hooked up the first line and began performing tests on it to make sure it was properly installed. Suddenly, the phone began ringing.

"Hmm," the repairman murmured, "that's odd."

"Is something wrong?" I asked, anxiously. The phones had to work, even if no one would call me until the following year. Intercom phones were very expensive in those days. If they were defective, I was too broke to buy another set.

The repairman picked up the receiver. "Hello?" he said, hesitantly. He listened for a few seconds, then handed the phone to me.

"It's for you," he said, smiling.

My first client was on the line. She had gotten my new number from Rosemarie at Legal Aid. My phones were indeed working, and I wouldn't need to wait for the next year's telephone book. My clients were determined to find me!

I'd like to think this was due to my skill as a lawyer, and maybe it was, to some extent. But I'm fairly sure the real lure was the fact that everyone knew I was accustomed to being a *free* lawyer. And, in truth, I was determined to *keep* being a free lawyer, for approximately half the time. There were too many indigent victims for me to stop doing that, because Legal Aid's new E D. had not hired anyone to replace me.

Judy Griffith stayed with me for a year, as promised. By then, my paying clients had earned me enough to hire a permanent secretary at the going rate. And I got very lucky. Susan Mitchell applied for the job.

From time to time when I was at Legal Aid, a violent defendant in one of my cases would express his fervent intent to kill me. I had good reason to believe that this situation would not end with my change of address, potentially endangering anyone who worked for me. When told of these threats, two highly qualified people who interviewed for the job politely withdrew their applications. Sue Mitchell stayed put, unfazed.

Sue also proved to be incredibly hard-working, efficient, and dependable. She was a whiz with numbers, with an uncanny ability to remember every phone number she ever dialed. I had hundreds of clients over the years, and interacted with a slew of attorneys, judges, court personnel, and other professionals. It was not uncommon for a single person I dealt with to have four different phone numbers: home, work, cell, and fax. Sue could remember them all. I doubt I could have accomplished many of the things I did for my clients without all the things Sue Mitchell did for me. We were a winning team.

During my years at Legal Aid, I'd been frustrated by the fact that federal funding guidelines strictly limited the kinds of civil cases—including family law cases—that we were permitted to handle. No longer constrained by those guidelines, I was free to represent clients not only in their protection from abuse, child custody, and child dependency cases, but also in their divorce, equitable distribution, alimony, child support, and spousal support cases.

Tackling the equitable distribution of marital assets was a whole new world for me. A non-recovering hippie from a struggling working-class family, I knew practically nothing about major assets and their valuations. I didn't own a house, didn't have a regular pension or a 401k, had never before owned a business, didn't own a bond or a stock, and had only a vague idea of what a stock option might be. I wasn't acquainted with anyone who owned a vacation home, a boat, a recreational vehicle, or a time-share in the Virgin Islands. The valuation of marital assets wasn't much of an issue in the divorces of clients who were poor.

But if I was going to be able to keep my office open, 50 percent of my clients needed to *not* be poor.

So every evening until early morning, throughout the month of September 1996, I studied assets and debts and the legal methodologies for equitably dividing them. As a result, I learned a lot about money and the things it could buy, and honed strategies for the division of those things that would benefit my clients. Yet I doubt I would ever have mastered the art of equitable distribution to the level that I did if not for Sue's gift with numbers. It was Sue, not me, who could decode complex tax returns and byzantine business documents, uncovering financial information that opposing parties' accountants had cleverly hidden from everyone else's eyes. Knitting our abilities together, Sue and I successfully obtained financial justice and economic independence for many victims of domestic violence and coercive control.

But protection from abuse, child custody, and child dependency were the cases that never stopped keeping me up at night, because lives were literally at stake.

In the early days of the Pennsylvania Coalition Against Domestic Violence, I helped with the drafting of progressive amendments to Pennsylvania's custody and protection from abuse statutes, and later testified before state legislative committees. I lobbied my congressional representatives and wrote letters to the editor and opinion columns for local newspapers. I taught everyone I possibly could—lawyers, district judges, child custody evaluators, police officers, parole officers, child advocates, domestic violence advocates, staff of non-profit organizations, hospital personnel, and county residents—about the dynamics of domestic violence and the many important ways that my audiences could become agents of change. Throughout, I schemed and plotted, struggled and fought, and worked sixty-plus hours a week, crusading for justice and the safety and happiness of women and children (and, every so often, a lovely man).

I often think back to the day when my mother advised me, "In three years you'll be 40, one way or the other. . . . You might as well be a lawyer." I've had countless opportunities to quote her wise advice as I've sat across from women who, facing new and frightening futures, questioned whether it was too late to further their education or to pursue some other endeavor that they had once dreamed of (or had never before dared to dream). And the irrefutable logic of my mother's words never failed to provide the supportive nudge they needed, to make them believe that it is never too late to be the person you want to be.

It is one of the special rewards I have reaped as an advocate for the poor and for victims of domestic violence, and one of the countless legacies from my remarkable mother, that so many women I have had the opportunity to counsel at the lowest points in their lives have gone on to earn advanced degrees or to cultivate untapped talents, and in doing so have achieved much-deserved security, serenity, and success.

By 2016, twenty years after I'd opened my office—and thirty-two years from the day I'd entered Legal Aid—I faced a painful reality: my physical stamina was beginning to diminish under the weight of my zeal. At the same time, the ratio of my free clients to my paying ones was tipping inexorably in favor of the former. I knew I needed to do two things: slow down and reduce my expenses. It was difficult to do, but after helping Sue obtain another secretarial job, I ended my lease and closed my office. I wasn't fully retiring. I moved my computers, phones, and files into my home, and greatly reduced the number of new clients I took on.

In early 2020, a global pandemic caused the Bucks County Court of Common Pleas to basically shut down. Forced by circumstances to cease engaging in courtroom battles, I decided it was the right time to stop accepting any new cases. Still, I did not fully retire. For a number of years, I had been volunteering (occasionally receiving a small stipend) as an on-call legal consultant for the national Domestic Violence Legal Empowerment and Appeals Project (DV-Leap). I advised some of the domestic violence victims who called the project seeking help navigating the legal system in child custody cases. I continued to do this whenever called upon. I have also continued being a legal consultant to A Woman's Place's (paid when the funding is available; volunteer when not), a job I have performed now for more than two decades.

In 2021, I began writing this memoir. The true stories I've told about the battles fought and the courageous clients I have had the great privilege to serve all occurred in the first six years of my long career. Stories still untold could easily fill many more books. I hope to soon embark on volume two.

Afterword:

Where Do We Go from Here?

T he events described in this book took place in two counties in Pennsylvania between the years 1983 and 1989. If these events seem like relics of the past, I have bad news. Everything that happened then and there not only *could* happen today but *is* happening today, in every county and in every state in America.

Domestic violence is an enduring scourge, and our legal system continues to do it injustice.

In 2021, when I began writing this memoir, 5,360 victims of domestic violence were murdered in America by an intimate partner or a family or household member; 109 were from my home state of Pennsylvania. I do not know how many of those victims were children, but I do know that child fatalities resulting from domestic violence have increased nationally by an average of 4.3 percent every year for the past decade.[1]

There was nothing unusual about 2021's fatality statistics. As always, differing totals from state to state were mostly in line with each state's population, the quality of its protection from abuse and child custody laws, the quality and quantity of its shelters and other services, and the strength or laxity of its gun laws. (An abuser's access to a firearm increases the fatality risk by 500 percent.)[2]

Abusers murder their victims in many ways. According to data from the Pennsylvania Coalition Against Domestic Violence, for instance, during the past ten years the majority of domestic violence victims in Pennsylvania have been shot to death, but others have been stabbed, strangled, suffocated, drowned, hung, poisoned, electrocuted, doused in gasoline and set on fire, locked in burning houses, pushed off cliffs, shoved into the paths of oncoming trains, flung out of windows, shot with bows and arrows, stomped to death, run over by motor vehicles, and bludgeoned to death with fists, baseball bats, hammers, heavy weights, and axes.[3]

That is not a complete list. The cause of death for some victims is simply described as "other." Before being killed, by whatever means, victims are often sexually defiled.

The true number of domestic violence victims murdered each year is likely far greater than the numbers recorded. Currently, no central data base exists for tracking homicides tied to domestic violence, so such deaths frequently escape proper identification. Further, when the murder is unsolved, as is the case in approximately 50 percent of the homicides committed each year, the crime's connection to domestic violence remains unproven. Also, when a domestic violence victim suddenly disappears and her body cannot be found, the "incident" is unlikely to be counted as a homicide. The victim becomes, instead, just one more of the many battered women and children who mysteriously vanish without a trace—or without enough traces to warrant a meaningful investigation by the authorities. The client who called Viola on the phone minutes before she was murdered by her husband did not make the count that year, because the officer on the scene chose to decide that *she* was the person who jammed a gun into her mouth and pulled the trigger. An untold number of murders each year are officially labeled suicides.

The yearly number of nonlethal incidents of domestic violence in America is staggering. According to the National Domestic Violence Hotline, an average of 24 victims of domestic violence are raped, physically abused, or stalked *every minute* in America. That adds up to more than *12 million* a year. More than one in three American women (35.6 percent) will be victims of domestic violence in their lifetime. For one in four, the abuse will be severe.[4] As with the death toll, the actual numbers are far greater. The majority of incidents of abuse are never reported. More often than not, victims don't tell. And even when they do tell, their reports are often discounted.

So the epidemic of domestic violence continues to rage, unabated. Why is it that the justice system has failed to contain it?

To get a full picture of the ways that family law statutes operate in the United States, we need to look back further than the 1980s. We need to view the long history of our legal system's treatment of women and children, especially as it pertains to its approach to domestic violence.

From the country's founding until the late 19th century, husbands had the *legal right* to beat their wives (and of course their children) to correct bad behavior. The laws did not employ the word "beat," however; that would have been unseemly. Instead, beatings were called acts of "chastisement" or "discipline," euphemisms still largely relied upon today for child victims of abuse at the hands of parents or caregivers. Although the practice was permissible, some limitations were loosely placed on wife-beatings. They weren't supposed to be severe enough to cause permanent injury or death. And if a whip or rod was used in the attack, it was better for the object to not to be overly thick. The width of a man's thumb was a commonly accepted standard.

In 1864, the justices of the Supreme Court of North Carolina perfectly summarized the attitude of our country's legal system when, in the case of *State v. Black*, they ruled that a husband was not guilty of assault after an attack on his wife that had left "her head considerably hurt" and "her throat injured and continued sore for several months." In its ruling, the Court stated:

> A husband is responsible for the acts of his wife and he is required to govern his household, and for that purpose the law permits him to use towards his wife such a degree of force as is necessary to control an unruly temper and make her behave herself; and unless some permanent injury be inflicted . . . the law will not invade the domestic forum, or go behind the curtain. [5]

The common law, which our young country had adopted from Great Britain, set the roles and rules of marriage and family life. Those roles and rules had long been considered immutable—in fact, God's will. Men were the kings of their castles and had the right to rule their households and the subordinates who lived within them: their wives, their children, their servants, their apprentices, and, to an even greater extent before emancipation, their slaves. The master could "chastise" or "discipline" these underlings any time he saw fit to do so.

Inch by inch, from the late 1800s into the early 1900s, laws governing the treatment of women started to evolve. Women were gaining a tiny measure of autonomy, and their "chastisement" was beginning to be less widely accepted as man's divine right. In 1919, after years of organizing and agitating, women prevailed over powerful opposition and won the right to vote. Gradually, officially sanctified violence against women became difficult to defend. Instead, the issue was portrayed, whenever possible, as a private matter, not worthy of intrusive attention from the public, let alone active intervention from the legal system.[6]

It took more than one hundred years after *State v. Black* for laws to be passed in America that protected female victims of domestic violence. Pennsylvania's 1976 Protection from Abuse Act, and others that followed in every state, were historic victories, despite their flaws.

But there were many flaws, and many flaws remain today. And today, the fight is not only to fix flawed laws but also to keep them from backsliding at the hands of those who think the rights of women and children have gone too far, to the detriment of men and the so-called sanctity of the family. Sometimes one step forward can lead to two steps back.

Every state now has a protection from abuse statute, but they vary in a number of significant ways. First, they vary in their definitions of what constitutes domestic violence. Some states recognize that beyond physical violence and the threat of physical violence, abusers utilize diverse tactics of coercion, fear, and intimidation to terrorize and control their victims. The statutes in states that recognize this fact offer expansive definitions of abuse. Other states have far more restrictive definitions of abuse, leaving large numbers of domestic violence victims ineligible to seek and obtain a protection order.

Iowa's current abuse statute, for example, defines domestic violence quite narrowly: as "Assault; threatening or causing physical injury; or pointing or firing a gun." Compare that definition to Delaware's current abuse statute, which states that domestic violence is any of the following acts, performed either "intentionally or recklessly: Causing or attempting to cause physical injury or a sexual offense; placing or attempting to place another person in reasonable apprehension of physical injury or sexual offense; damaging, destroying or taking tangible property of another; engaging in a course of alarming or distressing conduct in a manner which is likely to cause fear or emotional distress; trespassing; child abuse; unlawful imprisonment; kidnapping; interference with child custody and coercion; or any other conduct which a reasonable person under the circumstances would find threatening or harmful."

For domestic violence victims, the difference between those two state statutes can be the difference between life and death.

As inclusive as Delaware's list of abusive acts may seem, it is not comprehensive. Indiana and Tennessee currently include "abuse of a household pet" in the definition section of their statutes, recognizing the prevalence of this cruel tactic of fear and intimidation. And despite the increasing frequency of its use, only Mississippi and Rhode Island currently include "cyberstalking."

The duration of a protection from abuse order is another crucial feature that varies widely across state statutes. In a handful of states, the duration of an order either is, or can be, permanent. A permanent protection order is the only one that makes sense to me. Unfortunately, it is much more common for orders to last only one or two years. In Michigan, currently, the duration of protection orders is "not less than 182 days." Although a "no more than . . ." time span is not stipulated, I think the statute's wording leads to a belief that 182 days is a sufficient period of time for victims of abuse to receive the benefits of the law's protection. Only Arkansas currently sets a lower bar, allowing judges to issue orders that remain in effect for as little as 90 days. At least Arkansas offsets that strikingly inappropriate duration with a "no more than . . . " time span of ten years. In a few states, the duration of orders is left entirely to the discretion of the judge.

The protective provisions offered by protection from abuse orders are another crucial statutory feature that differs from state to state, and serves to either limit or increase the types of protection that an order can provide. All states prohibit abusers from threatening or physically abusing their victims, but the availability (or unavailability) of other protective provisions varies widely. In some states, protective prohibitions can be tailored, at least to an extent, to the victim's specific needs, while in other states only the most basic forms of relief are permitted to be granted.

Laws do change from time to time, so it is important for victims of domestic violence and their advocates and loved ones to check the eligibility factors, the possible protections offered, and the duration of orders currently in place in their own states. It is also important to note that judges everywhere have huge discretion—even when the law is inclusive and the evidence of abuse is strong—to choose whether or not to grant an order, as well as which of the law's available protective provisions such an order will include.

Sadly, better laws do not always equate to better outcomes in court for victims of domestic violence, as most states do not require that judges receive any training or education in the dynamics or dangers of domestic violence. (Pennsylvania does not even allow for such training to be legally mandated.) Even the best laws require knowledgeable judges committed to fully enforcing them, as well as strong advocates committed to working to strengthen and maintain them.

Thankfully, there are many determined advocates for victims and survivors of domestic violence, and protection from abuse statutes have, overall, improved since the 1980s. My state of Pennsylvania, as one example, has removed the strange "legal access" requirement that I referenced in chapter seven; has added "stalking" to its abuse definitions; has included protective wording concerning custody; and has expanded the duration of orders from "up to one year," to the current "up to 3 years." (I do not mean to overly praise Pennsylvania here. Neighboring New Jersey never had a "legal access" requirement in its statute, has always included stalking in its definition section, and has long granted permanent orders.)

Child custody laws have also seen changes, but progress since the 1980s has been met with intense resistance from advocates for "fathers' rights." The current status quo is too often tragic for women and children.

For hundreds of years, fathers had ownership rights to their children, making child custody determinations a simple matter. After women gained the vote, this practice began to give way. Gradually, the presumptive tender years doctrine emerged, based on a growing recognition that an early mother-child bond is essential for healthy childhood development. As a result, for a number of years, judges were likely to grant primary custody of young children to mothers. And because women were supposed to be in the home, taking care of children—not in the workforce, taking jobs away from men—mothers began winning primary custody the majority of the time. That outcome lasted until the later 1970s, when many states added an Equal Rights Amendment to their constitutions, making it unconstitutional for judges to decide the custody of children based on a parent's gender. "The best interests of the child" became the standard for decision-making.

However, "the best interests of the child" is a standard so nebulous that it gives judges little guidance and almost limitless discretion. The introduction of "factors" for judges to consider, to help them determine the best interests of the child, seemed like a positive step. In reality, whether it is actually a positive step or not is dependent upon what exactly those factors are.

Initially, the danger of domestic violence was not one of those factors.

During the years when the stories in this book took place, physical violence against the child in question might sometimes be considered in a best-interests assessment in custody cases, but the need for children to be "disciplined" usually explained physical violence away. Meanwhile, acts of domestic violence perpetrated by one parent upon another were considered irrelevant. After all, the parents were not living together anymore, so what difference did it make? (As documented by many studies, including by the American Bar Association's Commission on Domestic Violence, the motivation of abusers to intimidate and control their victims through their children actually *increases* after separation, in order to counteract the loss or lessening of other methods of coercive control.[7] Despite this reality, the myth that domestic violence stops when the parties separate is still widely accepted as fact.)

Nowadays, all states include domestic violence as a factor to be considered in custody determinations. That's the good news.

But there is bad news.

First, states list many factors to be considered in custody determinations. Pennsylvania, for example, lists 16. Very few states give the domestic violence factor more weight than any others.

Second, when a parent in a custody case is alleged to be a perpetrator of domestic violence, many states require a far higher standard of proof than the preponderance-of-the-evidence standard that is used to assess every other factor. In a number of states, a criminal conviction is necessary before the domestic violence factor can even be considered in family court. Needless to say, criminal convictions for domestic violence are exceedingly rare.

Third, there is one factor that, almost everywhere, is cherished above all others: the so-called *friendly parent* factor. It is a factor based on the comforting assumption that it is always good for children to have a close and continuing relationship with both parents post separation/divorce. In family court, this comforting assumption is an article of faith.

It is indeed good for children to have a close and continuing relationship with both parents—when both parents are loving, nurturing, and kind, and when the primary concern of both parents is the health and happiness of their children. Actually, when both parents fit this description, they are seldom seen in family court. They don't need to engage in bitterly contested custody hearings. These parents are able to negotiate, in the true best interests of their children, and reach amicable custody agreements. But abusers are not loving, nurturing or kind, and—especially after their partners flee—their children are handy objects and targets of their continuing determination to wield their power and coercive control. Abusers do not negotiate with their victims in the best interests of their children. Whenever possible, they take their victims to court.

The friendly parent factor is a powerful counterweight to the domestic violence factor, functioning to trump the importance of protecting children from the physical, emotional, and psychological damage they suffer when forced to remain in close and continuing contact with an abusive parent.

Florida currently has the following *two* friendly parent factors for its family courts to consider before issuing a custody order:

> The demonstrated capacity and disposition of each parent to facilitate and encourage a close and continuing parent-child relationship, to honor the time-sharing schedule, and to be reasonable when changes are required. [8]

And:

> The demonstrated capacity of each parent to communicate with and keep the other parent informed of issues and activities regarding the minor child, and the willingness of each parent to adopt a united front on all major issues when dealing with the child. [9]

When I first began practicing law, Pennsylvania's child custody statute, like those of most states, did not include factors. However, the statute began by proclaiming that it was the public policy of the Commonwealth for children to have ongoing, consistent contact with both parents. Many states, along with their friendly parent factor(s), still explicitly declare such a public policy today. Many states have even adopted a public policy that 50/50 custody is the parenting schedule presumed to be in the best interest of children.

The friendly parent factor is especially dear to untrained judges everywhere, who lack a fundamental understanding of the harmful impacts of domestic violence. They prefer soothing assumptions over disturbing realities. Don't we all know that it is good for children when their custody is shared and their parents get along? So if one parent refuses to "get along" with the other parent, she must not be a *good* parent and therefore she should not have primary custody of the children. In fact, if she seems *very* unfriendly, maybe she shouldn't have any contact with her children at all.

Abusers are quick to grasp the many advantages that friendly parent assumptions offer them, and they become adept at creating situations that cause the other parent to appear "unfriendly." This ploy, which I have seen exercised shrewdly and relentlessly by abusers on so many occasions, is one that few victims are able to defend against without the day-to-day assistance of a skilled attorney—an expense even fewer victims can afford.

Because judges and custody laws habitually deny or minimize the real dangers that victims and their children face, many victims are forced to spend up to eighteen years of their lives communicating weekly or daily with their abusers, while constantly being judged by how cooperative they are in their communication. Even worse, they are compelled by the law to repeatedly place their children at serious risk of harm.

As I have previously noted, victims of domestic violence are the only crime victims who, if they have children, are regularly required by court order to interact with their assailants, and risk losing custody of their children if they resist this mandate in any manner.

Studies have shown that between 30 percent and 60 percent of parents who abuse their spouses/intimate partners also abuse their children.[10] Furthermore, children who have been exposed to domestic violence may show levels of emotional and behavioral problems comparable to children who were themselves victims of physical abuse. [11]

In many cases, the very act of telling a judge that the other parent is abusive is enough to mark a parent as "unfriendly," regardless of the truth of the allegation. When a victim dares to ask that restrictions be placed on an abusive parent's contact with the child, for the child's protection, the request itself is seen as proof of her disposition *not* to "facilitate and encourage a close and continuing parent-child relationship" between the other parent and the child. As one would expect, a protective parent is likely to be unwilling "to adopt a united front" with an abusive parent "on all major issues when dealing with the child."

And when the *child* expresses his or her fear of an abusive parent, confirming the protective parent's reports, many family court judges think they know exactly which party to blame. (Hint: it is not the abuser.)

In most states, children able to speak maturely are allowed to meet with the judge, and their expressed preference is one of the factors to be considered. So when children tell a judge that one of their parents physically or sexually abuses them, or threatens to kill or harm them (or their other parent, or their pet), or subjects them to severe punishments for minor or imaginary sins, or habitually calls them dehumanizing names, or is violent and cruel towards others in their presence, you would think they'd be believed and their preferences honored.

You'd be wrong. Children who accuse a parent of domestic violence put themselves in great danger. The abusive parent will learn of the child's treasonous act; he will label the child a liar; and he will probably accuse the other parent of what is called "parental alienation."

Parental alienation is the theory that children who report being victims of physical, sexual, or other forms of abuse that cause their justifiable estrangement from a parent do so because they've been brainwashed by their other parent into falsely believing (or programmed by their other parent into falsely alleging) the traumatic experiences they have reported. Therefore, authorities should remove them from the other parent, dismiss whatever they say, and possibly further punish them for disrespecting the parent whose abuse they reported.

According to parental alienation theory, the "alienating" parent is trying to gain an upper hand in the custody case. Since it must be harmful for children to think one of their parents is abusing them, the quickest remedy is to remove the children from the alienating parent and place them in the sole or primary custody of the (supposedly wrongly accused) abuser. Accusations of sexual abuse are especially likely to trigger this result.

My experience with this terrifying conspiracy theory exactly mirrors that of Richard Ducote, Esquire, who throughout his brilliant career has focused primarily on cases where courts have granted custody of children to child molesters and domestic violence perpetrators:

> After twenty years in family law courtrooms throughout the country, I confidently say that no woman, despite very abundant evidence that her child has been sexually molested by her ex-husband or that she has been repeatedly pummeled by the violent father of her child, can safely walk into any family court in the country and not face a grave risk of losing custody to the abuser for the sole reason that she dared to present evidence to the judge and ask that the child be protected.[12]

The sordid history of parental alienation theory is worth knowing. The initial idea arose, in 1985, from the mind of Dr. Richard A. Gardner, an unpaid, part-time adjunct clinical professor of child psychiatry. Originally, Gardner named his brainchild "Parental Alienation Syndrome." He then self-published a number of non-peer-reviewed papers and books (along with cassettes and video tapes) heralding his theory and advertising his availability to testify at court proceedings. Before he committed suicide in 2003, Gardner was paid to testify, as an expert witness on behalf of fathers accused of sexually abusing their children, in hundreds of child custody cases.[13] In his view, the real culprits were always conniving mothers, who were somehow able to convince their children that their father had raped or molested them.

For a number of reasons, Gardner's parental alienation syndrome has gradually lost its luster over time. Maybe this happened because there was never any empirical or scientific evidence to substantiate it. Maybe it was because the American Psychiatric Association repeatedly refused to include it in its diagnostic manual (now the DSM-V). Maybe it was because the World Health Organization denounced it, or because the National Council of Juvenile and Family Court Judges soundly rejected it.

Other ideas that sprang from Gardner's head may have also played a role in the diminished use of parental alienation syndrome in family court—ideas like Gardner's insistence that pedophilia, sexual sadism, necrophilia (sex with corpses), zoophilia (sex with animals), and coprophilia (sex involving defecation]) are actually "natural forms of sexual behaviors. . ." According to Gardner, pedophilia is "a wide-spread and accepted practices among literally billions of people." He apparently blamed the Jews for failing to appreciate the obvious societal benefits of pedophilia. "It is of interest that of all the ancient peoples it may well be that the Jews were the only one who were punitive towards pedophiles," he noted, postulating that this wrongful attitude likely led to "our present overreaction to pedophilia."[14]

During parental alienation syndrome's heyday, there was little notice of the fact that the theory was also, at its foundation, a platform for the dissemination of Gardner's deeply misogynistic views. Even in child custody cases where the evidence of molestation was impossible to refute, Gardner held the mother responsible. Rather than acting in a "hysterical fashion"(which he thought women were innately predisposed to do), and "denigrating" the father by taking him to court, Gardner argued that the mother should be made to realize her culpability, and should give the father more of what he wants. "Her increased sexuality may lessen the need for her husband to return to [their child] for sexual gratification," he explained.[15] When a child tells her mother that she has been sexually molested by her father, Gardner advised the mother to respond: "I don't believe you. I'm going to beat you for saying it. Don't you ever talk that way again about your father."[16]

Besides blaming mothers in molestation cases, even when the crime was irrefutable, Gardner was not above occasionally blaming the child. Children, he believed, experience "high sexual urges" even in "early infancy."[17] Being "naturally sexual," they may "seduce" the adult, and, when discovered, may "fabricate so that the adult will be blamed for the initiation."[18]

Gradually—but not completely—Gardner's creative theory has fallen into disuse. Unfortunately, it has been seamlessly replaced by a subtle variation of the original, a feat accomplished by simply dropping one pesky word from its name. Now, children who report being victims of domestic abuse are doing so under the influence of "parental alienation," not "parental alienation syndrome." Now we don't have to reference Richard A. Gardner when we accuse devious mothers of convincing their children to fear and be estranged from a father who abuses them. We're even slightly open to the possibility that mothers don't always do this intentionally; sometimes they may do it without fully realizing it, possibly because they are mentally ill.

Let me be clear: there *is* such a thing as alienating behavior. I can tell you, from my years of experience dealing with abusers, that it is not uncommon for an abusive parent to very intentionally malign and demean the other parent to the child, in hopes of undermining the child's love and respect for that parent. Many abusers try to convince their children that the other parent is responsible for breaking up the family; that she doesn't care about her husband and children anymore; that she is selfish/incompetent/greedy/stupid/crazy; and, for good measure, almost always that she is a whore. (And that God says anyone who loves a whore will burn in hell forever.)

Abusers are notorious alienators. But their efforts almost never succeed in causing the children to *fear* their protective parent. I have certainly seen abusers succeed in chipping at their children's faith in the other parent's abilities, including her ability to protect them from the abuser's wrath if they reveal his behavior to a judge or doctor or other authority figure. But in three-plus decades of work in this field, handling hundreds of cases, I have only had two cases where an abusive parent was able to convince the parties' children that their other parent (a very loving father, in one of the cases) had become a "dangerous person." Yet even in those unique cases, the children never displayed any actual fear of the other parent.

And yes, some parents (even otherwise well-meaning parents) do sometimes say things—carelessly or unthinkingly—that might cause their child to view the other parent less positively. This can occur in intact families, too. Before the advent of parental alienation syndrome and its retitled progeny, this behavior was handled in custody cases by the insertion of a common provision in custody orders or agreements. We called it the no-bad-mouthing clause. It went something like this: "Neither parent shall say or do anything, in the presence or within the hearing of the child, that serves to denigrate the other parent in the eyes of the child, nor permit others to do so." The no-bad-mouthing clause was always framed as a mutual prohibition, even though in domestic violence cases it was almost always only the abuser who did the bad-mouthing.

Nowadays, the supposed harmfulness of "parental alienation" either dwarfs, absolves, or obliterates the dangers of domestic violence. A concept now firmly entrenched in our courts, it is embraced wholeheartedly by countless judges, child custody evaluators, mediators, and guardians ad litem—people who have the power, through their ignorance, to destroy children's lives.

Truthfully, women and children were often disrespected and disbelieved long before parental alienation syndrome and parental alienation arrived on the scene. However, these theories have magnified the influence of misogyny in our courts, providing a handy justification for the mistreatment women and children receive. This is a truth I have confronted many times.

The renowned legal scholar Joan S. Meier lists four major reasons why mothers' claims of abuse are widely denied in court: (1) A strong emphasis on shared parenting; (2) Gender bias; (3) Misconceptions about abuse; and (4) Unconscious psychological denial of the realities of violence against women and children.[19] I wish to stress that the psychological denial of violence against children is especially strong and deep-seated. (The one notable exception being when the accused parent is *poor*, and is therefore imagined to be less civilized.) Not understanding and not wanting to believe, courts turn to counter-explanations for ugly realities, explanations that serve to silence those who challenge their preferred beliefs.

Allegations of adult abuse are very often disbelieved, but not nearly as often as allegations of child abuse. When a mother and child make identical allegations of child abuse, their suspected collusion raises the stakes. Many children are court-ordered into the custody of their abusers as a result. Numerous studies have investigated and substantiated this fact. Here is a sampling.

A study led by noted sociologist Geraldine B. Stahly found that roughly 75 percent of mothers who reported child abuse lost custody of the child to the alleged abuser.[20]

In a Massachusetts study involving 40 men who were known to have abused their wives and children, 15 were granted either sole or joint custody of the children they had abused.[21]

Researchers in North Carolina, examining contested custody cases in their region over a five-year period, reported that 84 percent of the fathers were granted sole or joint custody. In 26 percent of the cases, the fathers were either proven or alleged to have physically and sexually abused their children.[22]

In a national survey to better understand the problems protective parents face, researchers at California State University, San Bernardino interviewed 100 mothers, self-identified as protective parents, 94 percent of whom had been their children's primary caretaker and 87 percent of whom still had physical custody of the children at the time of parental separation. As a result of having reported child abuse, only 27 percent kept custody of the children after court proceedings, the rest losing custody to the father. Ninety-seven percent stated that their reports of abuse were either minimized or ignored, and that they were punished by the court for having tried to protect their children. Forty-five percent were labeled as having parental alienation syndrome, and 65 percent were threatened with further sanctions if they "talked publicly" about the case.[23]

The National Institute of Justice funded a nationwide study of child custody outcomes in cases involving abuse and alienation, performed by a team of foremost experts.[24] The researchers examined 4,338 published custody cases. They found that when mothers who had physical custody of the children at the start of the litigation raised claims of abuse to themselves and/or the children, and fathers countered with alienation claims, mothers lost custody over 50 percent of the time—even when the courts issued no findings of alienation in their rulings. When the courts credited fathers' alienation claims, mothers lost custody 73 percent of the time.

Those percentages actually increased when cases that involved only abuse of the mother were removed from the equations. When mothers claimed that fathers had either physically abused the child, sexually abused the child, physically *and* sexually abused the child, or had committed both child abuse and domestic violence—and the courts credited fathers' alienation claims—mothers lost custody 87 percent of the time.

When fathers cross-claim that they are victims of alienation, courts are almost four times (3.9) more likely to disbelieve mothers' claims of child abuse than if no alienation claim is made. But even in cases where alienation is *not* alleged by fathers, mothers claiming that fathers had committed domestic violence, child physical abuse, child sexual abuse, or combinations of these offenses nonetheless lost custody of children who were in their custody at the start of litigation 26 percent of the time. Mothers who allege child sexual abuse lost custody 54 percent of the time when the father cross-claimed alienation.

The study's data confirms a reality I have had to battle my entire career: judges are rarely willing to believe that a father would sexually abuse his child. Despite overwhelming empirical evidence showing that most child sexual abuse accusations are true, the study found that courts credited sexual abuse claims only two percent of the time when alienation was cross-claimed. Shockingly, this number did not increase when there was corroboration of the sexual abuse the fathers had committed.

The Meier et al. nationwide study also found evidence of gender bias in these cases, including that when either parent is accused by the other of alienation (with or without abuse claims), mothers have twice the odds of losing custody.

Overall, this study, like so many others, reveals that an alarming numbers of children are being transferred into the custody of a (previously non-custodial) father accused of abusing them.

Only children and slaves are legally forced to be in the physical custody of persons who abuse them. The effects of these forced custody transfers on the health and welfare of children are devastating.

Joyanna Silberg, PhD. and Stephanie Dallam, PhD. studied 27 so-called turn-around child custody cases from across America. In 100 percent of the cases, claims of abuse by both the mothers and the children were disbelieved by the court. The mothers' reports were deemed not credible and the children's reports were dismissed as lies or exaggerations. Many judges believed the mothers had coached the children, even though *no evidence* of coaching was ever presented in court. (The researchers, independently, were also unable to uncover any evidence of coaching by the protective parent.) In 59 percent of the cases, the children were court-ordered into the sole custody of their abusive parent; in the remaining 41 percent of the cases, the abusive fathers were awarded either joint custody or unsupervised visitation. The children in this study spent an average of three years in the abusive parent's custody before another court reversed the initial courts' decisions. Eighty-eight percent of the children reported further abuse after being court-ordered into the custody or unsupervised care of their abusers. The new incidents of abuse tended to be more severe than the abuse they had suffered prior to the original court hearing.[25] These findings are consistent with many prior studies.[26]

Such an outcome is to be expected. When courts accept an abuser's assertion that his child and his child's mother cannot be trusted, the abuser justifiably grows emboldened. He can do whatever he wants to do now, and his victims will not be believed.

The children in the cases analyzed in this study all suffered multiple symptoms of distress documented in the court records, including depression; anxiety; dissociation; regressive behaviors; sexual behaviors;

school problems; nightmares; and suicidal ideation. Almost a third of the children threatened to commit suicide, and one child's attempt led to a nearly lethal hanging. Some of the children ran away from their fathers' home. Some were placed on psychiatric medications to help manage their anguish.

Myriad studies have documented the lasting detrimental effects of sexual abuse, physical abuse and exposure to domestic violence in childhood. The most recent study as of this writing (published March, 2024), was performed by a team of top researchers from Sweden and Iceland. A study of 25,252 adult twins, it found that those who reported having suffered one or more traumas in childhood—specifically, physical or emotional abuse or neglect, rape, sexual abuse, hate crimes, or witnessing domestic violence—were 2.4 times more likely to be diagnosed with a psychiatric illness as those who did not. Further, the odds of being diagnosed with a mental illness climbed by 52 percent for each additional adverse experience.[27]

Every year in the United States, pleas from protective parents and their children are vilified and ignored, and tens of thousands of children are court-ordered into the unsupervised custody of an abusive parent. Some of those children do not survive.

Between 2008 and June, 2023, the Center for Judicial Excellence (CJE) collected data on the murders of 944 children by a parent or parental figure involved in divorce/separation/child custody litigation. (Between the end of the study in June 2023 and January, 2024, forty more children had been killed.) Fathers committed these murders 71 percent of the time, mothers 17 percent of the time, and other parental figures (mainly stepfathers) 12 percent of the time. Research for the report was made difficult by the lack of a national data base, necessitating reliance on publicly available records and sources, primarily through local and national news coverage.[28] The actual number of children murdered by a parent of parental figure under these circumstances is likely to be much higher.

As with adult victims of domestic violence, abusers most often used guns (47 percent of the time) to murder their children. But also as with adult victims of domestic violence, child victims are killed in a variety of ways. Beating/blunt force trauma is the second most common method used, followed by stabbing, strangulation/asphyxiation, drowning, arson (typically by setting a house on fire and locking the children inside), vehicle, starvation, and drugs. Some of the murdered children died in "unknown" or "other" ways.

While all of the children were murdered in the midst of a parent's divorce or separation, CJE was able to access enough additional detailed information in 139 of the murders to irrefutably establish that (1) prior to the murder, a protective parent or parental figure had sought to restrict an abusive parent's access to the child(ren) due to safety concerns; (2) the parent who murdered the child(ren) had a history of domestic violence, child abuse, severe mental illness, or had threatened to harm the child(ren) or their other parent; and (3) the family court's actions or inactions were associated with the murder. When information about the court's essential role was obtainable, CJE categorized the children's murders as preventable. In fact, if society truly cared about and provided real protections for victims of domestic violence and their children, *all* of these murders would have been preventable.

Autumn Coleman, age three, was one of the children who was killed by arson. Just weeks before her death in 2019, her mother had gone to family court to beg for an end to the violent father's right to unsupervised visitation. The judge denied her request. On Autumn's second court-mandated unsupervised visit, her father FaceTimed her mother from his burning car so she could see her little girl being burned alive.

On March 31, 2021, as I was writing this memoir, a mother filed an emergency petition in a New Jersey courthouse, asking for sole custody of her six-year-old son, Corey Micciolo. Her petition described assaults and visible signs of abuse the child had endured at the hands of his father. One day later, without even bothering to hold a hearing, the family court judge denied the mother's request. One day after that, Corey's father beat him to death. The autopsy showed multiple blunt force impacts to Corey's small chest and abdomen, and bruises all over his face and body.

The emergency petition filed by the mother of Greyson Kessler, age four, was also denied by a family court judge, despite the father's long history of abusive behavior and mental illness (which had been documented in 250 pages of evidence in the court record). The next day, Greyson was shot to death while in his father's custody, the victim of his father's planned murder/suicide.

In 2023, Om Moses Gandi, age sixteen, was shot to death by his father. The father had been awarded sole custody of Om after he charged the boy's mother with parental alienation. The mother had reported her ex-partner's acts of domestic violence for many years, but his alienation claims were deemed more relevant.

Also in 2023, just two days before her first birthday, Willow Clare was stabbed to death by her father. And Zevaya Flanagan, age two, was strangled and beaten to death by her father; Ariana Fair, age three, was shot to death by her father; Noah Combs, age unlisted, was shot to death by his mother; Jaevion Riley, age seven, was burned and beaten to death by his father; Eleanor Carey, age three weeks, was shot and killed with a crossbow by her father; and JoJo Washington, age eight, Jayla Washington, age five, and Avery Washington, age three, were burned to death when their father locked them in a house and set it on fire.

This is only a small sampling of the children murdered by an abusive parent in 2023, as documented in the public records that CJE was able to locate. I would fill hundreds of pages if I enumerated the year and manner of death of each murdered child that CJE uncovered during its 24 ½ years of record-keeping. Just know, and remember, that hundreds and hundreds of children were intentionally killed after their protective parent went to family court to try desperately, in vain, to protect them.

I want to tell you about one more murdered child. Her name was Kayden Mancuso.

Kayden lived where I live, in Bucks County, Pennsylvania, with her loving mother, Kathy Sherlock. Her mother did everything in her power to protect Kayden from her father, who had a long, documented history of violent and erratic behavior. He threatened to kill family members and himself; punched the family dog; was barred from Kayden's elementary school for stalking and harassing a teacher; and was convicted of aggravated assault after he bit off part of a man's ear in a bar brawl. Nonetheless, after a custody hearing in December 2017, during which the father's dangerousness was clearly established, the judge ordered Kayden to spend alternating weekends in her father's unsupervised custody. Kayden's mother had no choice but to hide her own anxiety about her daughter's safety as Kayden wept in fear when the weekends approached. Violating a custody order, the mother knew, can easily lead a mother to lose primary custody.

During one of those court-ordered weekends, Kayden, age seven, was bludgeoned to death by her father. Before he killed himself, he left a gloating, triumphant note on his daughter's body for her mother to find.

Kathy Sherlock describes her little girl as "kind, caring, fun, witty, athletic, and sassy." Although I never met Kayden, I can attest to the sweetness and vibrancy visible in all her photographs. After she was murdered, I met Ms. Sherlock a number of times. She has become a powerful advocate for the protection of children, and I have great respect for her.

I felt honored when invited by Danielle Pollack, cofounder of the National Safe Parents Organization and policy manager of the National Family Violence Law Center, to play a small role in the final drafting of a series of proposed custody amendments in Pennsylvania, given the title of Kayden's Law, which have finally become law.

Kayden's Law mandates prioritizing safety factors over all other factors in child custody litigation. It redefines friendly parent factors, stating that a party's reasonable concerns for the child's health and welfare and efforts to protect the child shall not be considered alienation, nor shall a child's negative relationship with one party be presumed to be caused by the other party. When the court finds a history of abuse or a present risk of harm to a child or a parent, and it grants any form of custody to the abusive parent, the order must include reasonably necessary safety conditions, restrictions, or safeguards to ensure the protection of the child and the other parent. In that regard, custody may need to be professionally supervised or non-professionally supervised, with supervisors signing an affidavit of accountability that acknowledges their legal obligation. In addition, limitations may be set on the time of day and/or the number of hours or days that custodial contact will be permitted.

Further, Kayden's Law recommends the development and implementation of a program that provides ongoing education and training for judges, district judges, guardians ad litem, counsel for children, custody conference officers, and mediators regarding child abuse in all its forms—sexual, physical, implicit and explicit, trauma and neglect—and the impact that domestic violence has on children.

Every state in America needs to adopt a version of Kayden's Law.

In 2022, a version was included in the federal Violence Against Women Act (VAWA), where it is cited as either Kayden's Law or Keeping Children Safe From Family Violence. Included in its provisions is the availability of federal funding for states seeking to develop and implement education and training programs about abuse that rely on evidence-based, peer-reviewed research by recognized experts and are taught by experienced domestic violence or child abuse professionals.

As for the current practices of child protection agencies across America (like Bucks County's Children & Youth Social Services Agency), they have remained basically unchanged since the years I battled them in court. There is nothing I encountered then that is not being encountered now by lawyers for the indigent and for victims of domestic violence. In every state's child protection statute, the definition of neglect includes one or more factors that are directly related to poverty. And in response to this poverty, rather than providing aid, the agencies too often snatch children from their indigent families and put them in foster care. More than 250,000 children are forced into the foster care system every year. That translates to one child every three minutes. More than four-fifths of the removals are *not* based on physical abuse.[29]

Individual state statistics regarding child protection agencies do vary. For example, in 2019, 98.1 percent of the children placed in foster care in Montana were placed there due to neglect. Only 0.8 percent were placed due to physical abuse and only 0.5 percent due to sexual abuse. The same year in New York, the numbers were 90.9 percent placed due to neglect, 1.1 percent placed due to physical abuse, and .08 percent placed due to sexual abuse. In Idaho, the numbers were 83 percent placed due to neglect, 16.6 percent placed due to physical abuse, and 0.1 percent placed due to sexual abuse. Vermont was a distinct outlier, with the majority (66.6 percent) of its placements due to physical abuse.

Parents dealing with homelessness or housing instability are at special risk of being considered guilty of child neglect and having their children taken from them. Solely for that reason, 25,000 children were put in a foster care residences or facilities in 2019 alone.[30] Unless these indigent parents can promptly acquire what's considered suitable housing, they are in grave danger of losing custody of their children forever.

At the behest of child protective services in 2019, courts permanently terminated the rights of the parents of nearly 61,000 children.[31] In a large percentage of those cases, the terminations were due to the parents' inability to stop being poor. As a result, every day, year after year, children of the poor are removed from their homes and placed in residences or facilities where they are often subjected to abusive treatment and even intentional neglect by overseers who are paid to house them. As noted by Human Rights Watch and the ACLU in their 2022 report:

> Despite recognizing that access to resources and social supports . . . may prevent unintended neglect and protect children . . . , state and local agencies within the child welfare system spend nearly *10 times* more on the foster system than on services that would support families in reunifying with their children.[32]

After their parents' parental rights have been terminated, some children will eventually be adopted. But thousands upon thousands of children, transformed into orphans by the power of the state, will wait for years for an adoption that never occurs. Every single year in our country, more than 20,000 youth age out of foster care on their 18th birthdays, and are released from the system, on their own, without any family connections or network of support to help them.

As one would expect, given the many studies on the long-term damaging consequences of traumatic events on children, children removed from their homes by child protection agencies experience a plethora of negative outcomes. One study of adults who had been in the foster care system found that 54 percent had at least one mental health disorder, 20 percent experienced major depression, 25 percent had post-traumatic-stress disorder, and 22.2 percent experienced homelessness after age 18.[33]

Other studies have found that children who survive foster care are also more likely to become teen mothers; more likely to be incarcerated;

more likely to have suffered harm to their cognitive development; and more likely to have substance abuse disorders.34

Our child protection statutes are as much in need of major reform as they were when the events in this memoir took place. The evils they perpetrated then continue to be perpetrated now, every weekday in family courts across our land.

As for the larger society, funding and services to help domestic violence victims are still wholly inadequate nationwide, and government programs to protect the poor, which have always been underfunded, were further cut during the years of the Trump administration. Efforts by Congress to curtail or end other aid programs are ongoing. Food stamps have been taken away from hundreds of thousands of impoverished people. Thousands of hungry children have been deprived of free school lunches, which were often their only assured meal of the day. Recent federal allocations of summertime financial assistance for indigent families, to help mitigate the loss of free school lunches for their children, have been turned down by a few state governors. One governor refused federal allocations for supplemental stipends for food for poor children in his state with the claim that he wanted to shield them from obesity. Another governor refused the money because he "doesn't believe in welfare." Fortunately for that governor's children, their family isn't poor.

The Affordable Care Act (also known as Obamacare), which did not exist in the 1980s, has allowed millions of people to receive medical care. But millions more who need it are not eligible. The cost of subsidized housing keeps rising as its availability grows scanter and scanter, and it is increasingly difficult (and sometimes impossible) for poor people to be deemed eligible to receive the most token of welfare grants. Throughout America, Legal Aid offices providing free civil legal representation to low-income people are forced, by deficient funding, to further limit their limited services.

Nonetheless, the ongoing struggles for legal and social justice have not been in vain. Despite all the forces working against progress, there have been victories. Precious lives have been saved. Some people living in poverty have gotten a desperately needed helping hand. Some societal

biases have budged in the right direction. Some judges have been educated. Some bad laws have been amended. Some good laws have been
enacted.

There is still much work to do. I plan to keep fighting for justice for
victims of domestic violence and the poor, buoyed by the knowledge that
so many others, everywhere in America, are doing the same. Because the
words of Jacob Riis, the reporter, photographer, and social reformer who
fought to improve conditions in the New York slums, continue to ring
true:

> When nothing seems to help, I go and look at a stonecutter hammering
> away at his rock perhaps a hundred times without so much as a crack show-
> ing in it. Yet at the hundred and first blow, it will split in two, and I know
> that it was not that blow that did it, but all that had gone before.

Acknowledgments

First I want to thank my clients, whose bravery, courage, strength and resilience has inspired me so greatly and taught me so much. I wish I could reveal their real names, as so many of them are heroes worthy of personal recognition and acclaim.

It was not until after I had written this book that I discovered the Bucks County Writers' Group. Led by Adam J. Newton, a man beloved by all, BCWG is a vibrant collective of independent writers who meet weekly to discuss the craft of writing and share their work. Their thoughtful responses to the chapters I submitted for critique buttressed my belief that my true stories could stir readers to take a stand for justice in whatever ways they can. I want to especially thank our group's Paige Gardner, an excellent writer and extraordinary young woman, whose insightful advice improved my manuscript.

Thank you to Joan Meier, Professor of Clinical Law at George Washington Law School and founder and Director of the National Family Violence Lew Center at GW, who graciously read a first draft of this book and offered valuable feedback and support. Her lifetime of groundbreaking scholarship and advocacy on behalf of victims of domestic violence and their children has saved countless lives.

Thank you to Danielle Pollack, the National Family Violence Law Center's Policy Manager and the co-founder of the National Safe Parents Organization. Her steadfast dedication to the systemic reform of family law statutes and family court practices, on behalf of children and safe parents, is truly inspiring. Mere mortals cannot match her boundless energy.

Thank you, too, to Sasha Drobnick, the Director of Appellant Litigation at the Domestic Violence Legal Empowerment and Appeals Project (DV Leap). Sasha is a life-long advocate for social justice, whose impeccable legal research skills helped me win a crucial Superior Court appeal on behalf of the clients of AWoman's Place.

The late David Tilove is owed special mention here. The Executive Director of the Bucks County Legal Aid Society throughout all the years I worked there, David was deeply committed to our mission of providing free, high quality legal services to people who could not otherwise afford a lawyer. Legal Aids have always lacked sufficient funding, and it was said of David that he held our agency together "with bailing wire and string" as we fought, with all our might, to achieve equal justice under law. David was more than a boss to me; he was a gifted lawyer, a mentor, and a friend.

After I finished writing this book, I belatedly learned that no one in the publishing industry wants to review the manuscript of a memoir authored by a non-famous person. Some may be willing to read a *book proposal*, but certainly not the book. It seemed crazy to me, to be forced to write a book proposal when I had already written the book. But crazy or not, it was true, so I gave it a try. It turns out that I have scant talent for writing book proposals. It took me longer to write one than it took me to write this book, and the final result was . . . I think "lousy" may be the kindest word for it.

Enter Karen Wolney, founder and independent editor of Narrative Instincts. Karen explained what a book proposal was supposed to accomplish and guided me firmly and cheerfully toward accomplishing it, always expressing her confidence that my memoir would in fact be published. Then she did me a final great favor: she told me she thought Karl Weber, the publisher of Rivertowns Books, would like the manuscript. As always, Karen was right. After reading it (along with the book proposal!), Karl proclaimed his wholehearted enthusiasm for publishing it. He then promptly suggested changing many of my chapter titles (it turns out I'm also lousy at writing chapter titles), corrected all my typos, skillfully ironed out any awkward places, proposed that I write an Afterword, did another hundred and one things, and educated me through the multifaceted process, one important step at a time. His skill and patience every step of the way made it all seem easy. (Well, almost easy.) Every author should have a publisher like Karl Weber.

And every author should have a dedicated and caring publicist like Betsy Keller. This hasn't just been a job for her, but a passionate advocacy campaign to promote a message of my book: the desperate need for family court reform and laws that truly protect domestic violence victims and their children.

I also want to thank my beautiful big sister, Diane Laison, Ph.D. (she prefers "big' to "older"), artist and mathematician, who has always been my cheerleader. And much thanks to my brilliant daughter, Ruth Porter Groff, Ph.D., political theorist and philosopher, who sometimes questioned why I couldn't pursue a less dangerous profession but was always proud of my work nonetheless. When my memoir was still untitled (as noted above, I have no talent for titles), it was Ruth who reminded me how often, in my cases, I was heard to vow: *"Not if I can help it!"*

Finally, I am grateful for my incomparable mother, Helen Satinsky Splaver. How lucky I was.

Meg Groff
Doylestown, Pennsylvania
February 2025

To Learn More,
To Get Involved

Advocacy Organizations

The following organizations are dedicated to research, education, and advocacy on the issues of domestic violence, child custody law, and the rights of women and families.

American Bar Association (ABA)

The ABA works to promote the best quality legal education, competence, ethical conduct and professionalism, and pro bono and public service work in the legal profession. Provides practical resources for legal professionals, law school accreditation, model ethic codes and more.

Address: 321 North Clark Street, Chicago, IL 60654 (Headquarters)
Phone: 800-285-2221 (ABA Service Center Hotline, General Inquiries)
For legal assistance, go to website: www.FindLegalHelp.org

Website: www.americanbar.org
Email: Service@americanbar.org

Battered Women's Justice Project (BWJP)

The Battered Women's Justice Project is the national resource center on civil and criminal justice responses to intimate partner violence. A collective of national policy and practice centers at the intersection of gender-based violence and legal systems providing resource, training, consultations or research.

Address: 540 Fairview Ave N Suite 208, St. Paul, MN 55104
Phone: 612-824-8768
Website: www.bwjp.org
Email: communications@bwjp.org

Kyra's Champions & the Kyra Franchetti Foundation

The mission of Kyra's Champions is to stop child abuse and child murders. Advocates for policy changes that promote and protect children and families at risk of family violence. Focuses on legislative initiatives on the federal and state levels to ensure children and their safety are top priorities in our family court systems.

Address: 565 Plandome Rd., Suite 156, Manhasset, NY 11030
Website: www.kyraschampions@gmail.com

National Association to Protect Children

Seeks to increase transparency and accountability in the child protection and justice systems. Works to create legislation leading to stronger, tougher laws and the direct rescue of children.

Address: P.O. Box 2187, Knoxville, TN 37901
Phone: 865-525-0901
Website: www.protect.org
Email: info@protect.org

National Coalition Against Domestic Violence (NCADV)

A national organization that advocates for survivors of domestic violence and their families. No direct services/crisis. Provides education, trainings to local organizations, legislative activities; Hotline offers referral services/crisis information, education.

Address: P.O. Box 90249, Austin, TX 78709
National Hotline: 1-800-799-7233 or 1-800-787-3224
Administrative Line: 737-225-3150
Website: www.ncadv.org

National Family Violence Law Center at George Washington School of Law

The NFLVC serves as the preeminent home for national research and expert support for the growing movement to better protect children in contested custody cases. It provides pioneering quantitative and qualitative research, training and education, state and federal policy development, and selective litigation.

Address: 2000 H Street, NW, Washington, DC 20052
Website: www.law.gwu.edu/national-family-violence-law-center
Submit form online to contact the National Family Violence Law Center.

National Network to End Domestic Violence (NNEDV)

NNEDV is a coalition of domestic violence programs and advocates across the U.S. It works to end domestic violence through advocacy, training, and technical assistance.

Address: 1325 Massachusetts Ave NW, 7th Floor, Washington, DC 20005-4188
Phone: 202-543-5566
Website: www.nnedv.org
Email: info@hotline.womenslaw.org

National Resource Center on Domestic Violence (NRCDV)

Works to serve those dedicated to ending domestic violence through technical training, advocacy to strengthen policies, and research.

Address: 2080 Linglestown Rd., Suite 106, Harrisburg, PA 17110
Phone: 1-800-537-2238
Website: www.nrcdv.org
Email: NRCDV@nrcdv.org

National Safe Parents Coalition (NSPO)

A national coalition of survivor parents and concerned citizens in the U.S. advocating for evidence-based policies which put child safety and risks at the forefront of child custody decisions.

Website: www.nationalsafeparents.org
Email: media@nationalsafeparents.org

Safe Housing Partnerships

Provides resources and tools for those addressing survivors' housing needs due to domestic violence, sexual assault, and homelessness. Work collaboratively to ensure local program systems, institutions, and laws and policies are responsive to the unique challenges and opportunities at the intersection of domestic and sexual violence and housing.

Website: www.safehousingpartnerships.org
Submit form on-line to reach the organization with general questions relating to domestic violence and housing.

Service Organizations

If you or someone you know is dealing with a problem related to domestic violence, a child custody dispute, or legal protections for families and children, the organizations listed below offer resources and information that may be helpful. State, county, and local government agencies in your area may also provide such support.

Alliance for HOPE International

First and largest online and mobile searchable directory of domestic violence programs and shelters in the U.S. and a leading source of helpful tools and information for people experiencing and working to end domestic violence.

Address: 101 W. Broadway, Suite 1770, San Diego, CA 92101
Phone: 888-511-3522
Website: www.allianceforhope.com
Email: info@allianceforhope.com

Asian Task Force Against Domestic Violence (ATASK)

A safe, confidential, private organization that can be called even if the caller or the caller's family have no immigration papers. Help is available to all women, whether single or married, pregnant, childless or have children. The caller does not need to speak English; services are available in many Asian languages.

Address: P.O. Box 120108, Boston, MA 02112
24-Hour Multilingual Hotline: 617-338-2355
Website: www.atask.org

Childhelp National Child Abuse Hotline

The National Child Abuse Hotline (24/7) counselors support those concerned or affected by child abuse and provide appropriate individualized guidance to those who reach out. Staffed by live crisis counselors with master and doctoral degrees and life experience in working with child abuse, neglect, and maltreatment.

Address: 6730 N. Scottsdale Rd, Suite 150, Scottsdale, AZ 85253
Phone: 480-922-8212
Hotline: 1-800-422-4453
Website: www.childhelp.org; www.childhelphotline.org for live chat with professional counselors

DomesticShelter.org

DomesticShelter.org works to make more people aware of the services available for those experiencing domestic violence and make it faster and easier for victims of domestic violence and their friends/family, as well as program and shelter providers, to quickly find services and information best suited to their location, language and needs.

Address: 501 W. Broadway, Suite A #625, San Diego, CA 92101
Website: www.domesticshelters.org (enter your zip code to locate a shelter)
Email: info@domesticshelters.org

Domestic Violence Legal Empowerment and Appeals Project (DV LEAP)

The only nonprofit providing legal appeals to survivors of domestic violence in all 50 states. Founded in response to an urgent need for expert appellate litigation to reverse unjust trial court rulings and to protect the legal rights of women and children victimized by family violence.
Address: 6955 Willow Street NW #501, Washington, DC 20012
Phone: 202-742-1727
Website: www.nvrdc.org

Justice for Children

Call Center helps when the child protection system fails to protect a child. Offers information, guidance and assistance to adults who are trying to keep the child safe. Our Pro Bono Legal program provides free legal help when it appears that a court or agency will return a child to an abusive situation.

Address: 3518 Emancipation Ave., #200, Houston, TX 77004
Phone: 713-225-4357
Website: www.justiceforchildren.org

Legal Services Corporation (LSC)

The Legal Services Corporation is the single largest funder of civil legal aid for low-income Americans in the nation. It promotes equal access to justice and provides grants for high-quality civil legal assistance.

Address: 3333 Water Street NW, Washington, DC 20007
Phone: 202-295-1500
Website: www.lsc.gov. For Legal Help, type in your address or click on the map to find a Legal Aid organization in your area.

National Domestic Violence Hotline

Free and available 24/7. Advocates listen without judgment and help callers begin to address what is happening in their relationships.
Phone: 1-800-799-7233

RAINN (Rape, Abuse, Incest National Network) & National Hotline

Provides support, education and advocacy for survivors of sexual assault and their families. The largest anti-sexual violence organization that operates the National Sexual Assault Hotline in partnership with more than 1,000 local sexual assault service providers across the country.

Address: 1220 L St. NW Suite 500, Washington, DC 20005
Phone: 202-544-1034
National Sexual Assault Hotline: 800-656-4673. Provides confidential 24/7 Support.
Website: www.rainn.org

WomensLaw.org

Plain-language legal information for victims of abuse. Select the state you live in to find information about restraining orders, custody, divorce, immigration, preparing for court, and more.

Website: www.womenslaw.org
Email Hotline: hotline.womenslaw.org (provides legal information related to domestic violence, sexual assault, or stalking)

Source Notes

[1] Bureau of Justice statistics; Study published by JAMA Pediatrics, December 2020.

[2] Bureau of Justice statistics.

[3] Pennsylvania Coalition Against Domestic Violence, https://www.-pcadv.org/about-abuse/domestic-violence-statistics/.

[4] "Domestic Violence Statistics," National Domestic Violence Hotline website, accessed July 2021, https://www.thehotline.org/stakeholders/domestic-violence-statistics/.

[5] *State v. Black*, 262, (1864).

[6] "'The Rule of Love': Wife Beating as Prerogative and Privacy," Reva B. Siegel, *Yale Journal* (June 1996).

[7] "Ten Myths About Custody and Domestic Violence and How to Counter Them," American Bar Association Commission on Domestic Violence website, accessed July 13, 2024, https://www.ncdsv.org/uploads/1/4/2/2/142238266/10mythsaboutcustodyanddv_aba.pdf.

[8] Fla. Stat § 61.13(3)(a) (2022).

[9] Fla. Stat § 61.13(3)(l) (2022.

[10] The American Bar Association's Commission on Domestic Violence, Quarterly E -Newsletter, Volume 4, 2006.

[11] Ibid.; Jaffe, Wolfe & Wilson, *Children of Battered Women* (1990); Joyanna Silberg & Stephanie Dallam, *Abusers gaining custody in family courts: A case series of overturned decisions* (2019).

[12] *Exposé: The Failure of Family Courts to Protect Children from Abuse in Child Custody Disputes*, ch. 1, Richard Ducote, "What I Have Learned at the Courthouse," p. 11 (1999).

[13] "Richard Gardner's Opinions," The Leadership Council on Child Abuse & Interpersonal Violence website, https://leadershipcouncil.org/richard-gardners-opinions/.

[14] Gardner, R. A. (1992). *True and False Accusations of Child Sex Abuse*. Cresskill, N.J: Creative Therapeutics.

[15] Ibid.

[16] Joan S. Meier, *A Historical Perspective on Parental Alienation Syndrome and Parental Alienation* (2009), citing Gardner's recorded statement in a filmed interview (Waller, 2001).

[17] Gardner, R. A. (1992), *op. cit.*

[18] Gardner, R.A. (1986). *Child Custody Litigation: A Guide for Parents and Mental Health Professionals*. Cresskill, N.J: Creative Therapeutics.

[19] Joan S. Meier, Denial of Family Violence in Court: An Empirical Analysis and Path Forward for Family Law. 110 GEO. L.J. 835 (2022).

[20] Shahly, G.B., Krajewski, L., Loya, B., Uppal, K. German, G., Farris, W. et al (2004), *Protective Mothers in Child Custody Disputes: A Study of Judicial Abuse.*

[21] California Cognitive Behavioral Institute: *Que Sara Sara—Family Court Attitude Regarding Custody Issues* (2022).

[22] The Committee for Justice for Women and the Orange County, North Carolina Women's Coalition (1991). *Contested Custody Cases in Orange County, N. Carolina, Trial Courts, 1983-1987.*

[23] California Cognitive Behavioral Institute: *Que Sara Sara—Family Court Attitude Regarding Custody Issues* (2022).

[24] Meier, Joan S., Dickson, Sean, O'Sullivan, Chris, Rosen, Leora, and Hayes, Jeffrey, *Child Custody Outcomes in Cases Involving Abuse Allegations and Parental Alienation* (2019), National Institute of Justice.

[25] Joyanna Silberg et al., *Crisis in Family Court: Lessons from Turned Around Cases, Final Report to the Office of Violence Against Women, Department of Justice* (2013).

26 Saunders, D. G., Faller, K.,C., & Tolman, R.M., *Child Custody Evaluators' Beliefs About Domestic Violence Allegations: Their Relationship to Evaluator Demographics, Background, Domestic Violence Knowledge and Custody-Visitation Recommendations* (2011), citing Kernic, M.A., Monary-Ernsdorff, D. J., Koepsell, J. K. & Holt, V.L., "Children in the Crossfire: Child custody determinations among couple with a history of intimate partner violence," *Violence Against Women*, 11(8), 991 (2005); Saccuzzo, D. P. & Johnson, N. E., "Child custody mediation's failure to protect: Why should the criminal justice system care?" *National Institute of Justice Journal*, volume 251 (2004); Neustein, A. & Goetting, A., "Judicial responses to protective parent's complaints of child sexual abuse," *Journal of Child Sexual Abuse* (1999); Faller,, K. C. & DeVoe, E. & DeVoe, "Allegations of sexual abuse in divorce," *Journal of Child Sexual Abuse* 4 (4), 1-25 (1995).

27 H.B. Danielsdottir, MSc, T. Aspelund, PhD, et al., "Adverse Childhood Experiences and Adult Mental Health Outcomes," *JAMA Psychiatry* (2024).

28 Center for Judicial Excellence, *Child Safety First: Preventing Homicides During Divorce, Separation and Child Custody Disputes* (2024).

29 *"If I Wasn't Poor, I Wouldn't Be Unfit": The Family Separation Crisis in the US Child Welfare System*, Human Rights Watch and the American Civil Liberties Union (ACLU), November 2022.

30 Ibid.

31 Children's Bureau, "Trends in Foster Care and Adoption FY 2010-FY 2019," June 23, 2020.

32 Ibid., p. 9, italics added.

33 Peter J. Pecora et al., *"Improving Family Foster Care: Findings from the Northwest Foster Care Alumni Study,"* 2005 (accessed October 2022).

34 Joseph J. Doyle, Jr., "Child Protection and Child Outcomes: Measuring the Effects of Foster Care," *American Economic Review Journal*, vol. 97, no. 5 (2007); Laura Bauer and Judy L. Thomas, "Throwaway Kids: Star investigation reveals stark outcomes for America's foster children," *Kansas City Star*, December 15, 2019; Sarah Font and Marina Haddock Potter, "Socioeconomic Resource Environments in Biological

and Alternative Family Care and Children's Cognitive Performance," *Sociological Inquiry*, vol. 89, no. 2 (2019); Daniel J. Pilowsky and Li-Tzy Wu, "Psychiatric symptoms and substance use disorders in a nationally representative sample of American adolescents involved in foster care," *Journal of Adolescent Health*, vol. 38, no. 4 (2006).

About the Author

P rior to opening her own law office in 1996, Meg Groff was a family law attorney at the Legal Aid program in Bucks County, Pennsylvania, for 12 years. A recognized authority in the commonwealth on issues of child custody and domestic violence, Groff has focused on representing victims of abuse and the poor for more than three decades, handling huge caseloads and winning countless cases. She has been a legal consultant to local and national domestic violence organizations, and is a fierce advocate for social justice. She has taught thousands of people—lawyers, other professionals, and laypersons, in groups of all sizes—about domestic violence and family law, and has trained police departments in the dynamics of domestic violence and the proper handling of abuse calls. She assisted in the drafting of crucial amendments to Pennsylvania's Protection from Abuse Act and to Pennsylvania's Child Custody Act, and designed and implemented a project in Bucks County that ensures free representation, regardless of income, for all victims of domestic violence seeking protection orders.

Since settling in Bucks County in 1984, Groff has been closely affiliated with A Woman's Place, the county's battered women's shelter, and has served on the boards of numerous nonprofit agencies that assist women, children, and/or the indigent. She has received many awards and accolades for her staunch advocacy and *pro bono* services. Since retiring from trial work a few years ago, she has concentrated on legal consulting, on hands-on mentoring of young attorneys and advocates, and on writing this memoir. Two of her children's stories have been published in *Highlights for Children* magazine. A short story about one of her legal cases appeared in the January 2024 edition of *After Dinner Conversations*, and the full story of the sock factory incident (mentioned in chapter two of this book) was published in the summer 2024 edition of *Dandelion Revolution Press*.

Groff lives with her husband, a retired carpenter and leather craftsman, and their two dogs. Their daughter Ruth Porter Groff is a professor of political science and philosophy at Saint Louis University.

www.ingramcontent.com/pod-product-compliance
Lightning Source LLC
Chambersburg PA
CBHW051508120626
46551CB00012B/825